The School Counselor–Consultant

The School

Counselor–Consultant

Daniel W. Fullmer
UNIVERSITY OF HAWAII

Harold W. Bernard
OREGON STATE SYSTEM OF HIGHER EDUCATION

HOUGHTON MIFFLIN COMPANY · BOSTON
New York · Atlanta · Geneva, Illinois · Dallas · Palo Alto

Library of Congress Catalog Card Number:
78–146877

ISBN: 0–395–11960–X

Contents

Editor's Introduction

In "Canary in a Coal Mine" Culver H. Nelson has written:

. . . "Until very recently we elders could say to our children: 'I have been young and you have never been old.' Today's youth replies, 'You have never been young in the kind of world in which I am young and you never can be.' . . . Our youth will see more than we ever saw . . . they will watch history unfold at an even faster pace, . . . They will—in terms of sheer quantity of human experience—live longer than ever we have lived. . . . For they have seen time increased, experience telescoped, . . .

Because of all this we shall be tempted . . . not to be more flexible to change but, in our uncertainty about the future, less flexible. . . . I predict sadly that there will be a turn toward forms of religious fundamentalism, political extremism, and social monasticism. Why? Because most of us do not like an uncertain and unpredictable future. We want a rock to hold on to, however dead it may be. We want inflexible certainties, frozen assurances, something that at least appears infallible and solid and substantial."

What Dr. Nelson has said regarding present-day youth and present-day society has an impressive significance for our schools. Today's youth are in schools which prepare for the possible future not at all, the present with hesitancy, and the past with assurance. Few schools are half as aware of the world ahead as are their students. Schools are best at preparing youth for a stable and technological world—which no longer exists. They prepare least well for an unstable and changing post-technological world. This will be a world in which psychological needs and human relationships will be our center of concern, not technological development, a tighter organization of society—and a meticulous understanding of the past. In the face of the "safe" attitude of communities and the "practical" focus of administrators, who can expect teachers to move into the main current of youth's criticisms, realities, and longings? Moreover, they certainly won't do this without help on the specifics at the working level, without encouragement from colleagues as well as leaders, and without leadership in understanding the changed student of today.

Hence, the emerging role of the counselor as counselor-consultant, working both with teachers and administrators, as a consultant, as well as with students as a counselor to improve the learning climate of the total school experience. The counselor is still a competent specialist in human behavior, his goal is still the improvement of the student's sense of personal worth and achievement, but his scope now includes all who influence the learning environment of the student as well as the student himself. On the manner in which the counselor-consultant contributes to a realistic and supporting learning environment, Fullmer and Bernard write: "Improving the learning milieu is the key item in the counselor-consultant's concerns. It means focussing upon the processes of becoming and growing rather than on prescriptive doing." Thus, the emerging role of the counselor is consistent with the developing practice in education of focussing upon the process rather than the product.

These two authors are well-known for their emphasis upon the utilization of group processes in education. Their central approach to the development of a meaningful learning environment is the improving of communication through thoughtfully designed group experiences. Group concepts and procedures are analyzed fully and then applied to improving communication among all school personnel. In particular, group experience is seen assisting both teacher and student in their respective learning roles, as well as contributing to better teamwork in the development of achieving students in a healthy learning environment. The range of procedures used is wide—learning groups, behavioral counseling groups, encounter groups—small groups of every sort. All lead to better communication, particularly teacher-student communication and colleague to colleague communication.

This book is written by two obviously dedicated, mature writers. The courage of their dedication is evident throughout; it is an innovative and informed dedication to a learning experience that is contemporary in nature. The authors utilize the literature with discrimination. It is obvious that they have read ten times as much as they cite. They use literature to *support* ideas, not to introduce them.

This book presents the counselor-consultant as a major influence, using a most powerful tool, in the adaptation of the school to the learning needs of students in contemporary society. It is a book that will be widely quoted.

C. Gilbert Wrenn

Preface

Some prognosticators have warned that the school as an institution is in a last-ditch stand. They claim that the enormity of the job to be done is such that total repudiation and replacement of the present system are required. We do not share this view but we perceive that some marked changes are imminent. Neither do we believe that the development of an expanded role for counselors will be the sole way of making a successful stand for continued formal learning. We do feel that the "Why don't they...?" syndrome (meaning that administrators, school boards, society at large, and teacher education institutions should do something) ought not to excuse counselors from facing the question "What can we do?" Herein, we propose one approach: use of the counselor as a consultant.

A popular cry in the 1970's is relevance. It is suggested that the focal concern of counselors is the question "Is the school made for the child or must the child fit the school?" The question must be operationally (not theoretically or idealistically) answered in the way school personnel regard and interact with pupils and how they regard themselves. To the prior concerns of the counselor (individual analysis, guidance, counseling, programming, evaluation) must be added the task of dealing with the attitudes and behavior of adults (teachers, administrators, parents) who people the pupils' learning milieu.

This book is based on the premise that the professionally prepared counselor can have maximum impact on pupils by working with and through the key adults in the lives of those pupils. He can make his most telling contribution through group work in which parents, teachers, and pupils become recognized factors in the learning of other parents, teachers, and pupils. The evolving role implied is a "new life" more in the sense of growth and development than in the sense of a new conception of the ideals of the counseling profession.

The late Dr. C. Harold McCully was a significant element in the professional partnership of the authors of this volume. Some of his ideas have been pervasive in our work over the years and have come to be more and more meaningful as we tested their validity. Two of them are particularly important in the present book. One is that the professional worker possesses some specialized skills which enable him to perform services no other person can perform. We perceive these special skills and unique services of the professional counselor to be (1) the facilitation of interpersonal relations and (2) the clarification of communication. The professional preparation of guidance workers, as conceptualized herein, stresses a level of expertise and understanding in interpersonal relations and communication which goes beyond that required by a technician. It includes individual counseling and the skills of assessment but regards the pencil-pushing, schedule-making, record-keeping duties as a computer or clerical job which does not challenge the professional skill of human interaction and empathic communication.

McCully's second major idea is that a person defines his role by what he is and the competence he has. Administrators, school boards, even professional organizations do not define the counselor's role. An individual defines his own role according to the goals he envisions and the competencies he develops. The goals envisioned and the competencies recommended in this book are the development of professional levels of skill in social processes and communication directed to improving the school as a learning milieu.

The book is not a "how to do it" dissertation for those preparing to become counselors—though we believe that it should be a part of their conception of what they might become. It is concerned with finding out, through consultation processes, how what we know about pupil development and learning can better be implemented in various school communities.

We wish to acknowledge our debt to many colleagues and associates who helped us formulate, solidify, and test and evaluate the underlying concepts. Foremost among these are Ralph Bedell, John Guthrie, Wesley Huckins, Grace Irish, Rod Hilsinger, Dick Riley, and Earl Zwetschke. C. Gilbert Wrenn advised us during the preparation of the manuscript and did what he could to make sure that we were communicating. Those who really tested the concepts were the graduate students in counseling who, from 1962 to 1968, proved that the ideas are workable by those who believe in themselves. Since that period their reports have continued to be encouraging.

Daniel W. Fullmer
Harold W. Bernard

Chapter One

COUNSELOR-CONSULTANT: AN EMERGENT ROLE

Formal education, like other institutions of our society, has changed over the years. However, the change has not been spectacularly, or even noticeably, rapid, as it has been in business and industrial institutions. Indeed, while one might see little similarity between a store, a bank, or a factory in the 1970's and one in the 1900's, he would have little difficulty in recognizing a classroom full of fifth-graders or high school pupils. The same supremacy of teachers, the same task of maintaining order, the same uniform textbooks, the blackboards, the lined-up chairs and desks — all would be quite familiar.

Yet the task of formal education has changed in many and diverse ways — more, it seems, than in the case of stores or banks. For example, in the 1900's it was mainly the bright *and* motivated students who went to school, especially beyond the fifth or sixth grade. In fact, public high school education had been legalized by the Kalamazoo decision only thirty years. Today the statistical holding power, plus legal power, comes close to including 90 percent of normal school-age children and adolescents. There is considerable doubt, however, about the psychological holding power of schools. Many pupils are present only in the flesh (Silberman, 1970).

1

In the 1900's those who were successful in school had shared the experiences of others only through books, vicariously. Today's pupils have shared the experiences of others through radio, television, movies, and daily newspapers. Nowadays most pupils, including those in the late teens, have spent more time watching television than they have passed in classrooms. The pupils of the early 1900's believed, with adults, in the Judeo-Christian ethic of work. They were oriented to determine, seek, and strive for goals of achievement. Today's students are much less goal oriented but they are heavily role oriented; they want to *be,* they seek identity with peers, they must do their own thing (Glasser, 1970). The specters of the early 1900's — joblessness, penury, and fear of financial depression — have, whether wisely or not, been removed by unemployment insurance, organized unions which safeguard worker benefits, welfare, and social security. The struggle for survival has been replaced by the struggle for fulfillment.

There are those — Paul Goodman, Edgar Z. Friedenberg, John Holt, Peter Schrag, Jonathan Kozol — who see in the inelasticity of the schools an end of their usefulness; the schools' inability to change has doomed them to obsolescence. Others are not so pessimistic but they emphasize the need for marked change in school practice and policy — Jerome Bruner, James B. Conant, John I. Goodlad, Robert Havighurst, Martin Deutsch, Frank Riessman, Paul Woodring, to mention only a few.

The authors share the apprehension of the latter group of educators about the future of schools unless substantial changes are made. We hazard the guess that an effective approach to implementing needed change resides in a role conception for counselors that is beginning to be increasingly perceptible.

The Counselor-Consultant

A NEGLECTED RATHER THAN A NEW ROLE

The activities proposed for the counselor-consultant are not new. They are aimed chiefly at getting the parts of the school system to work together in a coordinated manner. For example, students and teachers are often regarded as being in two camps. The teachers are concerned with controlling the enthusiasm and obstreperousness of youth and with getting the young people to see the wisdom of mastering certain subjects or curricula. The young people, in the other camp, are concerned with circumventing or defying the other-imposed rules and with being their own person (Schrag, 1969). Another example is seen in the frequent conflict between counselors and teachers. In some cases this opposition limits the effectiveness of both teachers and counselors (Kushel, 1967). In other cases teacher-counselor communication is predominantly on the positive side, but there is still need for improvement (Sherman and Shapiro, 1969).

Home-school interaction may be either a problem or an asset to effective school functioning. Sometimes it is achieved through coordinated efforts; at other times it is regarded as a specialized function of an individual in the higher echelons of administration. Sometimes it is sought by the principal but is thought of as a matter of "interpretation" — explaining why what takes place does take place — rather than as genuine communication, which involves give-and-take. Home-school cooperation and communication have been a concern of school personnel for many years but recently have achieved a status which makes prior efforts seem virtually nonexistent. Consider the vital role parent participation has in educational programs for the culturally different pupil. One requisite for federal funding in many such programs is proof of consultation with and involvement of parents in planning and operating. In large measure this is the result of a growing realization that poverty is a pervasive problem. It involves all the members of a community *and* their attitudes toward people and "the system" as well as their attitudes toward, and perceptions of, themselves (Street, 1970).

The roles implied in the foregoing, and those listed below, have been attempted with varying success and varying awareness of importance by school principals. However, (1) the press of seemingly more important duties and (2) lack of specific training in the necessary skills have resulted in neglect of, or breakdown in, the communication required to permit the school to function as a coordinated entity.

INNOVATION

School activities should involve joint discussion, planning, involvement, and interaction — curriculum planning, program building, school financing — but one which looms large comes under the broad heading of innovation. If the schools are to serve the demands of the 1970's, they cannot continue to be so similar to the schools of the 1900's. Already many programs, *in some places*, exemplify the merit of innovation. In other places the *same* programs spell f-a-i-l-u-r-e. Excellent ideas seem to atrophy, and regression to tradition and prior habits occurs ("What's Wrong . . .?" 1970). Certainly there is no single and simple reason for this erosion, but a major factor is that not all the people affected by the innovation were involved in it.[1] There was literally no communication among the school principals during the planning, instituting, or implementing of the innovation. Because too few people really understood and accepted the reasons for change, they resisted the upsetting of their usual routines — or the interference with their own excellent but limited innovations.

It is true that some charismatic principals or university consultants "got something started" and took a number of enthusiastic followers along. Others went along with the crowd and participated for a while but lost interest because they were not frequently enough reminded of the goals or reasons.[2] The "gut level involvement" which is characteristic of successful innovation was lacking (Harrison, 1970).

One noticeable feature of successfully innovative schools is that whatever the specific innovation — team teaching, nongraded organization, continuous progress, elimination of competitive letter grades, programmed instruction, individually prescribed instruction, independent study, etc. — extensive and comprehensive planning was originally instituted and consistently continued (Bernard and Huckins, 1968).

Principals have performed these leadership roles in the past, but, despite protestations to the contrary, they have frequently acted in an authoritarian manner. They explained rather than discussed the programs. What they deemed to be discussion — and they verbally acknowledged the values of discussion — was a brief question-and-answer period following a description of the program or innovation. Some of the bolder teachers, specialists, and supervisors might ask a question or two, but genuine doubts were usually not voiced —

---

[1] Involvement here means that one's presence makes a difference, his voice is heard, he is — psychologically and practically — a cause.

[2] Specific examples observed by Bernard on school visitations in connection with I/D/E/A study. See Bernard and Huckins, 1968.

for many reasons, mainly because most people do not know how to deal with authority and because the authority is not accustomed to having its omniscience questioned.

A school principal admitted that, after promising himself to implement some innovations, he attended a workshop on continuous progress and decided that now was the time and continuous progress was the theme. He called his elementary school staff back a week early in the fall and presented the proposition. The twenty-eight teachers were divided into four discussion groups with the two part-time counselors and two appointed teachers as leaders. The principal was roving participant and answered questions relative to his intent, but he emphasized that decisions would be arrived at by consensus.

With the opening of school so imminent, it was decided that each group had better take a particular phase and, just before afternoon closing time, present its conclusions and ask for questions to be dealt with the following day. Topics for groups were:

Evaluation
Teacher aides
Curriculum content
Rationale for continuous progress

Parkinson's law seemed to operate, and the teachers felt that although they might not be "ready" the now-apparent necessary steps might as well be taken at once. Instead of going to Miss Blank's room, pupils were simply designated as primary, intermediate, and upper and assigned to teachers at random within these categories. Meanwhile the groups and teacher aides had enlisted the assistance of about forty high school boys and girls and five parents, each of whom worked from one to three hours a day. The groups continued to meet twice a week, once for small groups and once for total group discussion.

Toward the end of the semester the group on "Rationale" had its responsibilities shifted by the principal to parent and community relationships. These relationships were typically satisfactory to school personnel, pupils, and parents; but occasional individual problems did arise (one parent wanted her daughter to receive grades, despite the new policy of no letter grades).

During the second semester the weekly teachers' meetings were eliminated in favor of calling meetings when it seemed desirable. A credit university course, tuition paid by the school district, was offered. Twenty-three teachers took advantage of the course to

(1) provide new perspective on their experience, (2) improve their evaluative procedures, and (3) clarify plans for the future.

This community case study illustrates several aspects of the counselor-consultant function: (1) leadership without compulsion, (2) emphasis on process instead of preplanned product, (3) involvement and autonomy of teachers. It seems pertinent to suggest that the added dimension of interpersonal process groups dealing with "How you come across to me," led by competent facilitators, might have been a desirable feature.

SKILLS OF THE COUNSELOR-CONSULTANT

Consulting is a natural role of *professional* counselors because of their skills in facilitating communication and their understanding of the dynamics of interpersonal relations. The foregoing material indicates that improved communication between departments of the school and functionaries is essential to the successful initiation and maintenance of innovation. The skilled counselor who has a bold belief in himself is the professional to whom reference is made here. We have due respect for the beginning counselor and for the counselor who is serious enough to have the American Personnel and Guidance Association, or a principal, or a school board, or the state board of education define his role. However, we have in mind the highly competent counselor who defines his own role by virtue of his communicative skills — both individual and group. There can be no illusion that anyone is waiting with welcoming arms the creation of the role herein described. It will not be sold; it will be won in the sense that the proof of the pudding is in the eating. Results are the criteria (Harrison, 1970). Most parents, pupils, teachers, and administrators will readily admit that someone needs to do the job.

Danskin, Kennedy, and Friesen (1965) were among the first to see the need for a "radical redefinition of the school counselor's role." They postulated that less time should be spent in testing and individual educational, personal, and vocational counseling and more time with learning climates of the school, and with teachers and administrators. They expressed the belief that counselors are fully capable of (1) developing a frame of reference for human development, (2) searching for the significant determinants of learning, and (3) communicating to the school staff the human development stance. Their fourth emphasis was that a counselor should:

Demonstrate his human development stance by being authentically interested (a) in a teacher who is concerned for his own professional career, (b) in an administrator who has doubts about the school's image, (c) in a student who fears that he is not liked by his classmates, or (d) in the parent who is confused over and concerned for his child's attitudes and habits. This is to say, somewhat paradoxically, that the counselor can be free to invest a direct and personal interest in the growth and development of each of these — for that person's *own sake*, not primarily because this will lead to a better learning environment.[3]

Improving the Learning Milieu

EMPHASIS ON SELF

While one may agree that the person takes priority over actions which "will lead to a better learning environment," actually the two goals would not often conflict. That which enhances the ego concept also tends to facilitate learning. Because the purpose of the school is the encouragement of learning, improving the learning milieu may be a major function for the school counselor. Kehas stresses that a valuable kind of learning, all too frequently overlooked, is that of continuing development of intelligence about self. He regards facilitating the acquisition of this kind of intelligence as the unique professional responsibility and competence of the counselor (Kehas, 1969). The emphasis on self and self-knowledge as contrasted to knowledge about other things and people helps to clarify the difference in role of teachers and counselors. It does not, however, negate the fact that the pursuit of either kind of knowledge is aided by teamwork. Effective guidance and personnel work is most properly performed by a "hierarchy of personnel" (Howe, 1968).

BECOMING VS. DOING

Much of the unrest in high schools and colleges may be seen as centering about the notion of becoming vs. doing. It is unfortunate that this kind of polar thinking characterizes so many of man's prob-

---

[3] David G. Danskin, Carroll E. Kennedy, Jr., and Walter S. Friesen, 1965, "Guidance: The Ecology of Students," *Personnel and Guidance Journal,* 44:134. Reprinted by permission of the publisher.

lems, but the black-white (with no gray) phenomenon must be dealt with. Many young people seem to be repudiating the organized knowledge presented via the school curriculum as it tries to do the job society has conceptualized for it. The daily school tasks are branded as irrelevant and inconsequential. It is alleged that the curriculum is not concerned with the NOW and with the processes of becoming. This has been the reaction of lower-class pupils for a long time (Lynd and Lynd, 1929; Hollingshead, 1949), but students from all social strata are now voicing the indictment. Some scholars go as far as to say they are less interested in becoming than involved in the act of being.

Rather than taking sides in the argument about whether the "traditional" curriculum or the "whims of the pupils" — and their being — should take precedence, we prefer to agree with Goodman (1968) that, at least in the elementary school, any experience can be educative as long as the child wants to learn something further. Many factors in our culture point to the importance of emphasizing the process of education instead of becoming engrossed in the content or product.

Cultural and technological change is so rapid that college students have been warned that much of what they learn in their freshman and sophomore years will be obsolete by the time they have been graduated. Change is so rapid that the majority of pupils now in junior high school will work at jobs which do not yet exist. It has been predicted that the typical worker will make five or six major job changes during his lifetime. In view of the knowledge explosion — the body of knowledge currently doubling in less than ten years — the focus of education must be on process rather than content. Educators simply do not have the prescience to judge what students will most need to know. Hence, as suggested by Goodman, attention must be directed to an individual's enjoying the process of education to such an extent that he has an active desire to learn more. There must be an emphasis on the creation of such ego strength that an individual knows he is a worthy person quite capable of learning that which is new and demanding. The pupil must be helped to achieve enough independence to pursue his own education after the guardianship of a teacher has been terminated.

While immature individuals need not be indulged to the point of learning only what they freely choose, neither should their preferences of subject matter and their individuality of learning style be cavalierly ignored, as they have been in the past. Without being prescriptive as to content, we suggest that counselor-consultants assume leadership in discussions by students, teachers, parents, and administrators regarding both the content and the process of education.

Another factor that makes genuine involvement of the student in his own education a necessity is the declining demand for unskilled labor. One implication of this is that more and more pupils will be in school for longer and longer periods of time. There is simply no place provided in our culture for meaningful participation of young people. Hence the phenomenon known as prolonged adolescence — and there is no indication that the trend will be reversed. Already the recognition of having "no significant place in society" has contributed to unrest and, often, alienation. Again the implications call for study, especially in terms of the impact upon ego concepts. Teachers, counselors, and other school personnel need to study teaching methods, school policies, regulations, teacher-pupil relationships — all the things which tend to erode the ego concepts of youth as well as those which tend to fortify them. Except for taking a few courses in educational psychology and mental health, educators are not greatly concerned. Where the ingredients of the self-concept are studied, it is in teacher preparation programs and occasionally in in-service education. A few pupils gain recognition as being significant persons by earning high marks in school, but this avenue is of necessity limited to a few (Meyer, 1969). It seems inevitable that new concepts of success in the educational enterprise must be evolved if more students are to enjoy the sense of accomplishment that is requisite to continued participation. Adults who are not well coordinated do not *have* to play golf. Those whose memory span is short do not *have* to play bridge. But differences in aptitudes are largely ignored in school; the custom is to run the prescribed course in the prescribed time or consider yourself a failure. You may be tolerated but you will not be respected. Antidotes to this sadistic approach are at hand: the elimination of competitive grades, the provision of more alternative choices — and even tests that probe hitherto unacknowledged aptitudes.

IN-SERVICE EDUCATION

In addition to emphasizing ego concepts, improving the learning milieu means giving attention to the school's sociological environment. Boy and Pine (1969) present the view that if counselors were committed to changing the sociological aspect of the school the demand for individual and group counseling would be eased. Because sociology is the study of people living together, the matter of in-service education has pertinence when in-service work is schoolwide.

Too frequently in-service education is a matter of individual teachers' pursuing varied interests by means of summer school, evening classes, independent study, travel, and occasional schoolwide workshops. Except for the latter, these disparate activities have little pervasive effect and do nothing to improve the sociological functioning of the school. Even the workshops are "one-shot," inspirational approaches unaccompanied by periodic reinforcement or even evaluative follow-up.

In schools that have made notable improvement in the humane treatment of children and academic achievement the school staff as a whole, and often representatives of the community, have been included (Cottle, 1969a; Harrison, 1970). In-service education *involving the whole staff* capitalizes on factors which are known to make education and learning easier. Peer influences, for example, have an effect on teachers' as well as pupils' learning. Learning tends to be facilitated when one knows that he belongs and when he recognizes that his involvement is desired and may be significant. Learning tends to be facilitated when peers provide models, ideas, and suggestions. Learning is facilitated when significant persons in the environment observe and evaluate the processes and products of learning. In novel situations one's margin of comfort is expanded when the new can be approached in company with colleagues. In an experimental situation one's confidence is enhanced when day-to-day events can be discussed with and assessed by a colleague who shares the experience. The important factor of feedback functions in a group but may be absent when the experimental approach is tried only here and there. In addition, the results of learning, when applied by all staff members on a schoolwide basis, have a cumulative and corroborating effect.

Because feelings, convictions, and personal preferences are implicated in modification of school processes, one trained to deal with affect is in an advantageous position to lend help.

The mental outlook of the total staff is greatly influenced by the work that is done during the planning, investigating, and decision-making stages. Teachers will vary tremendously in their attitude toward an undertaking such as the nongraded school. Initially attitude will probably range from enthusiastic support to open opposition. Recognition of these varied attitudes is important in selecting those persons who will be most active in the investigation and planning stages; also, this recognition assures those raising serious objections that their concerns will be sincerely and conscientiously recognized and investigated. Those who offer serious objections can often provide appropriate dimensions to be included in the evaluation and appraisal phases which must be a part of the initial decision and of the plan which is inaugurated. It is important also to point out to these objectors that all possible alternatives will be investigated impartially.

There will be many discussions of the new plan in the informal organization of the school, and as the plan progresses, there will be many questions from students and from adult members of the community. Questions will not always be asked of persons best qualified to answer them. In these cases it is important that the attitude encountered by the questioning parent or student is one sympathetic to the project being undertaken. Administrators have learned from the National Science Foundations project that parents are very willing to have their children participate in a project that is clearly labeled experimental, if they can be assured that it has been carefully planned by competent persons who will thoroughly appraise the results.[4]

The function of the counselor-consultant as a facilitator of in-service education is further indicated by the part which sensitivity groups might play. Such things as are indicated in the above citation have been dealt with in a school system in Pennsylvania.

The situation was bad, but it could have been far worse. What helped was the sensitivity and understanding shown by adminis-

[4] Roy A. Larmee, "A Strategy for the Development of Nongraded Schools." From *Nongraded Schools in Action: Bold New Venture*, edited by David W. Beggs, III, and Edward G. Buffie. Copyright © 1967 by Indiana University Press. P. 82. Reprinted by permission of the publisher.

trators and teachers in their negotiating with students, parents, and community leaders. Somehow, punishment seemed far less important to them than communication, and somehow, too, these administrators and teachers seemed humanly prepared for the situation.

Behind their preparation was a valuable experience with a human relations training program from which the Intergroup Education Committee was an offshoot. The education leaders of Bristol Township had discovered the efficacy of this kind of training and during the winter of 1967–68 had asked Professor Max Birnbaum of the Boston University Human Relations Laboratory in New York City to develop a human relations training program for the school district. . . .

Public attention has focused increasingly, in recent months, on various approaches to "sensitivity training," and as public interest has grown, so has the confusion over just what such training is all about. There are, in fact, a number of different brands of sensitivity training, each with its own objectives, techniques, and outcomes in personal and institutional change. Professors Robert Chin and Kenneth D. Benne in their study, *The Planning of Change*, identify three different approaches. The first, based on the now traditional T-group (Training-group) experience, is designed to produce personal growth, understanding, and development. The second, aimed primarily at developing better intergroup relations, seeks understanding through radical confrontations in which members of hostile groups express their feelings, often in violent fashion, in an effort to encourage mutual understanding.

In contrast to an emphasis on personal growth and development, the third approach stresses interpersonal understanding aimed at improving work efficiency among employees or colleagues.[5]

Most counselors with recent or advanced training in various aspects of counseling will have had some kind of sensitivity training. Hence, as a group, they are in an advantageous position at least to introduce the use of sensitivity groups. If the prediction of Rogers turns out to be correct, the use of sensitivity groups will extend far beyond in-service education and permeate the entire school curriculum.

[5] Thomas J. Cottle, 1969, "Bristol Township Schools: Strategy for Change," *Saturday Review*, 52 (38):71, 79, September 20. Reprinted by permission of the publisher.

It is possible that education will continue much as it is — concerned only with words, symbols, rational concepts based on the authoritative role of the teacher, further dehumanized by teaching machines, computerized knowledge, and increased use of tests and examinations. This is possible, because educators are showing greater resistance to change than any other institutional group. Yet I regard it as unlikely, because a revolution in education is long overdue, and the unrest of students is only one sign of this. So I am going to speculate on some of the other possibilities.

It seems likely that school will be greatly deemphasized in favor of a much broader, thoughtfully devised *environment for learning*, where experiences of the student will be challenging, rewarding, affirmative, and pleasurable.

The teacher or professor will have largely disappeared. His place will be taken by a facilitator of learning, chosen for his facilitative attitudes as much as for his knowledge. He will be skilled in stimulating individual and group initiative in learning, skilled in facilitating discussions-in-depth — of meaning to the student of what is being learned — skilled in fostering creativity, skilled in providing the resources for learning. . . .

. . . Each child will learn that he is a person of worth, because he has unique and worthwhile capacities, he will learn how to be himself in a group — to listen, but also to speak, to learn about himself, but also to confront and give feedback to others. He will learn to be an individual, not a faceless conformist. . . .

His learning will not be confined to the ancient intellectual concepts and specializations. It will not be a *preparation* for living. It will be, in itself, an *experience* in living. Feelings of inadequacy, hatred, a desire for power, feelings of love and awe and respect, feelings of fear and dread, unhappiness with parents or with other children — all these will be an open part of his curriculum, as worthy of exploration as history or mathematics.[6]

ASSESSMENT OF POTENTIAL AND GROWTH

Long established as being within the competence of well-prepared counselors and still demanding greatly improved understanding by teachers is the area of testing and test interpretation. This problem has been approached only infrequently in "whole-staff" in-

[6] Carl R. Rogers, 1968, "Interpersonal Relationships: U.S.A. 2000," *Journal of Applied Behavioral Sciences*, 4:273, 274, 275. Reprinted by permission of the publisher.

service education. The continued misuse and poor use of tests, therefore, warrants considerable emphasis.

Tests are designed to reveal pupil differences and aptitudes and, it is hoped, to improve the teacher's understanding of unique pupil traits and proclivities (Ahmann and Glock, 1967, p. 6). In many schools there is noticeable lack of appreciation that (1) tests are samples rather than accurate measures of aptitudes and achievement, (2) profiles of subscores within a test have at least as much significance as total scores, (3) the concepts of validity and reliability must constantly be kept in mind and be used habitually in interpretation, and (4) the search is for pupil strengths rather than weaknesses. The value of tests resides in their assistance in "enlightened planning of the educational experiences of pupils" (Shertzer and Stone, 1970, p. 224).

Too frequently tests are used to categorize and sort pupils. This action has social and psychological consequences which may invalidate the carefully planned purposes of the test and abort the service envisioned by the test maker. Even test-naïve teachers have observed the feeling of shame and the acceptance of inferiority status of pupils whose scores place them in the lower categories. Teachers have sensed that some "late bloomers" have been denied opportunities for development (for example, participation in the college preparatory curriculum) because of their comparatively late start or comparatively deliberate rate of development. Noting these social and psychological consequences, they have been reluctant, or sometimes have refused, to use test results.

These harmful consequences of the misuse of tests have been summarized by Ebel (1970, p. 228) in terms of (1) placing an indelible stamp of superior, mediocre, or inferior intellectual status on a pupil, (2) developing a limited concept of pupil ability, (3) placing testers in the position of determining human destinies, and (4) rendering the process of decision making a mechanistic one. The antidote might well be the concern of schoolwide in-service education: (1) using tests to evaluate and improve status and developmental processes, (2) broadening the bases of achievement and widening the variety of talents probed by tests, (3) sharing with students, teachers, and parents the approximations indicated by tests, and (4) using test results as an aid and supplement to decision making.

A specific suggestion for the constructive application of tests is made by Taylor (1968b), who recommends giving more tests, rather than discarding them or using fewer samples. He posits this belief on Guilford's theory (1967) of the structure of human intelligence, i.e., that there are at least 120 subabilities or types of intelligence. It is possible to identify by tests over eighty of these, yet typical tests assess only eight — one-tenth of what can be tested and only about one-fifteenth of the theoretical possibilities. Taylor indicates that on any one test there must be, statistically, certain pupils who score in the upper 10 percent. If another test were given, another group of pupils (including a few of the first 10 percent) would be in the upper 10 percent. On a third test, again with some slippage, still another group would be the top 10 percent. Thus, with three tests, about 27 percent of students would be talented in terms of their position in the upper 10 percent on some test. With four tests, about 35 percent might be so placed. At a diminishing rate, as each new type of talent test was added to the battery, the term *talented* could be applied to a greater percentage of students. True, a number would probably not be in any top 10 percent, but most would at least earn the status of "above average" in one respect or another.

> The implications of this phenomenon are exciting because, if a variety of talents are tested and trained for, a student can learn a great deal about himself and his abilities and consequently become self-directed. He can steer himself throughout his life into activities that call for his best talents — a course that can well lead to optimum self-actualization and productivity.[7]

With such a view, tests could help teachers locate talents instead of categorizing pupils. Not only might this lead to the improvement of the learning milieu but the student's self-image would be enhanced. A new point of departure for capitalizing on the self-fulfilling prophecy would be made available to both pupils and teachers.

Another reason why test scores must be taken as indications and approximations is that there are no reliable tests of motivation to perform in an academic discipline. Experienced teachers are often

[7] Calvin W. Taylor, 1968, "Cultivating New Talents: A Way to Reach the Educationally Deprived," *Journal of Creative Behavior*, 2 (2):86. Reprinted by permission of the publisher and the author.

surprised to discover, after having a pupil in class for some time, how low his aptitude score is. They begin to doubt their own perceptions of the pupil's performance. Even on retest the score is substantially the same, and then the teacher begins to question the value of tests in general. The achievement of some pupils quite frequently leads to the conclusion that there are marked differences in the way pupils apply their potential, however low or high it may be. The clues regarding how one will use whatever aptitude he has come mainly from observation of prior performance. It is precisely for this reason that experts in the field of mental retardation refuse to name a precise range of scores to indicate feeble-mindedness, educable retardates, or trainable retardates.

In-service education devoted to the wise utilization of tests can be made to confirm the wisdom and limitations of the teacher's judgment. Both have a legitimate place in the assessment of development and both can be improved through the exchange of information, experiences, and personal beliefs.

The use of tests in providing "remedial" work classes to bring low scorers up to average in some area of achievement is highly questionable. If the classes are successful, the inevitable result will be to raise the average and there will still be some who are below average — and in the lowest 10 percent. If the remedial approach is unsuccessful, the individual's belief that he is an inadequate and incompetent person is confirmed. In such cases efforts to achieve in the deficient as well as in the more proficient areas may be reduced. This is not to say that attempts to improve reading skills or acquire other of the tools of learning should be abandoned. The belief of some is that the area of weakness can best be attacked indirectly by emphasizing the comparative strengths of pupils. Success in the area of competence, it is postulated, will so affect the pupil's self-concept that he can attack the area of weakness with more élan. Of course, some remedial efforts do succeed — through individual attention, recognition of varied styles of learning, individually tailored programs, and even comparison with others of approximately the same ability. Most successful remedial teachers, however, abandon comparisons and simply use the criterion of progress from one point to another. Tests so used, with sufficient frequency to show short-time changes, can provide a graphic representation of progress.

The burden here is not to answer questions about the wise use of tests. It is, rather, to suggest illustrative situations which merit investigation and discussion.

OPEN COMMUNICATION

From the beginning of its existence the human infant needs and demands communication. Unless there is communication — the mutual exchange of signals, gestures, and audible symbols — the infant literally becomes ahuman. His emotional potential fails to develop, and he becomes what Fraiberg (1967) calls a hollow person. Spitz (1949), moreover, has demonstrated that during certain critical early months of life normal intellectual and social growth atrophies in the absence of maternal communication. Successful kindergarten teachers establish the communication requisite to optimum learning by word, gesture, smile, and by *touching* (a hand on the shoulder, rumpling the hair, etc.). Bruner (1968) offers the proposition that the really essential element in the education of the young may be dialogue between the unsophisticated and the experienced person. The great cry of contemporary adolescents is for meaningful communication with parents, teachers, and other adults with whom they come in spatial contact. And the cry of citizens is that "the government" maintain communication with the governed (taxpayers). The "credibility gap" is a personal insult. One of the most common organizational problems of business and service institutions in the breakdown of communication between executives and grass-roots members (Lowry and Rankin, 1969, p. 323).

The "Why don't they . . .?" syndrome is a typical outcome of the absence of facile communication within an organization. For example, teachers ask, "Why don't the principals see that teachers use their sick leave properly?" Principals ask, "Why doesn't the central office get its notices out with a little lead time?" Pupils ask, "Why don't teachers let us know exactly what they want?" And everybody asks, "Why don't parents see that their children acquire some basic skills in citizenship?" The fruitful question, much less frequently asked, is "What can I do to improve the situation about which I am inclined to complain?" The "Why don't they . . .?" question is futile because the persons about whom it is asked seldom know that the issue exists. It is futile too because it tends to arouse and perpetuate hostility. On the other hand, the question "What can I do . . .?" is likely to be productive because that which is most amenable to influence is oneself.

Because any social or organizational question involves more than one person, the most fruitful communication usually takes place where all participants are involved. This participation may be even more productive than limiting action to the assumption of responsibility for one's own action. "Let's talk about it." Talking is so easy and natural that it is hard to say why "communication" is so difficult to initiate and maintain; perhaps feelings of safety come into play. A novel situation or one involving other persons — especially those in authority — seem to pose degrees of threat which vary from slight to overwhelming.

Barriers to communication have been schematized by Kline (1964, p. 194) in what he called a "paradigm of maturity" (Fig. 1-1). He found that persons entering a counselor education program (which included participation in interpersonal process groups) had varying orientations toward the situation. Most were at the lower end of the scale but not at the same level. That is, some were apprehensive while others were resistant, apathetic, or skeptical. The level at which one began the program was not necessarily related to how fast he climbed the ladder of maturity — if he climbed it at all. One might so quickly move from resistance to confidence and trust that the steps taken, by analysis of weekly diaries, were hard to identify. The major method of climbing the spiral of maturity was communication. The communication was implemented by (1) weekly sessions emphasizing interpersonal transactions (personal feelings, attitudes, and perceptions were discussed), (2) scheduled staff-student conferences, including criticism of staff and program, and (3) individually arranged, but not regularly scheduled, student confrontations of each other, and informal discussion of the meaning and implications of the interpersonal aspects of the program.

During the academic year a few students seemed to reach the top, and the open part, of the spiral. Some approached the top. Others, who were so closed that communication could not be established, remained at about the same level, and in a few instances there were regressions, e.g., from skepticism to vigorous resistance.

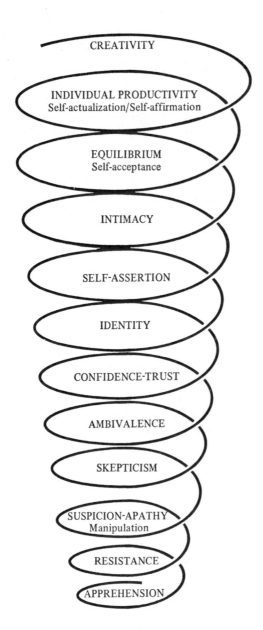

CREATIVITY

INDIVIDUAL PRODUCTIVITY
Self-actualization/Self-affirmation

EQUILIBRIUM
Self-acceptance

INTIMACY

SELF-ASSERTION

IDENTITY

CONFIDENCE-TRUST

AMBIVALENCE

SKEPTICISM

SUSPICION-APATHY
Manipulation

RESISTANCE

APPREHENSION

FIG. 1-1 *The Paradigm of Maturity According to Kline.
From* Counseling: Content and Process *by Daniel W. Fullmer and Harold W. Bernard, p. 194. © 1964, Science Research Associates, Inc. Reproduced by permission.*

It would seem that anything as basic and natural as communication would be easy to achieve. However, one can recognize that even such an effortless and vital phenomenon as breathing may sometimes be improved through conscious attention. Analysis readily reveals that early experiences, traumatic episodes, or experiences pretty much limited to an autocratic authority figure do much to inhibit significant communication. These resistances have been consolidated into the folkways and mores of formality and protocol that hamper communication even in the absence of personality reserve. Nevertheless, evidence is mounting that, under the guidance of competent facilitators, the efficiency of groups can be improved and personal satisfactions of the individual can be enhanced by the direct and conscious study of the dynamics of communication (Birnbaum, 1969; Shostrom, 1969).

A typical response to the dilemma of communication as it affects a school system is to designate it the responsibility of the principal. There are, of course, many answers to the question of whose responsibility it is. Traditionally it has been considered an administrative function. One handicap under which a principal suffers is that he must often make decisions without collaboration, and his role thus seems autocratic. As an authority he automatically inhibits communication on the part of some subordinates. This is the very reason the counselor-consultant should assume the role of communications facilitator. Communication is one of his specific functions. Several of the 1969 Senate Resolutions of the American Personnel and Guidance Association bear directly on this matter:

Resolution No. 1: ". . . the responsible involvement of student population in developing and improving guidance, curricular, and extracurricular programs in schools and colleges. . . ."

Resolution No. 2: ". . . to explore development and enactment of legislation . . . for the encouragement of increased employment of apprentice workers. . . ."

Resolution No. 4: ". . . to consider the local creation of committees . . . to advise on needs in the field, to offer consultation relative to [counselor] preparation programs. . . ."

Resolution No. 6: ". . . supports the principle of increased student involvement and participation in identifying causes of student unrest. . . ."

Resolution No. 7: ". . . to provide consultation, leadership, organization, stimulation, and assistance . . ." (in legislation and national and international concerns in guidance).

Resolution No. 10: ". . . calls upon practitioners of the education profession . . . to attend to the socially meritorious needs of disadvantaged and specially handicapped persons. . . ."

Resolution No. 14: Includes several statements on counselors as consultants in various capacities — all of which call for high-level skills in communication.

Resolution No. 16: Lists nine statements on human rights, including ". . . planning and implementing action toward expanding and guaranteeing human rights. . . ."

To these communication challenges to the counseling profession must be added the day-to-day need of facilitating communication between teachers and pupils, teachers and teachers, teachers and counselors, teachers and specialists, administrators and pupils, and administrators and teachers, and of making parents and citizens realize that their involvement in school affairs is not only needed but appreciated.

It may be necessary to concede that not all counselors are sufficiently skilled, at present, to meet the exacting challenge of expertness in communication. It also seems realistic to claim that counselors, by virtue of their professional preparation, have the best start on the development of the skills required to facilitate the open communication which is essential to effective institutional functioning.

> Preparation of the school administrators of the future will include the academic exploration of conflict as a phenomenon as well as skill training in conflict processing. New techniques currently in embryo will be refined: leadership capacities will be sharpened through simulation, sensitivity training and field experiences. Emphasis on group process, already prominent in leader training, will be extended through in-service designs that will incorporate all members of school organizations into training sequences.[8]

[8] Luvern L. Cunningham, 1967, "Leadership and Control of Education," in E. L. Morphet and C. O. Ryan (eds.), *Implications for Education of Prospective Changes in Society* (Denver: Designing Education for the Future), p. 192. Reprinted by permission of the publisher.

In the meantime, counselors already have access to some of the above-cited techniques. Moreover, they have an advantage over administrators in the facilitating of communication because of (1) professional preparation and (2) the fact that they are not in the authoritative position of having to execute policy.

SKILLS WITH GROUPS

Improving the learning environment means that with increasing years the student becomes less and less dependent on teachers — or other adults. Groups serve a transitional role as young people achieve independence in the shaping of their own future; i.e., peers instead of parents and teachers become the models. Furthermore, we live in a society oriented toward a democratic ideal rather than in an autocratic and stratified society. When groups have best served this transitional function, the child need never be arrested at the level of dependence on either parents, companions, or authoritarian demand. However, groups can be cruel and discriminatory. They can be limited in perspective and thus inhibit the development of the young (Aldridge, 1969). They can have limited perspective and thus be a source of maldevelopment (Meyer, 1969).

Anthropologists have learned that one who is not naturally a member of a certain group can become a part of the group if he does not seek to influence its structure and nature (Kimball, 1967). Sociologists have learned that delinquent or potentially delinquent groups can be transformed into constructive forces by skilled workers who earn acceptance into the group and whose influence is subtle (Sherif and Sherif, 1964). The need for subtlety is illustrated in the phenomenon that such workers are accepted by the group but their identity and purpose are not transformed. The anthropologist recognizes, deals with, and avoids the hazard of "going native."

Groups are significant avenues of achievement for the counselor-consultant for another reason. In many instances the group is a better teaching medium than is individual instruction. Although initially group work was used by counselors as a time-saver, it was quickly discovered that children sometimes learned better from one another than they did from "learned" instructors. The use of peer groups has been especially fruitful in teaching some disadvantaged children — those who have had a number of frustrating experiences with institutional adults, such as social workers, policemen, juvenile

delinquency probation officers. It may take considerable patience and persistence on the part of teachers to convey to young people that they are not "out to get them." And the effort is complicated by the fact that certain incompetent and frustrated teachers have just such a goal.

If counselors could perform no other unique service than expert work with groups, this would provide sufficient basis for widespread recognition. The counselor does not need to know the answer, or an answer, for perplexing school problems. If he possesses or acquires the skill to uncover and process the wisdom of the group, his contribution will be noteworthy. Probably there is no one best approach to educational dilemmas, in view of local needs and differing characteristics of individuals. Efficient group work can achieve the local answers that will, at least temporarily, lead to workable solutions.

Developing Professional Skill

PRE-SERVICE EDUCATION

Only within the past decade have counselor preparation programs consistently had counseling practicums as an essential feature. Prior to the 1960's many programs were devoted largely to studying motivation, personality theory, individual differences, socioeconomic class, vocational orientation, counseling techniques, the use and misuse of tests and inventories, and other academic disciplines related to human development and welfare. Only the outstanding programs provided practicum experiences. Furthermore, practicum experiences could be as sketchy as one or two counseling sessions with a coached client, a college student, or volunteer counselees from a school close to the university campus. Increasingly, the practicum has come to mean at least part-time performance of counseling in the school setting.

Practicum is vital in the preparation of school counselors for a number of reasons. It enables the enrollee to observe at first hand the nature of a helping relationship and to assess his ability to develop and maintain that relationship. It provides the enrollee with an opportunity to develop relationship (counseling) skills under the careful guidance of a competent supervisor. It enables the supervisor to protect student clients against inept practitioners.

And it enables the supervisor to detect those persons who are quite obviously unsuited for the school counselor's task.[9]

In the more exemplary programs counseling students may be assigned full-time counseling duties for a few weeks or a term in a school even at some distance from the campus. Group work under supervision is still an aspiration rather than a uniform requirement. Work with parents and family groups has not yet been widely accepted in counselor education programs. Pierson (1965, p. 64) asserts, as one result of his evaluative study of NDEA Counseling and Guidance Institutes, that "the purposes of counseling and guidance may often be served best by consulting with parents, teachers, and administrators, and by working with representatives from various community agencies." McCully too perceived that consultation was a major issue in planning counselor education programs. He cites the opinion of one observer that it is time to consider deemphasizing individual counseling sessions

. . . in the sterile vacuum of the counselor's office — replace by getting from behind the desk and moving out into the world; working with youngsters where *they* live: working with parents on their own ground; working with teachers and administrators; working with community agencies. The trend lies in the method — no longer do the professional protocols of social worker, psychiatrist, or school psychologist hold any magic. A whole new concept of consultation [is emerging].[10]

Perhaps one of the fastest growing trends in counselor education is that of sensitivity training groups or basic encounter groups for counselor candidates. The major reason for the emphasis is that, unless the counselor knows himself, his beliefs and perceptions will probably get in the way of his understanding counselees. If he cannot accept help from his professional colleagues in the school, he will be unable to help his clients (Pierson, 1965, p. 39).

Encounter groups are not a panacea, although when conducted

[9] George A. Pierson, 1965, *An Evaluation: Counselor Education in Regular Session Institutes,* Washington: Office of Education, U.S. Department of Health, Education, and Welfare.

[10] C. Harold McCully (quoting a respondent in one of his studies), 1969, *Challenge for Change in Counselor Education,* compiled by Lyle L. Miller (Minneapolis: Burgess Publishing Company), p. 152. Reprinted by permission of the publisher.

by competent facilitators they hold great potential for individual, group, and professional enhancement. As an approach to the improvement of human relations they are regarded by some as the most significant social invention that has occurred in many decades. Such persons as Birnbaum (1969), Rogers (1968), and Shostrom (1969) have great hopes for such groups, but they all warn that certain hazards must be avoided if the high promise is not to be transformed into apprehension by quacks, "ax-grinders," and inadequately prepared facilitators who create a bad name and reputation for all sensitivity groups — whether the facilitator is competent or incompetent. Among the hazards are the abandonment of reserves in communication before one has developed sufficient ego strength to withstand assault from others. The facades which inhibit communication, and which are often referred to condescendingly, have been built by much personal experience and serve a useful purpose. The facilitator must be able to recognize an incipient psychotic break and know how to handle it. The open communication practiced in an encounter group is not necessarily effective with persons who have not had similar experiences.

The precautions cited by Birnbaum, Rogers, and Shostrom are somewhat like those directed specifically to counselors by Beymer (1970), who makes eight recommendations: (1) Standard terminology should be developed. (2) The anti-intellectual aspects of some basic encounter groups should be balanced by insistence on facilitators who are not amateurs. (3) Participants should be screened in the hope of detecting those who might be harmed by the reduction of their defenses or facades. (4) The purpose of the group should be clearly defined — therapy, self-understanding, facilitation of communication, etc. (5) Facilitators must face the consequences of their "opening Pandora's box." (6) Better use must be made of existing knowledge in preference to constructing a brand-new behavioral science. (7) Participants must have volunteered and must be able to withdraw without criticism. (8) Focus should be primarily on outcomes rather than techniques.

Growth and change entail risk. While the counselor-consultant will be uncomfortable in many new situations, his temporary toleration of the discomfort will increase his reserves of comfort. One area of comfort that should be removed is that of continued functioning in what have been shown to be relatively unproductive fields. For example, it will involve discomfort to ask a teacher whether one may work with a child in the classroom to study his response to the learning milieu. But that discomfort is better than confining one's efforts to counseling with the pupil in the office. This emphasis is intimately related to the "Why don't they . . .?" syndrome. If the reader accepts the challenge that an important contribution of the professional counselor is related to the climate of the school and the climate for the facilitation of learning, he cannot be content to blame his own limited training. It is up to him to plan for change and to establish the role of counselor-consultant. One approach is in-service education.

IN-SERVICE EDUCATION

In view of the characteristic slowness of educational change and the characteristic speed with which other changes take place today, in-service education for teachers will probably increase rapidly. Typically, when reading about schools which had success with some innovation, or successfully faced down some crisis, one will find mention of a series of professional meetings which prepared the staff for competent involvement. Paving the way for such meetings and encouraging their continuation may be one service the counselor-consultant can render. An administrator can arrange in-service meetings, but they suffer the handicap of being demanded — the meetings immediately assume an authoritarian image. Counselors, with their skills in communication and their focus on pupil welfare, can implement in-service meetings by showing the need for cooperative staff involvement. It is the counselor who possesses established contacts with administrators, supervisors, specialists, parents, pupils, and teachers.

Formally organized in-service education will not usually be the fortunate lot of those who wish to create the role of counselor-consultant along the lines suggested herein. Lacking the preparatory experiences of laboratory and field work in his program of preparation, one will have to conduct his own in-service education. This can be done by trying it — asking a teacher whether she is willing to permit a classroom visitor so Frankie can be observed and so the two of you can plan some developmental experiences for him. Parents can be asked whether they would like to meet together to discuss their common perplexities with Sue, Jack, Don, Ed, and Sharon. Such meetings should suggest to the counselor-consultant articles and books to be read — or reread in the light of current transactions. The implication is that group meetings do not serve their maximum utility when they consist of the sharing of ignorance.

It may be that the counselor-consultant takes on his evolving responsibilities by initiating communication with the principal or with community agents and resource persons. The idea is that self-directed in-service education is, in the present milieu, a necessity. The precedents for the role have not been established.

Summary

The counselor-consultant function is not new in terms of what has been done in piecemeal fashion. It is new in that someone becomes responsible for giving attention to the total learning milieu of the school — as a primary concern. It is new in that the processes involved are based on communication and the perception of common destinies rather than being the result of administrative edict. Counselors may create the envisioned role by virtue of their skills in communication and group work.

Improving the learning milieu is the key item in the counselor-consultant's concerns. It means focusing on the processes of becoming and growing rather than on prescriptive doing. The necessary involvement in the process of continuous learning on the part of all school personnel may be achieved by in-service education based on the need for assessing pupil growth, establishing open communication, and facilitating group interaction.

Counselors on the job are not necessarily experienced in the suggested wider application of counseling skills. It is therefore recommended that they take initiative for making step-by-step progress toward the responsibilities involved. There is not enough time to wait for administrative edict or enactment of professional legislation.

SUGGESTED ADDITIONAL READINGS

Beymer, Lawrence, 1970. "Confrontation Groups: Hula Hoops?" *Counselor Education and Supervision, 9:75–86. The author criticizes sensitivity groups because they (1) are anti-intellectual,*

(2) *may produce change for the worse, (3) often shift in stated purposes to therapy, (4) are often led by facilitators who do not face consequences. In order to capitalize on the great potential of confrontation groups, he makes eight recommendations.*

Collins, Peter M., 1970. "Some Philosophical Reflections on Teaching and Learning," *The Record — Teachers College,* 71:413–421. *Basic topics such as the meaning of education, the distinction and relationship of teaching and learning, authority, and independence are discussed. All these seem quite relevant to the function of counselor-consultants.*

Harrison, Charles H., 1970. "South Brunswick, N.J.: Schools Put a Town on the Map," *Saturday Review,* 53(8):66–68+, February 21. *By making the principals within his district aware of their human relations impact, a school superintendent planted the seeds of trust, responsibility, innovation, and concern for children and provided impetus for improved learning climate. This is an indication of the role projected in the present volume for the counselor-consultant.*

Hart, Leslie A., 1969. "Learning at Random," *Saturday Review,* 52(16):61–63, April 12. *Many items relating to the creation of a favorable learning climate are discussed. The propositions which are stated would provide an appropriate agenda for discussions instigated by the counselor-consultant.*

Schrag, Peter, 1969. "Gloom at the Top," *Saturday Review,* 52(33):50–51, August 16. *The demands of students to be heard are given lip service by teachers and administrators. The fact is that they do not even hear what the students are saying — or realize that they are not hearing. Communication, facilitated by the counselor-consultant, may not be the answer but it is an approach.*

Chapter Two

PSYCHOLOGICAL
BASES FOR
COUNSELING-CONSULTING

The *process* of learning is emerging more clearly as a major emphasis in the professional work of educators. In the recent past, content has, with justification, been a primary concern. This does not mean that the process of learning has ever been overlooked. John Dewey, William H. Kilpatrick, Frederick S. Breed, Henry Tyler, and certainly others have emphasized for several decades that education is a social process (Silberman, 1970).

Realization of the loss to the nation of failing to emphasize process rather than content when dealing with gifted and creative pupils is another factor bearing on the current interest in process. Jerome Bruner, Abraham Maslow, Carl Rogers, and Arthur Combs are contemporaries who have emphasized the centrality of both the person and the process in effective learning. Finally, the phenomenon of rapid change suggests the futility of emphasizing content to the virtual exclusion of process. When much of what one learns in school is obsolete by the time he has been graduated, the process — with stress on continuous learning — must become a central focus.

This chapter will describe emergent psychological emphases showing how proactive psychology has come to supplement the reactive orientation of psychoanalytic and behavioristic views. The thesis that the self-concept is central in optimum learning is developed. The self-concept, in turn, is a function of human relationships, and when the self-concept is robust, the individual is more capable of exercising responsibility for his own continuous learning — both in and out of school. It is postulated in this book that the counselor-consultant of the 1970's should be a resource person, to school personnel and pupils, in promoting the human relationships that are conducive to optimum learning.

The Merging Emphases in Psychological Orientation

PSYCHOLOGY OF THE SCHOOLS

The psychological tradition prevailing among school teachers has long been connectionism, postulated by E. L. Thorndike. One of the laws of learning emphasized was the "law of exercise." This meant that the more frequently a bond between a stimulus and response was exercised the stronger it became. Thus, teachers went in for drill, repetition, and review in their efforts to consolidate learnings. Our own ability to repeat the multiplication tables, the Pythagorean theorem, and the names of state capitol cities, or even to respond, when only half-aware, to our own name demonstrates the utility of the concept. It would seem that exercise will continue to be a valuable teaching approach, especially in the tool subjects of reading, writing, and arithmetic.

Thorndike also postulated the "law of effect." This meant that when a modifiable connection between a stimulus and a response was accompanied or followed by a feeling of satisfaction the bond was strengthened. The bond was weakened if the result was annoying or unsatisfactory. Later he modified this law because, although satisfaction strengthened the bond, annoyance did not seem to weaken it. Annoyance did, however, prompt the learner to seek a new response. Learnings are rarely simple, nor can they be explained on a single factor. Nevertheless, for multiple reasons, teachers typically seek to make classrooms pleasant and to provide pupils with various forms of satisfaction — even to pasting gold stars on the foreheads of successful primary pupils, giving high grades to exemplary high school pupils, and conferring honors on outstanding college students.

These practices merit critical evaluation, not because the law of effect does not operate, but because the law operates on all pupils — not just the academically successful ones. Connectionism was also founded on a third law — the "law of readiness." This stated that when the learner was mature enough to respond successfully his resultant learning brought satisfaction. To attempt a response before one was ready, or sufficiently mature, resulted in annoyance. This phenomenon is most clearly perceived in learning to be toilet trained, to talk, or to walk. It is familiar in the school setting in reading readiness; with some variance due to experiential background (motivation) and nature of the reading material, children can most easily learn to read if they have reached the mental age of about six and a half years. Bruner (1963, p. 12) raises a question about readiness by stating that any subject may be successfully taught at any age in *some form*. Again, learnings are complex and variable rather than single and simple. School personnel would be well advised to continue accepting the law of readiness in terms of psychological maturity, cultural milieu of the pupil, and unique perceptions of the individual.

Thorndike was by no means unaware of the exceptions indicated above. In addition to the three primary laws of learning he proposed five secondary principles. (1) The principle of multiple response meant that many responses might be tried before a satisfying one was hit upon. (2) The principle of mental set referred to the attitude of the learner. In the contemporary setting this is well illustrated in the desire of middle-class pupils to do assigned school tasks and the disdain of lower-class pupil for "Mickey Mouse" school requirements. (3) The principle of partial activity recognized that a response could be, and often is, made to only parts of a total situation. (Thus, it is contended in this book that the school — part of a total learning milieu — can be most effective when it functions in coordination with the family, another major aspect of the pupil's world.) (4) The principle of analogy or assimilation asserts that when a learner is faced by an unfamiliar situation he makes a response which resembles an earlier response to what appears to be a similar situation. Again, this principle has been successfully used by middle-class teachers for middle-class pupils but not so successfully when dealing with pupils who are culturally different. (5) The principle of associative shifting suggests that any response may be attached to any stimulation to which the learner is tuned or to which he is sensitive. Thus, a pupil who is viewed as a reading failure by his teacher has a tendency to see himself as a failure in art, or social relations, or athletics; Thorndike, it seems, might also have been one of the first to formulate the idea of the "self-fulfilling" prophecy.

BEHAVIORISM IN THE SCHOOLS

Although the early educational psychology texts were written largely from the connectionistic point of view, behaviorism is also a widely accepted orientation. John B. Watson's research, teaching, and writing dealt with the matter of conditioning. Very simply, indeed over-simply, this means that for an ongoing response a substitute stimulus can be made to become an adequate stimulus for a given response. The classic example is the case of a dog which salivates at the sight of meat presented as food. If each time, at about the moment the meat is presented, a bell is rung, the dog is conditioned to salivate at the sound of the bell. This may be diagramed as follows:

$$S \text{ (meat)} \longrightarrow R \text{ (salivation)}$$
$$\text{simultaneous}$$
$$S + S_2 \text{ (bell)} \longrightarrow R$$
$$\text{After a few responses } S_2 \longrightarrow R$$

The important thing is that reward or reinforcement strengthens an ongoing response. This aspect of conditioning has been emphasized by B. F. Skinner (1959, pp. 359 ff.), who has, in animal laboratories and classrooms, shown that immediate reinforcement of an action tends to consolidate that action. Thus, a pigeon can learn to play ping-pong by being given a grain of food each time it approximates and then gets closer and closer to the response sought by the experimenter. This is known as instrumental conditioning and is accomplished on operant behavior (that which is taking place). The classroom application is the use of teaching machines. *Each* time a pupil gives a correct response, the machine rewards him by figuratively saying, "That's right. Now go to the next item." Much teaching, Skinner (1954) suggests, is ineffective because it is not possible for teachers to give the steady schedule of reinforcement that is conducive to optimum learning. (He further states, pointedly, that cultural inertia keeps educators from making more use of machines which would provide the requisite frequent and immediate reinforcement needed.) Another advantage of the teaching machine over the teacher is that the lessons are individualized. The pupil can proceed at his own speed, fast or slow, because as soon as he responds correctly he may tackle the next item. In a typical classroom a pupil might work several multiplication problems incorrectly before the teacher discovered that his one error was in recording a product of 44 from the multiplication of 7×6. Moreover, a machine guides toward the correct response without making the pupil feel he is a fool in the eyes of classmates or teacher.

Even without machines behavioristic theory and its accompaniment — reinforcement — can be, and is, used by classroom teachers. Reinforcement is afforded by words of commendation, a nod of approval, a remark that the teacher is pleased with the social behavior and academic performance of the class. But in moments of exasperation words of censure and sarcasm may serve to reinforce a dislike for school and academic activities. Whether supported by hehavioristic theory or some other psychological principle, *the teacher as a person* is a factor in the "schedule of reinforcement." Sometimes, for instance, pupils are conditioned to dislike school because their rewards (grades) are unsatisfactory, or because of a cross, demanding, and nonunderstanding teacher. And the teacher may have been conditioned to behave as he does because of his parents, his teachers, and his supervisors. There is, in short, much to be learned from behavioristic theory quite apart from the possible wide adoption of machine teaching.

PSYCHOANALYTIC THEORY

Counselors owe much of their understanding of the development and background of personality to psychoanalytic theory. The very least that can be said of Sigmund Freud and his followers and colleagues is that the theory was never static — dogmatic at times, yes, but never lacking in further development and transition. This alone might constitute an orientation for the school counselor-consultant in the 1970's.

There are, in addition, many psychoanalytic emphases which deserve serious study, contemplation, and adoption by counseling and guidance specialists: emphasis on childhood experiences, which are not easily forgotten; emphasis on the importance of love and acceptance, which is recognized widely outside of the psychoanalytic aura; recognition that psychological trauma may deeply influence what one learns; acknowledgment that the sex drive is natural, normal, and powerful and that family and cultural conditioning may pervert and distort its normal expression; acknowledgment of subconscious or unconscious drives to behavior, which can advantageously be brought to the surface of consciousness in counseling sessions, can then be recognized by the counselee, and can be handled by appropriate methods.

Psychoanalytic theory, in addition to providing clues to the understanding of personality, suggests some counseling techniques which might well become part of the counselor's armamentarium. On occasion, when the counselee is *ready*, advice may be given, e.g., vocational advice in the presence of indecision (but not when the counselee shows an opposing tendency). More frequently the decisions should be those of the counselee — as the result of the catharsis of thought and doubts and as the result of talking, which is often a means of thought clarification. Free association is a psychoanalytic method. Strictly speaking, it means that the counselee responds with the first word that occurs to him when he is given a key word — *mother, love, steal, fight,* etc. In practice it means that the counselee is encouraged to talk freely so the things that are perplexing him most are allowed to emerge. When the counselee is prompted too much by questions he can, inadvertently, be led to talk about the things the counselor deems important. The long series of counseling sessions which characterizes psychoanalysis suggests that counseling is the purchase of friendship. This factor might be considered by the impatient counselor who is in a hurry to get results. It may be that an attentive ear is more conducive to learning than is the proffering of counsel.

Other psychoanalytic concepts directly or indirectly influence personality theory — sibling rivalry, mother-daughter rivalry, stages of development, birth order — but the purpose here is to suggest that there is value in studying the theory. Not only was Freud innovative, but so too are the neo-Freudians who are following him theoretically and chronologically.

OTHER PSYCHOLOGICAL ORIENTATIONS IN THE SCHOOL

The psychologies discussed briefly above are not the only theories influencing school practice. Robert S. Woodworth, in an orientation which others called dynamic psychology, gave more attention to the behaving organism than was popular at the time. A number of persons contributed to what is known as Gestalt psychology, which emphasized the totality of behavioral situations, the multiple forces that shaped a response — including the perception of the individual. The trend in recent years has been for psychologists and educational psychologists to deny adherence to any one particular "school" of their discipline. Despite disdainful accusations that such nonadherents are wishy-washy eclectics, psychologists are selecting their viewpoints from various sources. They are seeking for consistency even as they draw from the thoughts and writings of persons who focused on different aspects of the complex thing called human behavior. Eclecticism may be anathema to some but it is a professional way of life to others.

PROACTIVE OR HUMANISTIC PSYCHOLOGY

The one big point that distinguishes emerging psychological orientation from its antecedents — connectionism, behaviorism, and psychoanalytic theory — is the matter of perspective. The earlier psychologies tended to perceive the organism, the learner, as being acted upon by external forces. To a marked extent, man was seen as a victim of surrounding circumstances. A growing number of psychologists are developing and lecturing and writing about an orientation in which the person is understood to be an active force in his own life. This evolving orientation is called proactive psychology to indicate that man is more than the product of his past. He can dream dreams, make plans, set goals, foresee the consequences of his acts, and behave accordingly. He does more than react to the past and present; he himself has the power to influence the future. Proactive psychology is a synthesis derived from empirical science, the study of man as a being, and of humanistic insight (Bonner, 1965, p. 5). Man can choose, man can hope, and man can strive.

The evolving psychology deals with the individual. Differences, whatever their source — biological, cultural, perceptual — are recognized, and the danger of generalizations is acknowledged. Observations about behavior are made in terms of tendencies, probabilities, and contingencies. It was no doubt a humanistic counselor who said, "I can't tell you why boys steal apples, but I can discover why *a boy* steals apples."

Choice, freedom, and responsibility are points of interest to the humanistic psychologist. One must be freed, by parents and teachers, to choose, but because one is free he must assume responsibility. Because the counselor cannot always continue to be present at the time of counselee choice, and because one cannot learn independence through being dependent, the counselor must teach the counselee the operational meaning of choice and responsibility. Further, this can be done better when the teacher is functioning on a parallel track with the counselor.

The phenomenon of the self-fulfilling prophecy illustrates the tendency for one to be or become that which he believes and expects he can be. Rosenthal and Jacobson (1968) found that even school pupils with limited ability tended to achieve well when the teacher expected them to accomplish much. The prophecy also works in reverse: If little is expected and one has little hope for himself, then little is achieved. This tendency has been noted frequently in the academic behavior of children who are culturally different. What one believes about himself — his self-concept — is important to his learning efficiency.

The self-concept is derived from human relationships. Psychoanalytic literature provides many case studies of children who believed they were "no good" because their parents were, or appeared to be, chronically dissatisfied with them. It is theorized that hippies dress as they do and college students protest because they have had insufficient or inadequate contact with adults. They fail to develop a sense of identity because their peer associates are similarly lacking a sense of identity (Bettelheim, 1969). By presenting the challenge of the task and giving some leadership, the counselor-consultant can teach teachers and parents the reciprocal and contingent relationships which foster strong self-concepts in pupils. Self-direction is both a cause and a result of self-esteem.

Some Postulates of Learning Economy

The following pages present a number of principles of learning which have been derived from theoretical postulations and experimental evidence.[1] Somewhere, in some school, they have been put

---

[1] The postulations were formulated for the most part by conversations and collaborations with a colleague, Dr. Wesley Huckins, now at Wright State

into practice and the results have been gratifying. Mostly, however, they are discussed in educational literature and teachers' lounges more than they are applied in the classroom.

TEACHER PERSONALITY

A pupil's school learning is facilitated if he has teachers who are curious, openminded, innovative, and enthusiastic and who have faith in children. It has been known for some time that the method of teaching is less important to learning success than is teacher personality. A teacher who used "progressive" methods, for example, might be more successful than a teacher who used traditional approaches. Yet the first teacher, using traditional methods, would still get better results — in subject matter mastery and pupil behavior — than the second, who also switched methods. Some teachers, no matter what the subject or method, chronically have more difficulty with classroom control than do others. A panel on Innovation and Experiment in Education (1964, p. 13) stated that out of its study of new curricula in mathematics, science, and social studies came a promising conclusion: Effective learning occurs when there is a "contingent relationship" between learner and teacher — i.e., when the learner has some control over the pacing of information he acquires and over the nature of that information. The ideal relationship, says the panel, is dialogue between learner and tutor.

Professional educators cannot assume that teachers are born and not made. Just as knowledge is acquired and habits are learned, so too is personality acquired and steadily, even if slowly, altered. The characteristics of curiosity, open-mindedness, enthusiasm, faith in pupils, and desire to be innovative can be cultivated. Teachers can be encouraged to enjoy problem solving and, can in turn, teach pupils to enjoy the search for answers (Bruner, 1968).

Didactic instruction directed toward teacher personality traits has been only partially successful. The counselor, acting as a consultant and using the school staff as educator, can help teachers develop the characteritsics mentioned in this postulation of learning. The

---

University, Dayton, Ohio. They have been examined by several psychologists and educators from various universities, who agreed with most of them but asserted, and we concurred, that they are but one interpretation of the process of learning. The postulations are largely grounded in proactive, humanistic psychology but at many points are in at least partial harmony with some of the psychological viewpoints mentioned earlier.

characteristics can be modeled by the consultant's adoption of them. He can, for example, be curious and open minded about what teachers feel and say. He can practice those psychologically sound innovations which teachers propose. And instead of supplying the answers, he can provide a setting in which dialogue takes place. Both teachers and consultants teach what they *are* at least as much as what they *say*.

HETEROSTASIS VS. HOMEOSTASIS

The learning of pupils is facilitated when their natural, normal, and innate curiosity — their urge to grow and become and to exercise their capacities — is recognized by teachers. This postulation is given lip service. In practice, the homeostatic urge — to rest, to minimize effort, to take it easy — seems to be uppermost in the minds of teachers. To counteract the homeostatic tendency they rely on complicated systems of rewards, grades, threats, punishment, and verbal reinforcement. Yet given a chance, pupils show that they enjoy activity, find satisfaction in the mastery of facts, and proudly display their newly acquired knowledge. They demonstrate, until it is knocked out of them, that they respond to the heterostatic urge to grow, become, and pursue self-actualization. Menninger (1963, p. 84) contends that to ignore the heterostatic urge to effect change, to initiate disturbance, to seek newness, variety, and opportunity is to accept a one-sided interpretation of the causes of behavior. One learns to be passive and defensive when his heterostatic tendencies are consistently thwarted. With the heterostatic principle in mind we can understand why little boys climb trees and grown men climb mountains. We can understand why small children fight off the hands of solicitous mothers and protest, "I can do it myself." We can understand why teachers sometimes object to having a troublesome pupil taken from the classroom to the counselor's office.

Unfortunately, some adults have for so long been subjects of repressive regulations, slaves of a system, members of the establishment, and on the rolls of the gray-flannel-suit coterie that the heterostatic urges have given way to encapsulation by the system. The realistic consultant, therefore, cannot rely on the heterostatic urge alone to induce teachers to make changes in their personality and instructional methods. Smith (1967, p. 66) warns, as a parallel, that an educational program for pupils cannot be successfully operated on intrinsic motives alone. At least for some it will be necessary to counsel teachers individually, to seek administrative pressure or the pressure of peer groups in order to engender the desire to exercise heterostatic motives.

SELF-CONCEPT

The learning of school tasks proceeds most efficiently when teachers acknowledge, through attitude and action, that a robust self-concept is an integral part of a pupil's readiness for learning. The pupils teachers appreciate most are those who are confident and industrious, accept guidance, regard the teacher as their friend, and do not vie for extra attention. Such pupils think so well of themselves that they have no need to seek extra contact with the teacher and are not defensive in their behavior toward peers. They feel they are able, accepted by others, and of enough worth to maintain their individuality. Their sturdy self-concepts are a reflection of the way they have been treated by key persons in their lives — parents, siblings, teachers, and close friends. These self-concepts are also a result of the predominance of success over failure, and probably their failures were in self-chosen activities.

It is likely that a great mass of creative talent, not necessarily academic, is lost as a national resource because divergent thinkers are suppressed or criticized for their nonconformity (Taylor, 1968a). There is a concomitant lowering of the pupil's self-respect and confidence. These creative and divergent thinkers are slightly extreme illustrations of many other pupils who for reasons of low intelligence, physical unattractiveness, or defect are not readily accepted and whose self-concepts thereby suffer. A huge task of every school staff is to develop its own positive regard for a much wider range of normality so that more pupils can develop a stronger self-concept.

The challenge to the counselor-consultant has at least three dimensions. (1) He works as a team member with the teacher in the classroom to find ways to strengthen the self-concept of individual boys and girls who currently most need such help. (2) He finds and tries to correct school practices and interpersonal relationships that insidiously undermine the self-concepts of teachers and pupils. Specific instances of such undermining will be cited in interpersonal process groups by individuals, but a common example is seen in the person who "can't get a word in edgewise." On the other hand, the nonacademic talents of teachers are often not recognized (as the unique talents of the creative pupil are unrecognized) — the flair for organization, the quick defense of the helpless, the perception of the needs of "bad" boys. (3) The counselor-consultant must lead the way, developing a talent for discovering the gifts of teachers and casting aside his own defensiveness.

Persistence of Self-Concept. Learning processes will be facilitated when teachers recognize, and interrupt or encourage, the self-sustaining nature of the self-concept. There are no miracles which convert a weak to a strong self-concept overnight. The self-concept changes slowly because not all the conditions which affect its strength and nature change simultaneously. A most salubrious school environment may have to offset the pressure of a burdensome home or community influence. The self-concept changes slowly because it is a factor in the level of aspiration. The pupil who does not do well in a competitive grading system comes to believe that he cannot achieve so he works less diligently and still further lowers his self-concept.

> A hoistman in a mine said to a high school graduate who was working during the summer to get money for college, "Son, you're lucky to have brains. Keep on using them. Me — I'm just a knot-head. Stuck it out through the ninth grade but I couldn't keep up. It's rough being a dumb-bunny." The speaker controlled a two-ton cage which traveled over 2500 feet a minute. At 7:00 in the morning and 4:00 in the afternoon this man stopped the cage at floor level both at the top and at the bottom of the mine shaft. Each trip the cage made stretched the steel cable by which it was suspended and the hoistman had to make a different allowance at the top and bottom of the shaft for each trip. The ten-foot drum of the hoist had to be in a compensated position on each trip. In addition, the vibration of a tight steel cable in a 2500-foot shaft had to be taken into account. This was done by a "dumb-bunny" who was carrying through life a self-concept which was, in some degree, shaped by a school situation.

When one does not expect much of himself, others tend not to expect much of him. Insight into the self-sustaining nature of the self-concept can be achieved by citing (1) many examples via (2) many persons over (3) recurrent periods of time in (4) working groups.

Origins of the Self-Concept. The *self-concept most conducive to optimum learning is fostered in a milieu in which teachers capitalize on the fact that self-concepts originate in a social and psychological context.* The social context productive of healthy ego concept includes the factor of acceptance. Teachers should come to know, through self-examination and interpersonal discussion, what age and kind of pupils they prefer. Some like them docile and conforming; others admire self-assertive, curious, explorative pupils. Some like boys and some prefer girls. Some like them clean and neat and others like the grubby, devil-may-care type. Some prefer the kindergartner, others the middle grader, and some respond most positively to the adolescent. Study of these preferences is not so much designed to alter them as to make teachers aware of them. Through such awareness teachers will have taken a step toward acceptance of a greater variety of pupils.

Pupils also have preferences, as is shown by their choice and cultivation of friends, and these have been graphically illustrated in sociograms. Teachers find that heeding the clues provided in sociograms in their arrangement of working groups, seating patterns, and laboratory partners results in more productive work. Some pupils are revealed by the sociogram to be unchosen (isolates). They can be placed with the much chosen pupils (stars), who by being much chosen demonstrate their aptness in social relationships.

It is suggested that sociometry is a topic worthy of consideration in in-service education. By using the process in in-service classes teachers can appreciate its application in the classroom. They can examine their own feelings as they work in the small group most congenial to them.

Psychological factors that enhance the ego concept include success, involvement, recognition of differences, freedom from anxiety, identification, and opportunities for play (Almy, 1968). None of these is to be achieved through a simple prescription — especially one formulated outside the particular school and region concerned. Fortunately, a typical school staff possesses ample corporate wisdom to devise practical classroom approaches to constructing a milieu favorable to ego enhancement. The counselor-consultant's role is not to teach but to highlight the teachers' successes and to involve them by (1) seeing to it that their opinions and actions *make a difference,* (2) recognizing *their* differences, and (3) reminding the staff of *their* achievements and victories — thus making identification with the staff a matter of pride.

STYLES OF LEARNING

The processes of learning will be improved when teachers recognize and provide for the unique styles of learning which exist within a classroom. Many passing references to "learning styles" are made in professional educational literature, none of them particularly definitive. Riessman (1964), without suggesting that all styles were included in his discussion, mentions people who learn primarily by reading, by hearing, by working quickly or deliberately, by seeing, by doing things physically, by working steadily for long periods, by working sporadically in short sessions; moreover, some people are flexible while others seem to have a one track mind. Nations (1967) adds to this list styles that can be grouped under sensory orientation, responsive mode, and thinking pattern. Sensory orientation relates to whether a pupil learns best by seeing, hearing, or touching. Responsive mode considers whether a pupil learns best in a group or by himself, whether he is a physical participator or an observer, whether he relates most easily to teacher or peers, and whether he is supportive or argumentative. Thinking pattern describes a pupil in terms of whether he gathers details or makes intuitive leaps, whether he gets the overall picture first or constructs it bit by bit out of cumulative data.

It may be that Guilford (1967) comes closer to defining the wide variety of learning styles, but under another heading. In investigating the nature of intelligence he constructed what has come to be known as the "periodic table of the mind." By combining three basic items and their subdivisions in the shape of a cube he postulates the existence of 120 possible human talents — far beyond the rudimentary concept of intelligence held by the typical person. Specifically, in Guilford's view the item "Operation" has five subdivisions, "Product" has six, and "Content" has four. It has been suggested by a number of scholars — Hallman (1967), Taylor (1968b), Williams (1967) — that there are multitudes of ways of expressing creativity, and that these variations must be acknowledged and accepted if more pupils are to find going to school a challenge and source of satisfaction.

Recognition of styles of learning does not preclude the teaching

of basic curricula. It may, in fact, make mastery of subject matter —
be it learning skills, history, or higher mathematics — a source
of achievement satisfaction. It does preclude uniform assignments
and the expectation that pupils will advance at the same rate or in
the same manner.

A start in the recognition of learning styles may be initiated by the
counselor-consultant's asking teachers to inventory their own learning styles. They can then capitalize on their particular style by using
it to make contributions to in-service education seminars.

MOTIVATION AND CHALLENGE

*Motivation for learning is magnified when the task is sufficiently
difficult to call for maximum effort;* AND *when task accomplishment
represents a significant achievement.* A common and inadvertent
error is for teachers — or tutors in any activity — to say, "Oh, that's
easy." If it really is easy, the child can have no sense of mastery in
completion of the task. If he fails, then, for sure, he is a nincompoop.
Pupils, both bright and slow, have demonstrated repeatedly that
doing difficult tasks is a source of gratification and a stimulus to
tackling another difficult problem. Consequently, and because what
appears to be easy in the eyes of an adult may be perplexing to a
pupil, it would be more sound psychologically to say, "This will be
hard, but I believe you can do it." But the proposition goes farther
than words. Teacher-pupil planning should be such that the goals,
though difficult, are possible of achievement.

This proposition of learning is related to concepts of success and
failure. It was stated above that a healthy self-concept was encouraged by a predominance of success over failure experiences.
However, success is relative. To some pupils it means getting a top-
ranking grade. To others it means passing the course, getting
average grades, or even "just getting by." Instead of measuring
success in terms of interpupil comparisons it would be more practical
(in attempting to achieve the goal of creating in pupils a love for
continuous learning) to think of success as improving each pupil's
present status. Thus, there would be a practical implication for the
use of, or fostering of, the heterostatic impulse. In addition, if
growth were the measure of success, attention would be given to
intrinsic rather than extrinsic factors in motivation. No longer
would it be realistic for bright pupils to stop short of maximum

achievement with the words, "You can't do any better than to get an A." No longer would it be reasonable for a slow learner to "retreat from the field" because he knows, from years of experience, that he cannot succeed in terms of getting a high grade. The motivational challenges for teachers, administrators, and counselor-consultants do not have to be concocted. There are so many of them that it becomes a matter of deciding which is most pressing in the locality concerned. In the summer of 1969 the Advanced Administrative Institute at the Harvard Graduate School of Education dealt with such problems as the following (Schrag, 1969):

> The youth revolution and high school student strikes
> Inept teachers and pupils listening to "drones"
> Hall passes and after-school detention
> Inaccessible administrators and counselors
> The generation gap
> Lack of communication between pupils and school staff members
> Lack of moral conviction by parents and school personnel
> Equality, opportunity, and independence

The counselor-consultant will find, as did Prescott (1957, p. 23), that some teachers are overwhelmed by the enormity of the task. Some draw back from the vision of opportunity for service. This is one reason why counselors are fitted to become consultants. They know from experience that many troubled counselees shrink from acknowledging their own inadequacies. The other side is that the successful *and satisfied* professional, no matter what the field, is the one who chronically takes the next steps.

LANGUAGE AND BEHAVIOR

Learning is facilitated when teachers take advantage of the dynamics of the verbal-symbolic approaches to solving problems and actualizing self. Words — verbal behaviors — are powerful learning media and goals. They become more powerful as they are tested in action and supplemented by other behavior, and when the things words symbolize can be seen, heard, and felt (Murphy, 1965, p. 13). Communication with others is largely verbal *and* abstract. It is a major determinant of the development and maintenance of the positive self-regarding attitude essential to effective learning. While the tone and inflection used when one is told that he is an acceptable person cannot be ignored, the words convey the message.

Technology, speed of communication, mass media of communication, and population pressure are shifting man's environment from a physical to a psychological one. It is less and less necessary to deal directly with the tangible and concrete and more and more probable that man will deal in the realm of ideas, symbols, and abstractions. Man can, with the verbal-linguistic mode, handle problems, dream and talk about them, before acting them out physically. Mistakes can be made without the suffering of serious consequences. Freud, Rogers, and those who endorse interpersonal process groups appreciate the fact that if one can talk something out he has less need of acting it out.

An authority on communication, Becker (1962, pp. 103–104) indicates that the self is primarily a linguistic phenomenon. A strong self is one who has firm control of words. The proper word, the apt phrase, the clear message — these are the highest manifestations of human interpersonal power.

Somehow schools have missed the boat in the verbal-linguistic area. Children are talked *to* rather than *with*. In the typical classroom, if talking is going on, 70 percent of the time it is the teacher who is doing it (Flanders, 1965, p. 1). Furthermore, children are expected *not* to talk with one another in many classrooms — fortunately this notion is changing. Although in many high schools silence is expected as pupils pass in hallways, some high schools are being built with extrawide passageways and alcoves so pupils may converse.

Bruner (1968) contends that one of the most crucial stimuli to intellectual growth provided by the culture is dialogue between the tutored and the untutored. The courtesy of conversation, he says, may very well be the major ingredient of effective teaching. The gap between the generations is characterized by the inability of the elders to converse with the youngsters. The "put-down," patronizing tones, fake sympathy, and "you'll find out" manner of the elders is responded to by youth by their "tuning out" (Schrag, 1969). Goodlad (1969), Hart (1969), Smith (1967), and Woodring (1968) are among others who have called attention to the importance of verbal-symbolic approaches to learning and education processes. Rogers (1968) claims that skillful dialogue, especially as it relates to feelings, emotions, and interpersonal transactions, may be one of the chief advances of social science by the year 2000. The counselor-consultant provides a setting for the practice of dialogue.

SELF-FULFILLING PROPHECY

Motivation will be increased and learning will be facilitated if both pupils and teachers believe that pupil capabilities are such that the tasks can be accomplished. Until recently this proposition was largely an impressionistic one. According to Rosenthal and Jacobson (1968), when teachers were told that certain pupils had shown, on a new test, that their intelligence was about to "blossom," this actually happened to the indicated pupils — yet the test scores initially had been haphazardly assigned. In this case pupils were not informed of their expected "blossoming." The variable was the teacher's expectation. The statistics of the study have been severely criticized (Thorndike, 1969), but the report will have some impact on teacher-pupil interaction.

Some teachers beginning a new school year prefer not to know which of their pupils have low test scores because they are aware of children's tendency to act dumb if they are thought to be dumb.

The self-fulfilling prophecy is given widespread recognition in the education of culturally different pupils. There is growing resistance to the use of conventional intelligence tests because the culturally deprived youngster is not so well acquainted with *school* language, stories, crayons, paper, etc. His intelligence test score tends to be comparatively low. Teachers do not expect much of him and he develops doubt about his own ability. Those who recognize the phenomenon think it would be better to avoid the use of intelligence tests in educating such children.

The self-fulfilling prophecy constitutes a reason for expecting pupils to be honest during tests, to behave during the teacher's absence, to conduct themselves as gentlemen and ladies at parties. It constitutes a reason for paying attention to styles of learning. If one can be successful using a style of learning not typically considered to be of an academic nature, the experience tends to give him a feeling of confidence that carries over into other activities. Thus, the existence of distinctive skills in drawing, athletics, leadership, organization, music, or talking, when recognized and aproved, might become the avenue to more zest and higher expectation in arithmetic, reading, and writing. This is a bold step away from the requirement that the pupil must first finish his composition, reading assignment, or whatever *before* he may play, join the chorus, or go to the gymnasium.

This postulation is related to the one which endorses making schoolwork challenging. It also suggests that remedial education (where emphasis is on weakness) and special classes for slow learners already have two psychological strikes against them.

HUMAN AFFILIATION

Learning is facilitated when the teacher and the pupil's peers show by word, attitude, and behavior that he is accepted, that he belongs, that his involvement is desired and appreciated. In most lists of basic human needs, the matter of belonging, affection, and affiliation receives mention in some terminology. "A sense of security" crops up frequently in literature dealing with child rearing. One must feel secure if he is to possess the openness for learning which makes him an able student. It is the secure pupil, already an established member of the group, who can risk the hazard of change and the uncertainty of the novel. It is the accepted person who can express his doubts, challenge dogmatism, and break the pattern of sheeplike conformity.

The teacher's demonstration of the fact that the pupil belongs must go farther than the words "Differences are recognized and accepted in this class." It clearly shows that the pupil's presence *makes a difference.* The fact of making a difference is the essential aspect of involvement; it means, "I am recognized," "I am a cause," "I have power." The dropout and the potential dropout have said and are saying, as are the student protesters, "I am (or was) never a part of the school." The word *alienation,* much used in discussing adolescents and youth, means being without a base, having no identity, being treated as an outsider (Erikson, 1964, pp. 83 ff.).

Children are not naturally cruel. They do not naturally discriminate. The song words from *South Pacific* say it succinctly: You have to be carefully taught, before it's too late, before seven or eight, to hate and to fear those of another color. *Somebody* teaches that the blacks, and the browns, and the reds, and the yellows do not belong and are not involved in many schools.

Perhaps the matter of showing human affiliation in the classroom means that the teacher's role will be drastically changed. It is a change being suggested by the same persons who endorse the use of dialogue. The shift is from the teacher as tutor, preceptor, and instructor to the teacher as resource person in the guidance of pupils' learning activities. Thus, instead of clinging to the mode of teaching classes as a group and expecting pupils to cover the same ground at the same rate, we shall see the whole setting of interpersonal relationships change. Individuals will really be given attention, and the climate will be one of warmth and supportiveness (Goodlad, 1969).

The challenge to the counselor-consultant is clear and demanding. If teachers are to change, they must see models of what they are to change to. They must be able to *practice* the behaviors which they already accept on the verbal level.

PEER INFLUENCE

Learning progresses most efficiently when teachers accept and capitalize on the premise that peer influences are strong deterrents or reinforcers of classroom process. It has been stated or implied repeatedly above that one *learns* to be a human. One of Haskew's ten implications of recent social changes is "The individualizing humanistic content of schooling should be demonstrated to be *the most important reason for keeping schools in operation.*"[2] Coleman (1965), Erikson (1968), Friedenberg (1965), and Sherif and Sherif (1964) are prominent among those who have called attention to the power of peer influences. This power is so great that it came to be known as "The Youth Culture." Recognition is not only a matter of improved insight into the origins of behavior; it is also a matter of the increased strength of those influences. The latter is due to urban living and the consequent massing together of young people, lack of work opportunities and its concomitant lack of contact with adults, and the increased birth rate since World War II. (In 1964, 2.8 million persons reached the age of eighteen. In 1965 the number jumped to 3.8 million, and virtually that same rate has persisted since 1965.)

School personnel reveal their ignorance, or disdain, of peer in-

---

[2] Laurence D. Haskew, 1967, "Another Perspective," in E. L. Morphet and C. O. Ryan (eds.), *Implications for Education of Prospective Changes in Society* (Denver: Designing Education for the Future).

fluences when they teach, preach, and demand a mode of dress and grooming different from that endorsed by the peer group. The result of opposition to fads, modes of dress, and variation in moral conviction is the polarizing of teachers and pupils in opposing groups. The objective of one group is to impose "common sense" (the way *we* did it when we were young — forgetting some of the less savory manifestations); the objective of the other is to devise ways to circumvent the regulations (Schrag, 1969). In extreme cases the conflict between adult and peer perceptions of propriety supplies the fuse for protests, parades, and confrontations. Disdain for the peer group is shown when ridicule, reprimand, and sarcasm are used in the classroom. It is shown when, in the name of honesty and social justice, teachers expect pupils to inform on their misbehaving classmates. Perhaps most of all, it is shown by the high prevalence of teacher talk. On the other hand, respect for the peer group is shown by schools that use an "open campus" policy.

It would border on the ridiculous to suggest a simple, categorical classroom procedure which would solve the problems imposed by the importance of peer relations. It would be an oversimplification to suggest that school personnel working as a coordinated unit could solve a problem that belongs to society as a whole. However, it does seem possible to bring about some improvement if the wisdom of all staff members, meeting in in-service seminars, can come up with procedures and behaviors for meliorating certain of the contributing influences.

READINESS AND MENTAL SET

Learning occurs most expeditiously when the learner is appropriately mature and when he is psychologically and socially predisposed to master a given learning task. Earlier it was stated that the most familiar instance of readiness is reading readiness. Another example is readiness for learning a second language. Penfield (1967) has conducted researches showing that if the language center of the brain is not used before the age of ten or twelve it is taken over by other mental functions and later is not so adept at language mastery. Even a very little use in dealing with a second language serves to *commit* the center, and later the individual can more easily than otherwise master a second language. Many authorities believe that some parents these days tend to push children into heterosexual activities before they are ready — dating and dancing are frequently cited. Similarly there is the opinion that hurry to achieve academically, musically, and athletically may spoil the appetite for such activities when sufficient maturity has been reached. "Children under pressure" is a concern of some mental hygienists.

In addition to the maturational phenomenon of readiness there is the matter of mental set. This refers to a more transitory condition in which the learner is experientially oriented toward a learning. Some years ago Johnson (1946, p. 55) asserted that probably the most impressive indictment of education is that it provides students with answers before they are ready to ask the questions. The phenomenon has been noted in recent years in school programs for the culturally different child. The wisdom of dealing with things that form part of his background and of tackling problems with which he has some familiarity has been recognized. Of course, Dewey and Kilpatrick were saying the same thing in the day when *progressive* was not a bad word as applied to education.

Learning independence is another area in which parents *and* teachers have failed to recognize readiness and mental set. It is understood that a prolonged adolescence is advantageous in such a complex world as ours, but on many occasions both parents and teacher could afford more opportunities to exercise independence and could even permit the adolescent to make mistakes.

The counselor-consultant must deal with these concerns in his in-service work. It is unlikely that a teaching corps will strike up the band when improvement in methods and personality is suggested. Some consultants may wish to take a direct approach in getting teachers ready for the experience. Others will prefer indirection and approach the developmental plan for teachers by using the case of two or three particular pupils who are having difficulty.

Reinforcement

The learner tends to repeat and consolidate those knowledges and behaviors which for him are successful in terms of gratification or approval or attention from others. The pupil who is commended for his scholarly efforts by approval from his parents, good marks from his teachers, and the expression of admiration from his friends tends to persist in his studiousness. Pupils who are ignored, or who have an unusual need for recognition, will do things — talk loudly, create disturbances, or violate regulations — to get attention. Being punished is, apparently, often better than being overlooked. Pupil goals are often different from those sought by parents or teachers. One boy, hearing about the kind of activities taking place in a class for slow learners, deliberately did poor work in his class and finally asked in exasperation, "Just how dumb do you have to be to get in Mrs. C's class?" Conant (1959) expressed concern about the number of girls who failed to apply themselves in mathematics and science for fear of being called "brains" or "eggheads."

The fact of reinforcement, in terms of either individual perceptions or typical social endorsement, is related to many of the other learning principles stated above. Reinforcement may come from the pleasure of exercising one's talents or potentials. Instead of making athletes ineligible because of poor marks it might be better to recognize athletics as a legitimate aspect of high school life — society apparently does. Instead of depriving an artistic pupil of his clay and paints because of his scholastic indolence it would be better for the teacher to exercise ingenuity in correlating the artistic and the academic. Reinforcement may come from the peer culture; the values of the school do not always coincide with those of the younger generation. Reinforcement is related to the proposition that learning depends partly on belongingness and acceptance. It could be, but in practice often is not, related to variation in learning styles.

Acting as a counselor, rather than as a counselor-consultant, one might improve rapport with teachers by locating and defining perceptions of students which contrast with those of teachers. Recognition of the factors that *in an individual* constitute reinforcement would work to the mutual advantage of all concerned.

Process vs. Product

In a society characterized by rapid change the process of learning is more important than the product. Of the postulations cited herein, this one has most frequently been objected to. Perhaps it will be easier to "sell" to counselors than to teachers. In the experience of many counselors it was the contact, the fact of association, the warmth and acceptance which prevailed in counseling sessions that resulted in help — not the wisdom of a course of action devised. In fact, situations must often remain unchanged — an alcoholic mother, a withered hand — whereas friendship and the opportunity to talk and ventilate brought improvement.

It is contended that no necessary conflict exists between process and content or product. Primary emphasis should be on teaching pupils how to learn so they may continue learning *after* the teacher is no longer there to guide, compel, and direct them. Concern should be with developing a love for learning. The process of learning should be enjoyable. In a world of rapid change a liking for, a predisposition to, and the habit of learning are more important than facts. This is said in view of the assertion that 70 percent of students now in junior high school will work at jobs which do not yet exist. It is said in view of the fact that it took 1750 years to double the knowledge extant at the time of Christ but that — with much more to deal with — knowledge doubled between 1960 and 1967. Much that an undergraduate prospective engineer learns as a student will be obsolete by the time he receives his degree. Bruner (1968) feels that one of the more revealing ways of looking at school problems is to examine the shift from the relative importance of facts to the importance of principles.

It may be that the *process* of in-service education will be of greater value than the curricular changes or the teaching adaptations that result. The satisfaction of growth, the zest of additional insights, the feeling of a deeper awareness of others may mean more than the adoption of a plan for independent study or continuous progress. The belief that what the teacher is is more important than what he does must be reiterated. The postulation also has implications for the counselor. For him, quite as much as for teachers, the remark of McCully (1969) has significance; he in effect said, "What one knows defines his role. What one is defines his limits."

> The case of Jimmy is reported here to bring a real person into the consultation theme. What happened to Jimmy could not have been accomplished without the continued and sustained efforts of his parents, teachers, counselor at school, school principal, and district administration. The school counselor brought this case to us because of a long history of school failure. The school counselor was a member of the family group consultation program operated by us through the University. Many bases had to be touched to carry out the three-year treatment plan to rehabilitate Jimmy and his family academically.

The school accepted Jimmy as a special student in a special class on the condition that the family participate in family consultation.[3] Family consultation requires participation by teacher, parents, and school counselor. This relatively new professional role of the counselor usually calls for a small group because of the diversity of persons and concerns involved in creating improved learning environments.

Jimmy had never had a sustained successful experience in school. There are several reasons. Jimmy was born in a foreign country, Japan. His first language was Japanese. His mother could speak only Japanese. His father was an American of Japanese ancestry who went to Japan, married, had a son, Jimmy, and subsequently moved Jimmy and his mother to the United States. Jimmy had lived in the United States since he was three or four years old. He spoke fluent English and Japanese.

Jimmy had lived in isolation from other children. At age ten he had never had any age-mate playmates. No school had kept him for much more than one year. In spite of all of these things, Jimmy could read and write in two languages. His math was quite good. But social behavior was another story.

Jimmy had not learned to play with other children. He had spent almost all of his life with adults who had treated him more as a toy than a boy. Because his family was affluent, Jimmy had been given almost everything a child might wish to have, except playmates. It took two years to accomplish the minimum socialization necessary to claim that Jimmy had the social competence to handle interpersonal relationships with peers without special guidance. A more complete rehabilitation would take at least three years.

The parents gave generously the time and effort necessary to consultation. The fact that Jimmy improved in sufficient increments to sustain the parents' motivation to continue the treatment plan is the best evidence we have of the value of consultation as a professional role for a school counselor. Consultation helped the teacher to keep going through times that tried the very fabric of her character. Jimmy stayed for three years in the same school. This fact alone seems to support our claim for the efficacy of consultation as a professional role for the counselor whenever it is essential to coordinate diverse interests over

---

[3] Whether you see this condition as blackmail or insurance depends upon the position you hold relative to Jimmy. The rider on the contract was insurance for the school and the school counselor.

extended periods of time to create and maintain improved learning environments.

Summary

It is assumed in this chapter that an important task of the counselor-consultant is to improve the learning climate of his school. A first step is to appreciate the contribution of the several psychological orientations that have influenced and do influence teaching practice. Connectionism, behaviorism, Gestalt psychology, and psychoanalytic theory are among the viewpoints that prevail in school practice. Increasingly, what is known as humanistic or proactive psychology is coming to shape teaching procedures.

Some postulations derived from these various viewpoints are as follows:

What the teacher is, as a personality, strongly influences what and how the pupil learns.

Pupils possess an inherent, natural, and normal tendency to grow, become, satisfy their curiosity, and exercise their potentials.

Pupils are more efficient learners when they feel good about themselves — feel they are worthy, accepted, and able.

The self-concept, high or low, tends to persist but changes in the presence of persistent and pervasive influences.

The self-concept arises and is nourished in a social context — the home, school, and neighborhood.

Learning is facilitated as the styles of learning of different pupils are recognized and their use is permitted and encouraged.

Motivation is partly dependent upon the challenge and achievement of that which is difficult.

Verbal-symbolic behaviors are major causes and results of learning.

Pupils tend to be and behave in ways that are expected of them by key people.

A pupil's learning is deeply influenced by the behaviors, values, and attitudes of his peers.

A pupil learns best when his peers and teachers manifest their acceptance and appreciation of him.

A pupil must be *ready* and mentally set for certain learning experiences before learning can occur economically.

The learner tends to learn those behaviors which are, for him, successful.

The process of education is more important than the product — but the two are not contradictory.

SUGGESTED ADDITIONAL READINGS

Goodlad, John I., 1969. "The School vs. Education," *Saturday Review*, 52(16):59–61+, April 19. *While taking a realistic look at some of the changes needed in school, this author suggests that the institution of education should not be abandoned when we are just beginning to try it.*

Gordon, Ira J., 1966. "New Conceptions of Children's Learning and Development," in W. B. Waetjen and R. R. Leeper (eds.), *Learning and Mental Health in the School*. Washington: Association for Supervision and Curriculum Development, NEA. *Gordon contrasts two ways of conceptualizing human beings: the linear causation model and the transactional model of man.*

McCully, C. Harold, 1969. *Challenge for Change in Counselor Education*, edited and organized by Lyle L. Miller. Minneapolis: Burgess Publishing Company. *A prominent counselor educator expresses views of and challenges to counselor preparation and function. He was one of the first to envision the role of counselor-consultant.*

Rogers, Carl R., 1969. "A Humanistic Conception of Man," in H. W. Bernard (ed.), *Readings in Adolescent Development*. Scranton, Pa.: International Textbook Company. *Among other things, the author emphasizes the directional and actualizing (heterostatic) growth tendencies of human beings.*

Schrag, Peter, 1969. "School Administrators and Angry Students: Gloom at the Top," *Saturday Review*, 52(33):50–51+, August 16. *The article presents a terse summary of the differences between the adult's and the young person's point of view. Their inability to communicate is indicated.*

Chapter Three

GOALS OF
CONSULTATION

In a professional relationship the counselor needs to be in communication with many persons at many levels in multiple ways. It is proposed that this relationship be with society at large and with all individuals within the structure of the school.

The professional practitioner knows both why and how behavior takes place in a given life situation. By way of contrast, a technician works prescriptively by following formulas. The technician does not know the ultimate consequences of what he is doing. The professional does know. The short-term consequences are frequently desirable but in the long-term the same behavior may lead to a destructive outcome. The alcoholic and the smoker are examples in contemporary society. The first drink or another cigarette is no big thing — except that for the addicted it leads to destruction (Blachly, 1970).

The professional counselor is competent in all aspects of counseling relationships. He can use the strengths in people to build up deficiencies and thus bring about more effective human living. The combining of strengths through the method of consultation is the apogee of professional counseling. Conventionally the concern has been more with remaking or reshaping the personality in the therapy model; consultation is a process for planning and developing action.

Counseling is the preparation for next steps; consultation is the process of encouraging the individual to take immediate steps now. When consultation is successful, the consultant is made obsolete, but the consultant role thereby gains impetus because the long-term consequences are constructive. This pattern is in sharp contrast to the behavior modification techniques in use in the late 1960's, in which short-term gains are impressive but in the end the consequences may lead to satiation of drive for external rewards (Liddell, 1956).

Consultation: An Aspect of Professionalism

Consultation is a small group process. Two to eight persons in a group create a learning and teaching device. Family group consultation has revealed that access to human resources beyond the isolated individual is extremely difficult to achieve. In the small group, information flow is vital to effectiveness. Information flow has become complicated in at least two respects. (1) The evaluation of the quality of information is difficult because in a complex society we have almost no firsthand information. (2) Sources of second-hand, or symbolic, knowledge make the process difficult because one may get the information needed but not know how to apply.

The counselor in his consultant role becomes the facilitator of information flow by bringing together individuals of diverse backgrounds. The specific goal in consultation is always made explicit ✓ by the counselor. Everyone knows the agenda. No hidden agendas exist, legitimately. However, the group will usually gain access to new knowledge rather the way a symphony orchestra creates overtones beyond the written score.

In the small group a person may learn to evaluate information by separating authentic data from spurious data. Because much information is secondhand, it is also necessary to learn to evaluate the source of information. The small group is a safe place to learn the skills and knowledge for each of the above.

Goals and Implications

Premises Basic to Consultation

Premise: Relationship is a life condition out of which behavior is formed to communicate with self and others. The relationship defines the relative status between an individual and his environment and/or another individual. The triangle of person, other person, and context will give the basic model in use here. Examples include parent-child, professor-student, child-child, superior-subordinate, etc. The relationship is always defined at the level of the social system — i.e., the classroom, the physician's examining room, or the corner bar. At the person-to-person level, relationship seems to be subject to constant modification, even if only one member moves through a significant age change. An example is Daddy's little girl who becomes a young woman. The relationship is changed.

Premise: The culture uses complex message systems to define relationships. Hall (1959, p. 45) lists ten primary message systems, only one of which, interaction, utilizes verbal language. Interaction includes both nonverbal and verbal levels of communication. The nine additional message systems help to qualify and redefine existing interpersonal and impersonal relationships.

Premise: Individual behavior comes out of a relationship. The person responds to his perception of a relationship. The response is an act of behavior to communicate his perception of the moment to a significant other person (Fullmer, 1969a).

Premise: The relationship itself communicates all-at-once with each and all participants. Hall (1959) claims that each culture defines relationships. Each person learns the same meanings for the same relationship in a given culture. Therefore, each person has the same messages and meanings in common with everyone else, instantaneously (all-at-once).

Premise: Behavior is a form of communication which is highly organized into isolates, sets, and patterns just as is any verbal language. We can illustrate, for example, by pointing to what happens at a football game when the referee signals an event. A set is the hand patting the top of the head followed by another signal to indicate the infraction response and disposition (penalty declined, imposed, etc.). An isolate is the whistle blown once. A pattern is the relationship between the isolates, sets, and events in communicating between referee and scoring officials, and fans (spectators).

Premise: The functions of a counselor remain determined by the relationship defined between himself and other persons (Watzlawick et al., 1967).

Premise: Consultation permits the counselor to act outside the relationship and thus to go beyond the relationship; to make big changes instead of little ones. This is a significant difference between counseling and consultation. In counseling, we have hoped for big changes while promoting a gradual shift over a long period of time. Consultation strategy is designed to produce massive changes more immediately (Fullmer and Bernard, 1968).

Premise: Consultation permits the counselor to escape the limiting model of counseling and encounter and deal with higher levels of discontent. In consultation high-level complaints are encouraged and responded to, while counseling has been aimed at reducing complaints to zero (Patterson, 1969a).

GOALS IN RELATION TO PREMISES

It is postulated that the most important change in the future operations of the counselor in the school setting will revolve around the model for his work. We think the consultation method is particularly well devised to serve as a future-orientated model.

Counseling and guidance have always maintained that the future should be planned rather than descending upon us as a surprise, and much current American thinking seems to agree. Dr. Thomas Greene of Syracuse University reported in May 1968, at Phoenix, Arizona, that all of us are writing the history of education for the year 2000. His thesis was precisely that of planning the future rather than having it just happen. The counselor-consultant can fit into the future by working in a new model that allows him to transcend the limitations placed upon him in his traditional counselor function.

The individual will need to become self-renewing as well as self-determining (Gardner, 1963). In order to achieve this goal he will have to be exposed to a method of work that will exemplify the way he can utilize human resources to acquire the necessary knowledge and skills on a future-oriented basis. Since most of what one will need to know ten years from now has not yet been discovered and much present knowledge will soon be technologically obsolete, it behooves us as counselors to come up with a model for working that will provide the means and the end for achieving a continuing renewal and determining the relation between self and society.

The notion in consultation that contributes the most to the futuristic orientation is that one's neighborhood constitutes a considerable resource if the individual can learn to utilize its talents and opportunities and to create conditions providing access to other people. The latter do not have to be experts or professional specialists in order to proffer the kind of assistance needed by most people. This notion has been expanded in recent years to include the idea that the organizational structure for dispensing professional services, particularly in school counseling, could be improved if somehow target students were involved in delivering the services. The training of tutors from upper grades to assist children with learning difficulties in lower grades has worked exceptionally well, for example. Tutorial programs, mostly volunteer, exist in nearly every major school system.

It is desirable to tie the counselor-consultation method to the counselor's function in its wider aspects. We want to escape the restrictions of the counseling model without abandoning all that is good in the counseling function.

Improved professional competence is the ultimate goal for all participants in the consultation process. The counselor's competence level will set the limits for his efforts in consultation. Competence in his field includes the "why" as well as the "how" of behavior. At the beginning of this chapter we mentioned the technician. The technician is like the person who learns to use a telephone without needing to understand its internal circuits. He has a useful and worthwhile function and avoids the hazards of dichotomous thinking (Watzlawick et al., 1967). The teacher may be a professional or a technician, depending upon the level of competence he exhibits in actual behavior. But the counselor *must* be a professional, and probably some counselors will be reluctant to enter the consultant relationship. Others may be overenthusiastic.

SPECIFIC GOALS OF CONSULTATION

In this section eight goals of consultation are briefly stated, each with an explanation of its implications for developing a counselor-consultant opportunity and responsibility. The basic task is to enhance the flow of authentic information within the small group consisting of counselor-consultant, teacher, parent, pupil, and other behavior specialists.

Goal 1. The overall goal of consultation in school counseling is to improve and enhance the learning environments for children, teachers, parents, and administrators. The counselor-consultant achieves this with the assistance of all the human behavior specialists and resource persons he can convene. There are two levels of consultation: (a) consultation with the resource person and (b) consultation with the target person. It is most productive to put resource persons and target persons in the same group.

The milieu in which learning occurs is primarily a people environment, though there are some physical facilities, materials, and equipment. We are concerned more with people than with things in the consulting function.

Implication: Counseling has been and will continue to be concerned chiefly with the learner, teacher, parent, administrator, and counselor — or other specialist — as a person in the environment. The relationship helps focus attention. The relationship is frequently determined by forces in the environment, i.e., family status, peer pressure, drug scene, personnel of the "establishment," poverty, affluence, etc. Group and consultation methods make it possible to break out of the restricting limits and create a new model for the counselor to use.

The task of improving the learning environment centers upon the issue of change. What needs to be different? How much different? How soon different? By what time schedule? The answers add up to: big change now. Big changes can be put into action immediately. This is the powerful dividend from consultation. The counselor had to be satisfied with gradual change in small increments until the consultation method developed.

The learning environment at home, at school, and in the community is very largely composed of people. Even the machines are programmed to put across people messages and images. The big change can be simply the addition or removal of one other significant person. For example, in an urban milieu one other person may be an "only friend" or "the only one who knows me."

Consultation takes us into the future because the strategy is as paradoxical as are the problems it solves. A paradox can be resolved if one can step outside the confines of the relationship. Consultation is the strategy for moving beyond the relationship into the milieu of other persons and events.

Goal 2. Consultation is intended to improve communication by enhancing the information flow among the significant persons in the learning milieu.

Implication: The improvement of communication by facilitating the information flow among significant persons in the learning milieu is notable in group work. Consultation is primarily a group strategy. Significant persons are permitted access to one another on a neutral level as contrasted to the informal level of the teachers' lounge or the formal level of the faculty.

Here is one of the major unsolved problems in institutional and community structure. The operation of getting information to flow — from the expert to the target person — has never had great success. The genius of consultation as a method in human communication resides in the fact that people do engage their counterparts when the social system rules permit them to. Much of the literature about consultation treats only the information flow from expert to target person(s). It would seem preferable to include all the persons concerned with a given life situation or learning environment.

Goal 3. Consultation is designed to bring together persons of diverse roles and functions to engage in the common task of enhancing the learning environments of significant others, i.e., children, parents, teachers, and administrators.

Implication: Bringing together persons who have diverse functions is important in improving the learning environment, but diversity at the operations level has a common purpose at another level too. The task is achieved whenever one significant other person learns that the culture uses complex, but primary, message systems to define relationships. When it is desirable that someone's behavior change, the relationship out of which it comes must change. Consultation is a learning environment focused on learning how to learn.

Goal 4. Consultation extends the services of experts. The human behavior specialist is a scarce resource. In many schools professional services are totally inadequate in view of the need for help. If the counselor consults with the resource specialist *and* the teacher, parent, or administrator, the resource person is in effect speaking to a wider audience. Continuous supervision by the professional specialist is essential to safeguard the obvious vulnerabilities in the process of consultation.

Implication: One expert may serve only a few other persons in his entire career if he stays with the model of direct service. The counselor may be an expert or may utilize other experts. The method of consultation is used whenever direct service is unavoidable, as in a crisis, or when the counselor must become the expert because "expert" services have been delayed beyond a reasonable time.

Goal 5. Consultation can be an in-service education function for teachers and administrators. The goal is to increase the ability of these persons to deal effectively with a wider range of differences among students. Grouping procedures in many schools tend to militate against differentness. Children with learning disabilities and social control problems are grouped together, for example.

Implication: Innovations in education have been at least as important for their personal communication value as for the direct improvement of instruction (Bernard and Huckins, 1968; Cottle, 1969a). The payoff of improved communication is increased competence. Teachers learn from each other and carry group interaction beyond the original assignments. Consultation can release the potential for development in much the same way. Behavior comes out of relationships. Relationships are defined, in part, by the sharing of a specific task.

Tasks are identified by the counselor in consultation with teachers and administrators. Tasks for in-service education projects are those identified as needed by most faculty to meet a common concern.

Goal 6. The consultant is charged with helping others in the process of learning how to learn about behavior (Hall, 1959; Watzlawick et al., 1967). The consulting method lends itself to being both a process toward learning and a vehicle for learning. The counselor can gain access to the teacher's classroom as a consultant — the vehicle function. He can involve the teacher in a sharing of information — the communication flow toward learning. The parent and administrator may be engaged in a similar manner.

Implication: The major premise of learning to learn about behavior is based upon the culture's pattern of beliefs which defines the nature of relationships among people and things. The system seems to account for most of the self-fulfilling prophecy so common in every culture (Dundes, 1969). Shared beliefs in a given culture will lead to universal ideas about certain phenomena, which in turn will prescribe the behavioral response to any given event. The system inevitably leads to confirmations that will not stand up outside the particular culture. Learning to learn is perhaps our most complex concept. It has the power of changing mysticism into understood and predictable phenomena. Learning to learn leads to intriguing insights about established counseling systems, behaviorism and phenomenology included.

Goal 7. Consultation hopes to create a milieu containing all the significant components of a good learning environment.

Implication: The consultant works with whatever configurations of persons are available. His task is to bring together as many contributors to a good learning environment as possible. People are the chief resource.

Creation of an environment which contains all significant components for learning is perhaps the most difficult goal in consultation. It is tempered by the entire cultural program for behavior, definition of relationships, and flow of communication among people. The culture program is a system of rules and conditioned behavior responses already internalized by each individual member of a given social system. This is, indeed, the planned outcome of the socialization process maintained in the family, school, and community.

Goal 8. An overall goal of consultation is to trigger self-help organization. Our society will probably never get enough professionals. If it did, they still would not be so effective as are people who help themselves. This is the big change that consultation aims to produce.

Implication: Consultation leads toward self-help forms of social interaction. The idea is to teach the skills and knowledge to any teachers, parents, and administrators with whom the counselor-consultant works. Most of the readily learned skills require only brief exposure. Knowledge and complex skills take more time to achieve. The aim of the consultant is to eliminate the need for his presence by establishing self-help capabilities.

More implications: Goal 1, to repeat, is to improve and enhance the learning environments for children, teachers, parents, and administrators. The counselor needs to remember that the social system of the school has already defined the relationships he will have with these people. In order to undertake the consultation method, he will have to recognize that verbal language is only one small part of the communication system. The counselor may redefine relationships if he can involve the significant other persons in working with him on the innovation of consultation. The consultation may occur in a group or individually with one other person.

The overwhelming majority of consultations involve more than one other person — often neighobors — and so are classified as small group consultations. In order to achieve the goal of improved communication among all principal adults in the school setting, the counselor will need to pay close attention to the conditions under which the group is convened. The relationship itself communicates all-at-once,[1] and each participant will be intensely engaged in the process of communication. The counselor-consultant must structure the situation in a way that will allow the individuals to clarify for themselves the nature of the relationship and the communication messages being exchanged.

If our society is truly in search of new models for organizing its personal and social interaction, the idea that counselors should limit their concerns to the relieving of complaints or the reducing of complaints to a zero level should be examined carefully. In consultation we have come a long way toward the development of a new level of encountering the usual behavior complaints lodged by youngsters, parents, and teachers against the school social system. The initial sessions in most consultation are flooded with a large variety of minor and major complaints. The issues surrounding the life conditions out of which these complaints come are frequently

[1] All-at-once describes the condition encountered when a person enters a new situation. Instantaneously, he is aware if everything is all right or amiss. This is the impact of nonverbal and contextual (external) cues coming into awareness.

in the context of a school. In this situation the most productive attack is encouraged; alternatives are discouraged. The complaints give some hint about the direction to be taken. In brief, the policy is to attempt the possible and bypass the improbable alternatives.

The counselor turns his attention to one specific issue with which there seems to be some possibility of rendering assistance. He listens carefully to reports of the family to estimate whether the failure to resolve the issue is a matter of ill-defined strategy. If a family has poor skills and inappropriate behavior, there is little hope that they will manage any event well. They may not know how to solve the simplest of problems. It is necessary to know this sort of thing before attempting to help them to resolve even a moderately complex problem.

One discovers frequently that if parents, children, teachers, administrators, and other human behavior specialists can be helped to consider a problem at a different level from that traditionally or recently utilized they can usually eliminate many minor complaints. Then they may be more successful at resolving an issue that is more complex and at a higher level because resources do exist to assist them. If they are disgruntled at a low level of complaint, there is very little others can do.

Here, for example, is a child who will not study at home. Maybe he would study at the library. His anxious mother wants her child to get good grades in school, but he is flunking. Can you get the mother to consider another level? The larger issue of whether the son may commit suicide, or whether he may not finish school at all, is an alternative. What difference does it really make if the alternative seems to be final?

Because consultation is much less limited by the internal orientation of a counselor, it can be focused upon the external components of the environment. The counselor is sometimes restricted to acting only in the relationship and only in a counseling session. In the consultant role he can act when he is away from the relationship, actually working directly with other significant persons to bring some resolution to the conflicts that have been identified. Even here, however, it is important to remember that the function of the counselor will remain determined by the defined relationship between the counselor and the other persons.

The Counselor-Consultant Function

THE HELPING RELATIONSHIP

Make-believe is fun for all. When Lucy hangs her shingle to inform her friends that "Psychiatrist is in," the sign also appropriately defines the relationship: "Five cents." In keeping with the genius of Lucy's creator, this is a most "realistic" definition. The helping relationship is sometimes worth less than a nickel even though it costs much more! Consultation is an evolving helping relationship that directly involves other significant persons in the life of the counselee — parents, teachers, principals, and so on who deal regularly with the counselee and/or his social-economic environments.

The goal of consultation is to multiply the effectiveness of the helping relationship by increasing the numbers of people coordinating the treatment of a counselee. All other goals are subordinated to the main one.

To achieve the goal of consultation, it is necessary for the counselor to go to the geographic location of the significant other persons. He leaves his office and ventures into the classroom, where the teacher is in charge. He is in alien territory. To be a consultant the counselor learns to work in alien territory because there may be no neutral ground. A counselor is counseling whenever he works in his own territory. Consultation may proceed in alien or neutral territory.[2]

Territory defines relationships. Think of the classroom, bedroom, or city street as examples. Place is a definite concern. Time is important too, but for different reasons.

COMMUNICATION

Communication is the central concern in all helping relationships. The message and meanings exchanged between two interacting individuals are the objects of all data-taking in research. Observation of behavior is limited to (1) the communication and (2) the relationship definition.

Consultation attempts to affect the communication between child

[2] For remarks on territory and nine other Primary Message Systems, see E. T. Hall, 1959, pp. 45 ff.

and adult. Relationship is the determining life condition that limits what is communicated. Because the relationship has already (all-at-once) communicated meanings by the definition of each person in the given relationship, there is no such thing as not communicating. Therefore, the frequently encountered idea of improving communication is a false trail. The communication is already accomplished (all-at-once) by the relationship definition and consequently need not be improved. We need to know (1) what was communicated and (2) what may be communicated. Of course, the skill to "read" the behavior and to send additional messages and new meanings becomes the test of credibility.

Sophistication in manipulating the symbols of communication allows one to convey multiple messages and meanings. The double message system is one variety encountered in consultation. For example, a teacher gives much kind attention and deference to the counselor each time they confer. Later, the counselor discovers his reluctance to report negative messages to this teacher. The counselor's credibility may come into question. What has happened? The teacher has communicated at more than one level simultaneously. The content level has been: "See how interested I am in what you [counselor] have to offer in the way of help," and also "Because I am nice to you, you would violate our relationship if you did not defer negative criticism." The relationship definition is more subtle but is no less virile in its effect upon subsequent behavior. What is communicated influences what may be communicated (Watzlawick et al., 1967, p. 211).

The difference seems to revolve around the idea of how the counselor behaves in his role as consultant in the school. The consultant function is in both an individual and a group context. The counselor goes into the classroom to work with the teacher on all social control problems with the children. The teacher and the counselor work on an individual basis in relation to a specific problem with one of the children. This relationship is extremely close to the counseling relationship, but the other children in the classroom are also involved. Social control problems become a central issue in all learning environment concerns in the classroom. The counselor-consultant deals with learning environments in school, home, and neighborhood.

The counselor may handle the learning environment (consisting of teacher, parents, and youngsters) in one or more of several arrangements. The consultant function is used to transmit to the teacher those things which might modify the learning environment in order to facilitate a given child's learning experiences.

The authors' hypothesis is that the role of counselor-consultant is simply another role for the counselor to play; there is no dichotomous construct between counselor and consultant. The counselor would continue to carry on his traditional functions in the school. The consultant function would be an added dimension to an expanding counselor role.

GROUP AS A MEANS OF APPLYING THE COUNSELOR'S PROFESSIONAL COMPETENCE

The counselor may convene a group containing all the significant persons in the life of the child (including the child and his parents, siblings, teacher, and whoever else is significant) and ask it to consider the specific life concerns of the child. If these concerns are learning difficulties, behavior control problems, or simply the preoccupations of anxious parents, consultation may take place. Consultation becomes a means of working with numbers of people for brief periods of time and allowing them to consult with one another. The widely diverse range of concerns, talents, and resources represented in such a group is an indication of the type of function the counselor is performing when he brings it together.

One orientation to school consultation is that it involves only school personnel (Faust, 1968, p. 23). The position taken by the present authors, tested in ten years of practice, is that it is possible to work with parents and that it is feasible, timewise, to consult with the entire family. Our experience in working with families in groups has given us a different view of the function of the counselor in consultation from Faust's. We have been less concerned with the fine-line description and the discrepancy between consultant and counselor as professional persons. In the first place, it is unnecessary to dichotomize the professional person. The counselor does consultation as a part of his total personal professional job. Therefore, the consultant per se is acting a professional role of the counselor. The rationale for using the counselor as a consultant with families and teachers grew out of the need to expand the effective working relationships of the counselor in the school. The test of the effectiveness of consultation as a method is the expansion in the numbers of people who are brought into the helping relationship. The most significant contribution of the counselor-consultant function is the ability to use the method to focus diverse elements upon the learning environment in the classroom, family, and community in some kind of unified effort. In the initial work with families attention was directed to the learning environment, the family, and the home. Working extensively with the learning environment in the home and family is a major test of the counselor's professional competence. However, families cannot be excluded arbitrarily from the environment of learning.

Behaviorism and Counselor Consultation

LEARNING MODELS AND COUNSELING

Therapists identified with behavioristic treatment models apply learning theory and principles rather than interaction theory and principles. The context in which their treatment is carried on is essentially monadic isolation. That is, they treat one person at a time and have concern only with one highly specific behavior event or symptom. The isolation is what marks the difference between behavioristic treatment and counselor consultation, for principles of reinforcement and conditioning abound in every social interaction arena (Krumboltz, 1966, p. 13).

Consultation implies open interaction among a number of persons collected together. The task is to know what the consequences are for each member or significant other person when behavior changes in one of the participants. We are encountering the part-whole phenomenon. Whenever one person changes behavior, the others respond. The nature of the response depends upon the prior relationship definition. For example, treatment of one member of a symbiotic mother-son relationship in isolation is extremely disturbing to the other member. Not infrequently the untreated member becomes disorganized as a personality and passes into a psychotic condition. We prefer to work in groups and include all significant members in the family or interaction linkage. The behaviorist would typically treat the new patient in monadic isolation. The choice of words is less important than the purposes to be served in treatment and/or research. There is no argument at the philosophic level because the results would not resolve anything. Behaviorist models use a strategy identifying specific goals and applying reinforcement and conditioning principles in the treatment process. They ignore the relationship variables, as they do all informal culture systems. The data better fit the design used in behavioral science research.

The milieu treatment strategy, on the other hand, focuses upon the input and output, to borrow computer jargon. Behavior is assessed for current status and recorded as data. These data are stored, and the treatment strategy is applied over a given time period, after which behavior is assessed a second time. The data — pre and post — are compared. Changes may be assumed to have been caused by the treatment process. Behaviorists claim that this procedure is too speculative and uncontrolled. Milieu treatment professionals claim that the behaviorist fails to account for the host of intervening variables.

Both groups are probably right — for different reasons. The stage of our knowledge being what it is, we may all be wrong. However, current practice provides for use of both major strategies when conditions seem to indicate that a specific course in treatment plans can be established. For instance, the need for psychiatric treatment may be so great that it is a temptation to wait for such help because the case is too tough; yet the client cannot postpone his suffering.

Consultation is the opposite of the controlled environment methods. In a completely controlled environment there is nothing to consult about. In an environment rich in choice alternatives, each of which is essentially of equal apparent value, the consultation process is meaningful. In the school, a child may move in and out of environments of various degrees of control as a part of the total treatment strategy.

LEARNING TO LEARN

Every culture has preferred ways to learn how to learn. One might assume that anyone of normal character with average or above mental (cognitive) facility will have learned most of the useful knowledge and skill permitted by a given style of learning how to learn. Therefore, it can be argued that a possible method in counseling-consulting is to teach the other person one or more additional styles of learning to learn.

The method of teaching might stress rote memory, demonstration, logic, or the American principle of doing (experience). Our systems for education are as tied to a belief about learning as is the language.

THE GAME OF LIFE

Play is universal role playing in our culture (Hall, 1959). Play and learning are closely interrelated. Make-believe is an exact simulation process that gives anyone "playing" an out. A way of avoiding the uncompromising real-life consequences offers a situation in which learning takes place — this is the "magic" of play.

The defense system used in our culture is closely related to play and learning. The ways we devise to protect ourselves from others are intricately woven into the informal leadership system Americans use (Berne, 1964). Every institution, every community develops an informal system which parallels, but is rarely a duplicate of or concomitant with, the formal system. The counselor who learns to use the informal leadership and social system in the school is assured a measure of success. An example, on the broad social-economic and political dimension, is the poverty program. The strategy is to establish grass-roots power systems. The power in American social structure is entirely informal and therefore out of sight (awareness). The formal system is subordinate, operating only with the consent of the informal system. These are extremely complex forces that do not show up on organization charts. Fiction may be the only safe medium for writing about the advise and consent functions. Counselors who act as consultants move in similar complex social systems within the school, community, and family. The hazards to the counselor's credibility are ever present. The credit-discredit continuum is a source of concern because a counselor will lose his effectiveness or gain in effectiveness in relation to his credit quotations on the "big board" of community (informal) opinion.

Play, defense, and learning are central issues for the counselor when he applies the method of consultation. The rules of behavior defining the relationships are already accepted by the culture's social systems. The aim is to learn to use the systems.

Counseling, Consultation, and Group

CONSULTATION: A NOVEL DIMENSION

Consultation as an application of group counseling is new to the decade of the 1970's. The counseling model employed in the past has been such that a series of progressions has now led to the function of influencing the environment of the counselee. The intent was there in the counseling point of view, but the method was missing. When family consultation was developed in the early 1960's, the toughest resistance encountered was among professional counselors. The idea that an entire family unit — father, mother, children, auntie, uncle, even close friend — could meet all-at-once was almost too revolutionary. Today, the practice of including the family in the counseling milieu is much more common. Counseling with an individual in isolation may still be done, but it is considered desirable for significant others to have a place (on a consultation basis) in the treatment milieu.

Counseling and consulting are compatible and complementary professional methods. Consultation arose out of a need to affect more people in the counseling treatment milieu. The method of consultation provided a way to define relationships within a group in acceptable forms of commitment and made involvement a positive venture instead of a tentative unknown. Counseling defines relationships on a complementary one-up or one-down basis (Shostrom, 1967), which is particularly restricting to people in need of help. Vulnerable persons seem able to accept the consultation relationships definition. In group process jargon, the facilitator is less threatening as a concept than the counselor. The dilemma of being safe and benign or risking is not completely resolved by the method of consultation.

Consultation is a direct encounter with the central issue of access. Because most of the resources in a human organization are other people, the process of utilization of "my" talents needs both knowledge of the problem and the skill to solve it. Knowledge is shared in consultation. Skills are developed in the group practice arena. In group consultation the two major functions of knowledge and skills are handled all-at-once. Individual consultation between the counselor and the other person limits the practice arena to a verbal model. Individual and group consultation is used in the same way individual and group counseling is used — namely, in the configuration best suited to the task confronting the professional helping person.

Consultation is one method of working with people. It requires an expert with fully developed professional counselor competence.

AMBIGUITY IN THE CONSULTATION RELATIONSHIP

Consultation is an interactive form of work with other people. Social control is a matter of self-control and permission to enter the life space of these "others." Because the formal structure typical of principal-teacher or supervisor-teacher relationships is missing, the consultation encounter is frequently ambiguous. The process of imposing some familiar structure is an initial task, for consultation is essentially an encounter between equals instead of superiors and subordinates. Thus the usual social power of the expert authority is eliminated, and the counselor has to use his knowledge and skills for building relationships. There is some difficulty because the situation is novel and at first without structure (ambiguous).

Ambiguity is usually stress producing. The counselor may feel the stress too. It is especially helpful to acknowledge the emotional climate and begin with some honest sharing of feelings.

DEFINING THE TASK IN CONSULTATION

Task definition has several levels of complexity due to the varying abilities of the participants. The teacher will typically define an initial task that is familiar and in vogue — i.e., learning disability, brain damage, dyslexia, etc. Clinical labels serve to absolve the responsibility of the teacher from taking any action. The counselor needs to have enough professional competence to determine the task and to decide what is possible. Diagnosis may require clinical referral. Such decisions would be part of the initial problem solving. Consultation provides for other professional specialists to be brought into the situation. There is no need for monadic (simple single-focus) treatment.

WHAT DOES THE COUNSELOR-CONSULTANT DO?
THE CASE OF JENNY

The counselor-consultant reverses the field of activity in the traditional counselor role. Originally, the counselor was defined as an extension of the medical model of privacy, shut away in an office and maintaining an exclusive one-to-one relationship over time. This psychotherapeutic practice became part of the school counselor role, and it marks an essential change in the pattern of guidance in student personnel programs. The change came about primarily because of the influence of Carl Rogers's *Counseling and Psychotherapy* (1942). For some twenty years this psychotherapeutic model dominated counselor education programs and the counseling practice of professional practitioners.

Beginning with the NDEA counseling institutes in 1958, the number of professionally trained counselors markedly increased. They were initially taught the psychotherapeutic model. But about 1960 a new trend in school counseling, called "group," emerged. Group work was extended to consultation with families, teachers, and other significant persons in the life of the child and his learning environments. The inclusion of school administrators, supervisors, other counselors, teachers, parents, siblings, and even peers in the counseling milieu was slow in developing compared to some of the contemporary technological advances of the time (color television, for instance). Only now, as the 1970's open, are we able to say definitively that working with groups in any of the usual modes of the school and home environment is both a plausible and a desirable counselor function.

Leaving his office, the counselor enters the classroom with the teacher and the pupils to work with the youngster who has been referred for help. Several significant things are then set in motion. In the first place, people learn much more quickly by example than by vicarious means, including verbal definitions and descriptions. When the counselor applies his professional competence in the presence of teachers and pupils, they rapidly learn through direct exposure. In this case the teacher may learn the counselor's skill in working with a particular problem or a particular life condition or a particular child.

One of the authors was serving as consultant to a school district in south-central Arizona. The counselors, the assistant superintendent, and the school psychologist were sitting in the office of the superintendent discussing the dimensions and characteristics of the counselor-consultant role in the classroom with the teacher. The author was struck with the near impossibility of describing in the time allowed anything meaningful about the counselor-consultant role. So he suggested that he give a demonstration in a classroom situation. Arrangements were made to visit a first-grade class made up of fifteen youngsters selected out of the regular classroom because they had some particular behavior control problem. (Discussing the wisdom of placing youngsters who are suffering from similar difficulties of behavior control in the same classroom with one teacher will have to go by the board.) The teacher granted us permission to conduct the demonstration in her classroom.

Immediately after lunch the eight adults took seats at the back and to the side of the classroom and observed as the teacher completed her lesson with the group of youngsters. All of the children except one were sitting in their chairs at their desks and participated actively in the teacher's lesson. One little girl, whom we will call Jenny, was lying prone on the floor beside the teacher's desk. This is how the demonstration began. The story will be told in the first person.

> I (Fullmer) sat very near Jenny and began simply to observe what was happening in this classroom. The addition of eight adults caused very little concern among the youngsters because they had been forewarned about our coming; they continued to participate with the teacher without any more than the usual amount of glances, smiles, and giggles. They and the teacher seemed pleased to have guests. As I sat close to Jenny she exhibited a few attention-getting signals which I ignored. After about ten minutes she quietly got up, folded her blanket, and laid it aside. I continued to stay out of touch with her, not responding to her directly or indirectly. Jenny then proceeded to behave in a way that duplicated as nearly as possible what she could observe of the teacher's behavior. This included patting youngsters on the back because they had done a good job on their paper, which she had first examined carefully. She did not have any candy to eat or give to the other children so she quietly went about the room collecting paper wrappers from the candy and depositing it in a wastepaper basket near me. I continued to watch without direct participation or overly solicitous responses although I did recognize Jenny as a person and made it plain that her behavior was part of the presence being observed in the room. Other adults followed my lead and observed but didn't overtly respond to Jenny.
>
> It should be noted that no preparation of what would be done

was made in advance verbally or communicated in the room nonverbally. I was as much at a loss about what would happen and how the demonstration would unfold as anyone else. I had asked to be permitted simply to move into the classroom without advance preparation in order for the people to see that the demonstration was not staged. After about twenty minutes from the time we entered the room the teacher had completed her lesson and came toward the group of adults to ask for direction for the next move. Questions were raised and suggestions made by the counselors and the teacher concerning which child I might work with. I declined to allow any selection of individual children to take place on the grounds that I would choose the child or situation for the demonstration. This immediately avoided two types of errors that may arise in consultation work. (1) If I select the child, I do not have to guess what the teacher wants done. The error is avoided because I can operate on my assumptions instead of having to guess. (2) If the teacher selects the child, the child with the most severe and immediate problem may be missed or bypassed. The teacher will be inclined to pick the child who is most disturbing *her*. Interestingly, she did not mention Jenny as a possible target. Her suggestion was a little boy whose behavior was overtly disruptive but emotionally stable and well organized.

I asked the teacher merely to introduce me to the class to make me safe for them to talk to. She was to tell them that I was a teacher too and would conduct the class for the next few minutes. She introduced me by name, the children answered, and I moved to the front of the room. These were first-graders, and since it was the month of October they were in their sixth week in school. When I asked to be given a chair, the response was overwhelming; I had four chairs. So I invited those who had brought the chairs to sit with me. The purpose of this move is to assume a posture that puts one roughly on eye level with the children. Jenny had been extremely active in helping to arrange my position in the room and to accommodate any desires that I expressed. My opening remark to the class was "What would you like to do?"

I turned to Jenny and another little girl, who carried a panda doll about the same size as she, and asked, "Would you like to help me?" Jenny's reply was an excited *yes* and a very gross body movement which led her all the way to the teacher on the opposite side of the room. We waited, and Jenny raised her head from the teacher's lap, circled in a wide arc, and walked directly back to me.

We were ready to begin. I asked her whether she would like to help me run the class and she said yes. Whereupon she took over the teacher role and began a lesson in arithmetic. This conduct included her writing on the blackboard and virtually ignoring the members of the class. After a very few minutes the bell for recess rang. The teacher then lined the boys up on one side of the door and the girls on the other, and they marched out in a double line. Jenny did not leave with the group; she had not been going to recess for the entire time she had been in school. Jenny was now left with eight adults including the principal of the school and two state supervisors, an assistant superintendant, a school psychologist, two school counselors, and the author. I asked her whether she would like to conduct the class now? Jenny's response was "I don't have any students." I said, "Could we be your students?" Jenny looked at us in studied concentration. "You'll have to sit in the seats," she said and motioned toward the rows of chairs in the front of the room. As we took these chairs, the relationship was clearly defined as Jenny-teacher and adults-pupils.

She began by tapping with a wooden pointer — just barely long enough — on a wall chart printed with pictures and significant sounds, letters *m, n,* and so forth. "Well, say them!" she commanded, whereupon, in unison, the adults responded. She was progressing through the second column of these sounds when she came to one she did not know. In true teacher fashion, she tapped the paper and said, "We'll skip that one." Everyone laughed, and we moved on through the list. Following this exercise Jenny introduced a couple more until recess ended. When the youngsters returned to the classroom and found the adults sitting in their seats, the teacher merely suggested they sit in the guests' chairs. Jenny continued her class, but she was now joined by three children who became her assistants. At the end of one more exercise she was asked to relinquish control but she refused and started another exercise. I considered it essential not to overpower her but to get her to relinquish control of the class, but she obviously enjoyed the power of holding. When I appealed to her in terms of the need to meet another appointment which involved catching an airplane to go home, she said that she would let us go after the present lesson. We all joined in vigorously to achieve closure of this lesson. I did not know how the closure would be accomplished. Jenny solved the problem. She merely followed the lead of her teacher by saying, "You are now to be dismissed. Line up by the door." We lined up by the door, but girls and boys were on both sides. "Well, line up right," she said.

"You won't get to go until you line up correctly." So we lined up correctly by getting the boys on one side and the girls on the other, and Jenny opened the door and held it open while we marched out.

The feedback on what happened in this session should be deferred so that you can speculate about it. But maybe you can pause now before reading on and ponder what the conditions were and what consequences might have been expected.

This is the story.

Jenny had been in two schools during the six weeks of the first-grade year. Unable to maintain the desired behavior at the first school, she had been expelled and subsequently enrolled in the public school and put in a special class. The teacher had described her behavior in this way: During the morning the child would come to school with her parents and join the activities of the class until about noon. Then she would curl up on the floor and remain there for the rest of the day. She would progress to tears just before going home, and her mother would have to come and pick her up. At home, her mother had reported Jenny would cry until she went to sleep at night. This was Jenny before the classroom demonstration. I did not know any of the story until after we had left the classroom. In follow-up reports the teacher said that Jenny participated in school from that moment on and no longer dissolved into tears. She went out to recess, went to lunch with the other children, rode the bus to and from school, and never again repeated her old pattern of behavior. Near the end of that school year she transferred to another state and entered a new school. One year later she was still progressing in the normal way in the new situation.

You may want to speculate again about the why of the change and some of the aspects surrounding my contribution, the teacher's contributions, the contributions of the school and significant others. As soon as you have decided who was responsible for behavior changes, I would like to speculate with you; we will never be certain because there is no way to determine cause and effect in this kind of setting. The speculation goes like this. I believe that the teacher learned enough in that one brief exposure to keep Jenny's new behavior pattern going the rest of the day and to continue it the next day — by responding in a way that would allow Jenny to operate in the style she had developed in that encounter.

Sharing skills through direct action is only one of the possible approaches in the counselor-consultant model. The all-at-once phenomenon of group behavior carries with it a greater potential for communication than does the sequential development of a verbal description of a life event. The elements were all present in the Jenny case. Each counselor-consultant should have his own Jenny. I wonder whether scientific writing will ever allow for the inclusion of the admittedly uncertain elements in human behavior. Differences between Faust's position and Fullmer-Bernard's position on consultation are essentially differences of language and differences of emphasis among all the possible emphases. We strive to achieve a meaningful mix between (1) the determinism of the behaviorists and the reinforcement principles that certainly operate in the conditioning inherent in the cultural structure of learning in human behavior and (2) the phenomenological and process-oriented learning principles. Our task is to attempt a clarification of the doctrinaire positions of the behaviorists and the phenomenological exponents and to show that in consultation there is room for both the behaviorist and the phenomenological concepts.

Summary

The counselor, as a professionally competent human behavior specialist, needed a method for going beyond the usual limits of counseling. The relationship was the limit and is the limit for developmental counseling and remedial and corrective counseling.

Consultation is the method devised to take the counselor beyond the relationship. The counselor-consultant works with environment — especially learning environment. Our foundation of behavior is culture patterns and rules. Our position reduces mysticism by introducing a rationale for understanding behavior based upon culture rules.

Behaviorism is treated in the culture context as a credible doctrinaire position. The limits of that system are pointed out much as milieu systems limits are pointed out.

The small group is used as the heart of the consultation method. Group is the idea of sharing and giving access in a society that is extremely restrictive because it has commercialized sharing and delimited access by rules of protocol: caste and socioeconomic class.

Our society has grouped people according to income, race, education, social level, etc. Children are grouped in school in a similar pattern. The consultation group brings diverse backgrounds together to stress differentness as an asset, not a liability — because uniqueness too is highly prized in our culture–social system.

Developments in the counseling profession have placed the counselor at the threshold of a new role. It is herewith proposed that consulting is one of the legitimate functions of the professional counselor. Consultation is primarily a group function and therefore occurs with a variety of different special skills and resources represented by the members of the group.

The chief task of consultation is the improvement of learning environments. This brings up a number of additional aims and goals for consultation, the priority and sequence of which we attempt to define and promote.

The counselor's concern is expanded and extended to the environments — largely people environments — of the learner. This is in sharp contrast to the early days, when the counselor focused upon the individual and small groups of individuals but paid little or no attention to the environment provided by the culture program for learning to learn and the context created by the participants in counseling — both individual and group.

SUGGESTED ADDITIONAL READING

Cottle, Thomas J., 1969. "Bristol Township Schools: Strategy for Change," *Saturday Review*, 52(38):70–71+, September 20. *Here is the way one school system has used the strategy of consultation. Counselors and students can see the significance of the big change compared with the small-increments concept.*

Faust, Verne, 1968. *The Counselor-Consultant in the Elementary School*. Boston: Houghton Mifflin Company. *The student of counseling and consultation needs exposure to as many views as possible. Faust gives his views for the counselor-consultant in the elementary school. As perspective for secondary and higher schools, the material is valuable.*

Fullmer, D. W., and H. W. Bernard, 1964. *Counseling: Content and Process.* Chicago: Science Research Associates. *Early reports about family consultation in groups signaled the new direction toward the counselor-consultant function. The major issue was a plea to make a big change in the function of the counselor. The hope has remained open and the present authors build on this earlier work.*

Lazarus, Arnold, 1969. "Relationship Therapy: Often Necessary but Usually Insufficient," *Counseling Psychologist*, 1(2):25–27, Summer. *Superstitions need to be trimmed from psychotherapy. Lazarus thinks the truly active ingredients should be identified. It is necessary, he claims, to go beyond the relationship parameter in counseling and therapy.*

Rogers, C. R., 1968. "Interpersonal Relationships: U.S.A. 2000," *Journal of Applied Behavioral Sciences*, 4:265–280. *The future of man's relations with others and the physical environment comes to mean the consequences planned for and those that were missed. More people means more crowding. Interpersonal relations are an issue now.*

Chapter Four

EVOLVING ROLE OF
THE PROFESSIONAL
COUNSELOR

This statement is often reiterated in educational literature: The one thing we can be sure of is that things will change. Older persons in our society can look back on a lifetime and wonder whether the things they remember actually constituted reality. The "generation gap" is attributed to the fact that the rate of change has accelerated so much that communication is difficult. It is as if occupants of two cars are attempting to converse as they proceed, in the same direction, at sixty miles per hour. Sign language might help, but it is hard to maintain the same speed. In any case the cars keep going — if either stopped to assess the situation, the gap would widen.

Whatever school counseling may be in a particular locality, it will not stop just for the sake of evaluating its status. Examination must take place as the daily transactions continue. There will be no cataclysmic changes. Whatever counseling becomes in the next few years will evolve out of what is being done now, and especially out of what is dreamed of and hoped for now. Whatever counseling becomes is probably being practiced in at least an experimental form by some adventurous counselor. A senior class motto says it well: "Today is yesterday shaking hands with tomorrow."

Occupational Guidance

THE ROOTS OF GUIDANCE

Frank Parsons is credited with being the father of the guidance movement. He was, as are many now, concerned with the rapidity of change, and he proposed, by developing an occupational counseling program, to help boys find jobs. As he worked in a Boston settlement house, ideas similar to his were blossoming in a few schools throughout the nation. For instance, in the same year that Parsons initiated his plan in Boston — 1908 — a plan for vocational guidance was instituted in Grand Rapids, Michigan. It included more than matching personality and position; other parts of the program were moral guidance, course selection, counseling for cocurricular activities, and the use of group guidance to provide instruction in social living (Mathewson, 1962, p. 88).

Leaders during the early days of guidance behaved as if they thought that jobs should match personality and intelligence. The belief is tenacious, and to many professionals and nonprofessionals the reasoning is extremely plausible. A number of exacting research studies have indicated that there is a correlation between job satisfaction and scores on the Strong Vocational Interest Blank and the Minnesota Multiphasic Personality Inventory. Undoubtedly the Strong inventory does identify interests, but it has been shown that these interests are often transitory. The Minnesota inventory does provide clues to personality orientation and thus contributes to an understanding of the problems of work and social adjustment. Neither measure has been successful enough to cause it to become an integral part of all school counseling programs.

BEYOND THE MATCHING OF JOB AND PERSON

Doubts about the correlation of personality traits and job selection and success were expressed in a study by Stewart (1947), who found considerable overlap in the intelligence of workers in top-ranking job classifications and in the lower ones. For instance, the miners (a low-rank job category) who rated highest in intelligence exceeded the accountants (a high-rank category) who rated lowest in intelligence among their colleagues. Similar perplexing discoveries have recently been made about intelligence and school success in relation to adult professional competence (Strauss, 1969). The personality of teachers has been studied frequently, but the conclusions are equivocal. While the ability to establish empathy with students is important, the approach to empathy varies with specific cases of teacher-pupil interaction. Some pupils like their teachers stern and demanding; others prefer friendly, permissive instructors. It seems likely that those deemed to be successful on the job would also vary with the orientation of the boss. Some supervisors require workers who are obedient and responsive to instruction whereas others would prefer the resourceful and creative worker. Thus there is considerable range in intelligence and personality among workers who are regarded as successful in any one job category. A good deal of evidence supports the notion that job success is as much a function of attitude as it is of aptitude (Herzberg, 1966).

Such complexities have led some counselor educators to pronounce an "epitaph for vocational guidance." Barry and Wolf (1962, pp. 181–192) concluded, as a result of their study and analysis:

> There is no sound theory which underlies vocational guidance practices.
>
> There is no justification for separating vocational from personal, social, and educational guidance.
>
> The assumption that there is a "single, early, wise, intellectual vocational decision" is invalid.
>
> Many widely used vocational guidance procedures defeat rather than promote the process of helping students.
>
> The delimiting and restricting aspects of vocational guidance necessitates new views and approaches.

In the opinion of Barry and Wolf (1962, p. 181) it is unfortunate that criticism of a practice is so frequently thought of as being negative. They state an issue which the authors of this volume recognize: Out of experience and practice come insights which chart the way to future developments. Much of the value of vocational guidance stems from the stimulus it gave to the wider movement called, simply, *guidance*. Similarly, it is hoped that the experience and insight gained by school counselors in working with individual pupils will show the way to a realization of the value of working with key adults in the life of the pupil. The job of the counselor-consultant is not so much a new role as it is an expanded function.

The waning role of vocational counseling was partly the outcome of the phenomenon of change and the rapidity of technological progress. Vocational guidance loses pertinency when it is realized that most children now in elementary schools will ultimately work in jobs not yet in existence (McCully, 1969, p. 10). On the other hand, counseling for self-sufficiency gains pertinency as it is realized that knowledge now doubles every seven years. Education for resilience to, if not eagerness for, change emerges as the unprecedented challenge to professional counselors.

Evolution of the concept of guidance and counseling, from vocational orientation to such things as communication and self-realization, is reflected in the name of the journal of the American Personnel and Guidance Association. At one time called *Occupations*, since 1952 it has been titled *The Personnel and Guidance Journal*. Thus it indicates the emerging emphasis on people and process. Steady increase in the number of divisions within the Association also reflects evolution by acknowledging the fact of differentiation of function and diversity of interests.

There can be little doubt that the view one takes of man will condition his perspective on vocational guidance. If one believes that an individual is what he is largely because of his heredity, that he is born with intelligence, it is easier to accept the notion that one should find his slot and become content in occupying it. If, on the other hand, one believes that an individual is born with the *potential* for developing intelligence and personality, he is less sure that as a counselor his task is to help a person find his proper place. This issue has not been satisfactorily resolved, and the debate has received recent impetus from the research and writings of Jensen. He concludes that about 80 percent of intelligence is hereditary and that, further, racial differences in intelligence bear on educability. Since these differences are due, at least in part, to selective breeding and reproduction, education should offer a wider range of "educational methods, programs, and goals, and of *occupational opportunities* . . ." (Jensen, 1969a, p. 117).

Certainly the matter of occupational guidance and training has not been neglected, nor is it moribund. However, if we shift from individual status or potential to social organization, a diminution of the vocational orientation seems to be warranted. McCully (1969, p. 10) refers to an "overdeveloped society," one in which there is a steadily increasing demand for highly trained manpower and a steadily decreasing demand for manpower at the lower levels of mental ability. In such a society, whether one's ability is largely inherited or represents a potential for development, it is vital that each person be "trained" to the highest level possible rather than that doors of opportunity be closed by premature predictions about ultimate destiny. Regardless of whether his intelligence is 80 or 20 percent heritable, there still remains the massive matter of motivation — how to use the intelligence he has. It is postulated here that many more persons are capable of capitalizing on the opportunities provided in higher education than has heretofore been appreciated. Support for the contention is provided by the large numbers who took triumphant advantage of the GI Bill for furthering their education. Continued development may occur as the social roots of motivation are turned to advantage through the process of counseling.

The Concept of Counseling

Role Determined by Competence

Concomitant with, if not a result of, skepticism about the role of vocational guidance is the recent growth in interest and competence in counseling. Prominent among the many descriptions of the unique function of counseling are such items as self-understanding, self-realization, autonomy, responsibility, and effective social participation. At least in some counseling orientations the objectives range from encouraging the mere ventilation of feelings — lending an attentive ear — to developing a plan for improving social relations. Often the objective is to seek remediation of some self-defeating pattern of behavior. Other school counselors attempt to avoid the therapeutic relationship and, through referral, have a psychologist or psychiatrist work with the seriously disturbed youngster.

As expertise is acquired (for example, through the counseling institutes sponsored by the U.S. Office of Education and the upgrading of counselor education in colleges and universities), the relief of emotional disturbances has had more attention than formerly. Such work, often showing rather dramatic results, attracts more attention than does counseling, which is designed to help ordinary youngsters actualize more of their potentialities. Whether for ordinary or disturbed pupils, counseling is directed toward developing the individual's attitudes and attributes in such a way as to achieve mental health. The ultimate goal is a well-integrated, appropriately maturing person who is capable of the successful pursuit of self-realization.

THE PROFESSIONAL ROLE

Counseling involves working with an individual to (1) bring about changes in the individual, (2) alter the situation so that adjusting processes are facilitated, or (3) alter the individual's perception of the situation so that he feels less pain or more success. For example, the counselor (1) tries to get the individual to take an easier or a more challenging course than the one he is now taking, (2) approaches the teacher to see whether some alteration of methods will reduce the pupil's anxiety or resentment, or (3) attempts, perhaps through reflective counseling, to get the counselee to see that his mother does love him or that his teacher is not out to "get him."

One perception of counseling is that it seeks active behavior change. This is done through interrupting self-defeating patterns of behavior, intervening in the life processes of the individual, and influencing the quality and direction of growth (Fullmer and Bernard, 1964, p. 118). Such a view of counseling presumes that the counselee is capable of, and must ultimately assume, an autonomous and effective way of life. Behavior is interrupted by removing him from the situation or confronting him with what he is doing. Intervention means that the counselor has entered, for a brief period of time, the stream of life events. After the behavior has been stopped and the counselor has been accepted as an understanding adult, he influences the next choices and the next steps.

Counselors have various orientations regarding the amount of confrontation or teaching that should take place. Krumboltz (1966) views counseling as a particular kind of teaching-learning situation. The counselor recognizes the self-defeating nature of a certain behavior and through praise or recognition reinforces behaviors he knows will be more effective. There are others who are less sure about their omniscience as persons, let alone counselors, or are uncertain that they know what the correct answers to problems should be (Shoben, 1966). Understanding, as contrasted to learning (where the counselor knows the answers), is the important factor in this orientation.

Wrenn (1962, pp. 126 ff.), reporting for the Commission on Guidance in American Schools, summarizes the goals of the counseling function in relation to work with students:

1. "To Contribute to Student Self-Understanding and Self-Acceptance" (p. 127).[1] The student is helped to see the realities of his personal characteristics and aspirations in relation to cultural change and developmental opportunities.

2. "To Be Sensitive to Cultural Changes Which Affect Student Self-Understanding" (p. 128). In order to aid the student in seeing himself in relationship to his characteristics and the characteristics of society, it is necessary for the counselor to appreciate and understand the nature of the world and of the individual.

3. "To Help Students to Make Informed Educational and Vocational Choices" (p. 128). Executing this function starts with the student's perception of himself but immediately includes, in a rapidly changing technological world, vocational choice as a lifelong process. Vocational choice is subsidiary to fostering tolerance for ambiguity and developing the flexibility to meet and deal with change.

4. "To Develop Group Learning Experiences for Students" (p. 130). This function goes beyond group counseling as a means of saving time or achieving psychotherapy. It means groups convened and led by the counselor provide a learning experience for each participant which will enable him to see himself in relation to the reaction of others toward him.

5. "To Increase Student Self-Reliance" (p. 131). One of the distinctions between guidance and counseling is highlighted in this statement. It is the counselor's task to help the individual clarify his understanding of himself and his goals

[1] Headings are quoted directly from C. Gilbert Wrenn, 1962, *The Counselor in a Changing World* (Washington: American Personnel and Guidance Association). Reprinted by permission of the publisher.

so the student can assume responsibility for the choice *he* makes. Wrenn states that "Counselors have no business making things easy for a student"; however (probably because they are taken out of context), these words and this idea would be debated by the authors of the present volume. To the extent that counselors attempt to improve the learning milieu, they are making things easier for the student, yet this need not imply any decrease in self-reliance.

6. "To Counsel Girls Realistically" (p. 131). Employment statistics reveal that the vast majority of girls, when they become adults, will perform the dual role of wife and worker. Thus, the counselor must face the issue of marriage-plus-job when thinking of the girl's self-respect, self-confidence, and self-realization.

7. "To Accept and Encourage Diversity in Talents" (p. 132). Although educators have long given lip service to this objective, the typical educational practice is to encourage conformity and subscribe to the tyranny of the average. Torrance (1969) has conducted research which substantiates Plato's statement that "what is honored in a country will be cultivated there." In schools where originality, creativity, and diversity are encouraged a greater proportion of pupils reveal those characteristics. Wrenn calls on counselors to provide some of that encouragement.

Later discussion (Chapter Six) will give more details about counseling theories; the purpose here is to show that counseling is in a process of transition — as the whole pupil personnel field is in a state of flux. The initial stance in the profession was quite properly called guidance. The student was literally led by the hand to make certain choices. His scores on intelligence, personality, and vocational aptitude tests provided data which influenced the guide. An analogy: When the big-game sportsman goes out with a guide, the idea is to get the meat. The guide might tell his client where to go and how to stand when he gets there. Moreover, in case there was a big night preceding the hunt, the guide might have to pull the trigger. Counseling places more of the responsibility on the counselee — though not all, as seen from the foregoing pages. Changes in the individual or in his perceptions are sought that will enable him to select his own goals and choose the routes toward them.

Consultation constitutes another phase: The orientation is in terms of changing the milieu of the pupil so that his hunting trip will be less hazardous. A degree of success at the "lower, more easily hunted areas" will make it more probable that the counselor can build the skill and confidence required to hunt the more rugged terrain. In terms of personnel practices this sequence may be conceptualized as follows: Guidance (dependent on guidance specialist omniscience) led to counseling (with emphasis on individual initiative, learning, and responsibility), which in turn led to consultation (with a view to restructuring the environment — especially the learning environment). None of these concepts is mutually exclusive, and counselors who have not thought of their role as consultation have in reality been consulting.

Rousseve (1969) has indicated that one issue facing counselor educators is that of making a candid statement of their own position and orientation. The authors of this volume agree despite the belief of some counselor educators that in some degree such a statement deprives the student of his own full autonomy and freedom of choice. Further, we believe that one's actions, if not his words, inevitably reveal his orientation. Because this book, more obviously than we wish, does reveal our position, we now emphasize only the more prominent of our basic premises. Pierson (1965), in an evaluation of counselor education as conducted in National Defense Education Act Counseling and Guidance Institutes, provided a framework for identifying the more salient issues in the work and preparation of counselors. There were initially nine issues, but in view of their overlap he condensed them into five: determinism and free society, mental health and individual responsibility, the role of science and supervised counseling practice, the relationship of teaching to counseling, and the role of the school counselor. These are used as the basis for clarifying our perspective.

Man is viewed as an organism which is open and ready for growth and development. He is simultaneously influenced by environmental conditions *and* by his perception of those conditions as well as by his hopes, aspirations, and visions. The individual has some control over his own behavior, and the counselor should be as well acquainted with the postulates of proactive, humanistic psychology as he is with the tenets of behaviorism and psychoanalysis. Man is not born with intelligence or personality but with a potential for developing it, in a social context. One becomes human by association with other humans.

Mental health is achieved as a by-product of involvement, being of some consequence in the lives of others, and tolerating the trauma of transcendence. Involvement and being of consequence emphasize individual responsibility. All persons, counselors included, exert their greatest influence through what they do to and with themselves. The mentally healthy individual is less inclined to manifest the "Why don't they . . . ?" syndrome than to ask, "How can I . . . ?" This posture is particularly apropos to the development of the role of counselor-consultant.

To go beyond being a technician to being a professional it is necessary that one be thoroughly grounded in the basic sciences of his field. The conventional approach would require personality theory, psychological assessment, differential psychology, counseling theory, and the like. Pierson (1965) found that most programs in counselor education were adding sociology, anthropology, and sometimes communications theory. Supplementing the basic sciences is counseling practicum. Required in only a few counselor preparation programs prior to the Institutes — even at the doctorate level — practicum is now universally required in accredited programs. We would add to such real-life experience the desirability of the professional candidate's being counseled. If one is to give help, he must be capable of receiving it. In addition, one gains a different perspective on counseling when he is on the receiving end. We believe that one should also live through the process of consultation — call it consultation practicum — before he can logically pronounce judgment on the desirability and scope of consultation.

Although we do not think that teaching experience should be a prerequisite to counselor preparation or certification, we do feel that counseling is a kind of teaching — teaching being defined as the guidance of learning. Pierson found that

> The presence in schools of some inept and inadequately trained counselors has justified the classroom teacher's concern about the

separation of guidance from teaching. Such unqualified counselors have often underestimated the teacher's competence in guidance and they have overestimated their own guidance abilities.[2]

It is our conviction that the professional counselor can maximize his influence on pupil growth if he works through the teacher with a view to further developing the teacher's competence in guidance activities and the application of such counseling skills as listening, encouraging pupil self-examination, examining the processes of learning, and encouraging pupil communication with peers and teachers. We are in accord with the position taken by counselor educators in institutes:

> The replies received from counselor educators in institutes indicate that they believe school counselors must support classroom teachers in their guidance efforts. They regard the school counselor as an important specialist available to students, parents, teachers, and administrators as the entire school community strives to achieve the goal of optimum development of the individual. They believe that school counselors should counsel students individually and in small groups and that they should serve as consultants to teachers, parents, and administrators. They point out that counselors must assume leadership responsibilities for the guidance program of the school, but that counselors cannot be responsible for all guidance or even all counseling.[3]

In spite of the efforts of APGA as a professional organization to define the role of the counselor, and in spite of the efforts of individual counselors to seek formal definition of their role by administrators or school boards, we believe that role definition is achieved through levels of competence. "What an individual knows defines his role and task; what an individual is establishes his limits" (Bernard and Fullmer, 1969, p. 3). If one is not prepared to do counseling, he will be found making schedules, planning programs, and keeping records. He will succumb to the temptation to become a pencil pusher in the school office. If one is a competent counselor, he will not have to demand a role. The

[2] George A. Pierson, 1965, *An Evaluation: Counselor Education in Regular Session Institutes* (Washington: Office of Education, U.S. Department of Health, Education, and Welfare), p. 38.

[3] *Ibid.*

need for the service is such that he will gravitate into it. Thus, the counselor's role cannot be predetermined or defined in a book because the person himself defines it in terms of his own competence.

The same can be said with respect to development of the consultant role. It must be experienced. Developing skill in it leads to expanding the number of contacts, and it helps to have feedback from colleagues, teachers, or administrators. In the absence of such feedback, acknowledgment from pupils or parents can provide support for continued development.

Consultation

CLIMATE FOR DEVELOPING THE CONSULTATION PROCESS

What the interests and functions of school counselors will be by the end of the 1970's is hazardous to predict. However, there is evidence of growing involvement in the process of consultation. Perhaps the 1969 Senate Resolutions of the American Personnel and Guidance Association provide substantial clues to developments in the decade of the 1970's (APGA, 1969).

In three of the seventeen resolutions passed by the Senate in 1969, consulting or consultation is specifically mentioned. Resolution No. 4 calls upon counselor education faculties to establish local committees to advise them of needs and urges them to *consult* with those committees and representatives of the American Personnel and Guidance Association in formulating new programs for counselor education. Resolution No. 7 calls upon the Association to exert influence on the U.S. Office of Education to establish a highy visible unit to deal with the functions of guidance and counseling, urging that unit to "provide *consultation,* leadership, organization, stimulation, and assistance" in ten specific areas — one of which is consultation with state departments of education in planning and evaluation of counseling programs. Resolution No. 14 calls for the APGA to establish a commission charged with the responsibility of cooperating with and helping division and branch offices of the Association and urges that commission to seek the aid of outside resource consultants and itself to *consult* with national and state divisions.

Seven of the seventeen resolutions deal with concerns that seem to come within the purview of the consultation concept — although the words *consulting* and *consultation* are not used in the resolution. Specifically these seven resolutions deal with the involvement and participation of persons, as people, in the further evolution of counseling practices. Resolutions No. 1 and No. 6 call for involving students in the design of curricular and cocurricular programs in schools and colleges, as well as for involving them in identifying and assessing the causes of student unrest. Resolution No. 3 proposes that the APGA endorse the establishment of age eighteen as the standard age for voting eligibility — clearly an engagement of adults with youth and of youth in their own and the adult world. Resolution No. 5 calls for state and national counselors in administrative positions to assist local counselors in protecting their rights as professional people. Resolution No. 9 deals with state executive officers' using funds available to provide *advice and guidance* on matters of vocational education — again a consulting capacity. Resolution No. 16 directs the APGA's Commission on Human Rights and Opportunities to serve as a *resource* for individuals and groups planning and implementing the expansion and guaranteeing of human rights. Resolution No. 17 *demands* that the APGA concern itself with the specific needs of nonwhite students and that nonwhite members of the Association be represented in those actions which deal with nonwhites.

Concern with people as people has always had high priority among guidance workers and counselors. What is new in the profession, and in the resolutions of 1969, is that people planning together, communicating with each other, and working cooperatively are made a focal point. It seems that the mystery of what goes on in the counseling cubicle is rapidly being replaced with an openness of communication and a recognition of the worth and contribution of people of all ages and degrees of responsibility. Quite candidly, the authors are disappointed that the resolutions do not deal more directly with the relationship of counselor-consultants and classroom teachers. Comfort can be taken from the hypothesis that resolutions dealing with cooperative effort of counselors at local, state, and national levels will probably reduce the distance from the counselor's office to the teacher's classroom.

Even though in 1969 the APGA Senate did not address itself to the role of consultant with teachers, the function has been anticipated by others in the profession. Danskin, Kennedy, and Friesen (1965) have recommended that counselors expand their function by becoming *consultants in human development*. At least some counselors, they say, have become disenchanted with the traditional guidance services of individual inventory, information, counseling, placement, and follow-up and have, little by little, taken on the responsibilities of curriculum planning, scheduling, and directing student activities in hopes of improving the students' academic menu. Now the time is ripe, they assert, for becoming experts in the area of human development and, by means of that knowledge, seeking to improve the learning climate of the school as a whole. This would involve an understanding about socio-economic class and what the pupils bring to the school from their families and social status. Such knowledge would include a perception of the role and influence of peer groups. It would entail acquaintance with the matter of teacher-pupil interaction. And this interaction is no unitary thing because the learning style of some pupils demands succor and that of other pupils is aggressive-competitive. (Similar differences might be noticed with regard to teaching styles: Some teachers are effective on a didactic level while others are just as effective using a guidance and resource persons approach.) The search for data on learning climates and patterns of human development would also require acquaintance with the subcultures which exist within a school. Although Danskin and his associates were concerned with student subcultures, others have taken note of such things as administrative subcultures, the curriculum culture, and the instructional subsystem (Beck et al., 1968, pp. 207 ff.). Of considerable pertinence in this volume are two observations made by Danskin and his colleagues. (1) Not all teachers and administrators are waiting with open arms and bated breath for counselors to take such a pervasive approach to learning and human development. (2) Perhaps many guidance functions will remain essentially as they have been conventionally defined. It may then be necessary to develop a new breed, and some counselors will themselves face additional career choices.

The Counselor as Instrument of Change

McCully, too, recognized the necessity and challenge of the counselor's upgrading his professional status by including the consultant function. He acknowledged the worth of the guidance specialist who works at the technician level but he envisioned the coming professionalization as the result of improved levels of competence rather than as an outcome of organization and pressure. His vision included the requirement that the counselor become a scholar of technological changes in human processes and interaction, and a scholar in the philosophy of the nature and potentials of man. Added to the responsibility for scholarship is responsibility for action. Two aspects of the action phase are outstanding. One is that a counselor must transcend the process of talking about change and experience it himself. Those who have lived through change and the dilemma of ambiguity during their preparation period know that the consequences are not fatal. Indeed, innovation and transcendence may be a way of life for some (see the postulation "Heterostasis vs. Homeostasis," Chapter Two). A second area of action, according to McCully (1969, p. 14), is that "the counselor of the future could become an effective consultant to teachers with respect to these conditions in the learning environment — a human instrument of change."

McCully justified the call for a different level of professional competence in terms of four broad social trends and on the basis of two challenges presented by current educational dilemmas. (1) Our society has suffered a loss of effectiveness in inducting youth into participating membership in adult society. (2) Because of rapid technological change, society experiences continuing difficulty in introducing youth into work careers. (3) Our society is overdeveloped; i.e., there is continuing decrease in the need for manpower at the lower levels. (4) Hierarchical, bureaucratic organization in corporate society tends to depress individualism. (5) Because the foregoing social phenomena will not disappear as the result of philosophical analysis, it is necessary for the schools to devise and encourage ways to protect the integrity and individuality of the learner (and again it is suggested that the postulations set forth in Chapter Two be examined).[4] (6) A corollary of (3) and (4) above is that schools cannot afford to scrap human

---

[4] Such examination will provide a small exercise in the reader's becoming responsible for his own learning, as suggested by McCully in the words "experiencing the process."

potential by countenancing the high incidence of school dropouts. Emphasis must therefore be on a total learning environment that focuses on freedom and responsibility. Student self-concepts must be developed which will allow students to perceive themselves *as a part of* their determining environment.

McCully considered counselors — with their knowledge and skill related to interpersonal transaction, human development, communication, and tradition of intervention in the lives of others — the most logical persons to make the changes needed in an evolving school.

Resistance to the Counselor as Consultant

Not all those who perceive the need for a new function in the operation of schools agree that it should be assumed by counselors. Boy and Pine (1969) see a place for additional service calling for social engineering or expertise in cultural architecture. This added service would seek to restructure the school environment in response to the sociological problems of pupils. Such restructuring requires a social analyst who will examine the social concerns of adolescents, the class and status system of the school, teacher roles and relationships, the learning climate, values existing (and conflicting) in the schools, and so on. Boy and Pine contend that this analyst should be a sociologist or an anthropologist, not a counselor. The counselor already has a legitimate and valued function, they maintain — that of helping individuals and groups with their problems — and this role should not be diluted or deflected. Rather, the function of counseling individuals and groups should complement the function of social analyst. Retention of the counseling role is especially important because administrators and teachers have only recently begun to accept it, and the reason for the delayed acceptance is that until the last decade there have not been enough *professionally prepared* counselors to demonstrate the effectiveness of their service. Moreover, the battle is not yet won; counselors are still engaged in the process of winning acceptance and achieving professional status. There is danger that skewing or distorting their hard-won role may cause counselors to lose their effectiveness.

The authors of this book agree with the logic presented by Boy and Pine. A professional is needed who looks at the entire school system and assesses its impact on both formal and informal learnings. Individual and group counseling should not be diluted or sidetracked. But we do not agree that a sociologist or an anthropologist is in a better position to implement the service. While he has expertise in social organization and social systems, he typically lacks the orientation toward intervention in the lives of others. The counselor could bring to the role of counselor-consultant his skill in communication, his understanding of group processes, his knowledge of the sources of motivation, and his posture of intervening in, and influencing, the lives of others. His orientation is one of action as contrasted to analysis. Nor do we agree that the additional function inevitably means dilution of an established role. Consultation is counseling, albeit on a base somewhat broader than that conventionally accepted. Experience has already demonstrated that not all counselors can develop the skills needed; often they do not have the inclination to develop them. Moreover, the number of persons who will qualify at the level of consultant — in terms of preparation and personality — will be so limited that the addition of "consulting" will not significantly dilute existing services.

Summary

The concept of counselor-consultant is a stage in the evolution of the total guidance movement. It grew out of, and is a part of, the challenges and problems constantly facing the counseling profession. Occupational guidance was the original germ out of which developed the broad movement of guidance. The early history of guidance almost immediately revealed that personal characteristics have to be studied in connection with job requirements.

Technological and cultural evolution and revolution kept emphasizing the need for new and additional pupil personnel services in the schools. Counseling was one of the answers to this insistent need. As experience with the skills of counseling was gained and some understanding reached of the meanings it might have, counseling evolved from an analysis of the individual to an attempt to influence patterns of personal development. Changing culture and growing appreciation of the dynamics of personality led to greater recognition of pupil need for autonomy, involvement, and freedom combined with responsibility. Increasingly decisions were left to the individual in hopes that he would become able continuously to meet and deal with changing cultural and occupational phenomena.

It is but a small step toward, perhaps even a part of, independence and autonomy to realize that in order to experience autonomy it is necessary to have alternatives from which to choose. Hence the concern with the total learning environment and with developing the skills and opportunity to involve and communicate with a wider spectrum of the human environment. Professional counselors have the basic skills to implement such dialogue between all who constitute the learning community.

SUGGESTED ADDITIONAL READINGS

Bernard, Harold W., and Daniel W. Fullmer, 1969. *Principles of Guidance: A Basic Text.* Scranton, Pa.: International Textbook Company. Pp. 3–24. *The chapter "Background, Status, and Future of Guidance" presents a brief history of guidance and counseling upon which the need for further research and experimentation is postulated.*

Boy, Angelo V., and Gerald J. Pine, 1969. "A Sociological View of the Counselor's Role: A Dilemma and a Solution," *Personnel and Guidance Journal,* 47:736–740. *Because the school counselor's role is still open for a defined identity, the authors look upon the proliferation of duties as a hazard. The function of consultant on the learning environment of the school culture should therefore be left to others than counselors — sociologists or anthropologists perhaps.*

McCully, C. Harold, 1969. *Challenge for Change in Counselor Education,* compiled by Lyle L. Miller. Minneapolis: Burgess Publishing Company. Pp. 8–15. The chapter "The Counselor — Instrument of Change" is also published in *Teachers College Record,* 66:405–412. *Changes in society and the failure of schools to prepare youth for those changes make it necessary to develop some new approaches. McCully regards counselors as the logical persons to effect the needed intervention and innovation.*

Pierson, George A., 1965. *An Evaluation: Counselor Education in Regular Session Institutes.* Washington: Office of Education, U.S. Department of Health, Education, and Welfare. Pp. 61–69. *On the basis of a study of pioneering work done in counselor education in NDEA Institutes, Pierson makes some recommendations for further action and experimentation.*

Thoresen, Carl E., 1969. "The Counselor as an Applied Behavioral Scientist," *Personnel and Guidance Journal,* 47:841–848. *"The swirl of change — instant history — coupled with contemporary human problems makes it imperative that counselors shed their complacencies and 'truths' in order to doubt, question, and examine all that they now do." No one model of counseling or of role definition will suffice.*

Chapter Five

CONSULTING:
A PROFESSIONAL FUNCTION
OF THE COUNSELOR

The *product* of education has become less important than the *process* by which the product is achieved. This shift is tantamount to giving an end to the means. It has also caused consulting to find a place in the current professional practice of counseling in the schools.

With from one-fourth to one-third of our population engaged in the process of education we can expect business and industry to continue, or even accelerate, interest in things educational. The complex paradox of product and process continues to consume our energies.

The science of human behavior confronts us with the paradox between the determinism in *objective description* of behavior and the free and responsible personal choice of the *subjective experience* of living. Understanding behavior as being determined by some prior circumstance which causes the current observed behavior is clearly evident when behavior is placed under objective investigation. The present status of our knowledge indicates that we may continue to live with this paradox between free-choice subjectivity and antecedent-objective determinism.

When economic planners seem to turn education into the elixir of human capital, it is essential to try to understand the nature of the paradox between product and process in the educational function.

Consulting is the process of bringing people together. When people are brought together, attention can be focused upon the *process* and the *product* of the task. Equally important is understanding in depth the nature of the processes that go on if indeed any product is to be achieved. When small groups of people are brought together, it is reasonable to expect more than one product to be achieved. Here again is a paradox: If you attempt to regulate the process in the small group in order to achieve the preordained product, the efficiency and efficacy are questionable. As the saying goes, a camel is really a horse put together by a committee. In fact, if one has specific tasks leading to a specific product, it is wiser to commission an individual and provide him with the resources necessary to turn out the product. The model may be described as the fine line drawn between the process by which many products are achieved (none of which has been designated in advance, but only approximated in theory and expectation) and the producing of a specific product that has been projected a priori.

When a counselor-consultant consults with a group, concern is with the process rather than the product. The product becomes a kind of secondary gain. This is one way to describe verbally the resolution of the paradox between product and process.

The Professionalization of Counseling

INITIAL STEPS IN PROFESSIONALIZATION

McCully (1969) was one of the architects of professionalization of the school counselor. Beginning in the early 1960's (McCully, 1962) the matter of professionalization of school counseling was before the professional association in journal articles, conference speeches, and major association programs. Throughout the 1960's the tide of unrest continued to expose the issues surrounding the occupation of counselor. Some leaders argued for commitment to education. Others proposed in-depth identification with established disciplines—e.g., psychology.

These issues continue to agitate professional leaders in the American Personnel and Guidance Association and in the universities and colleges involved with counselor education. A joint policy statement of the Association for Counselor Education and Supervision and the American School Counselor Association concerning a school counselor written especially for superintendents of schools and school boards was published in 1969. The professional association, American Personnel and Guidance Association, and the American Association of School Administrators combine their intent for the *expectations* and *commitments* of counselors in the schools. The statement covers direct individual and group counseling service to students. In addition, it considers two indirect expectations: consultation with significant adults and consultation with significant professional persons concerned with the emotional-cognitive climate of the school. These clearly support the thesis that consultation is a major responsibility of the school counselor.

McCully (1962) was one of the first leaders in counselor education to become concerned with whether the concept of a counseling profession, as it exists in the American social system, could survive at all under a totalitarian society. He felt that occupations aspiring to become professions must qualify by virtue of their unique services. The attitudes and expectations of the public would be the ultimate test. The parallel between the free society, the private enterprise concept, and the professions as they have developed is indeed striking. Professions carry more prestige than do occupations. The material rewards in a profession frequently are less in quantity than are those in some occupations, yet occupations seem to be considered of less value.

It is considerably more difficult to defend professionalism as an entity in a vacuum than to defend it with reference to the criteria for quality performance of a service to citizens in a free society. The latter approach is the intent of much of the literature concerning the professionalization of counseling. Since consulting is a professional function of the counselor, it follows that the counselor should indeed be a professional person. It is not enough to merely claim to be a professional. The society must show recognition commensurate with professional status, primarily through support by financial and/or social prestige of the positions and services of professional counselors. For example, professional status allows social service to be better performed than it could be by a technician at the occupation level. The utilization of an expert in a democratic society becomes more important when it is recognized that status difference is under the control of the consumer. The professional person is ultimately responsible and accountable to his public. Or rather, the professional is responsible to his colleagues or peers and is accountable to his public.

McCully (1962) was asking why the call for professionalization of the school counselor did not come. A number of reasons were advanced to account for the apparent lack of progress. All of them seemed plausible but of little consequence when one considers the nature of the school. The social system of the school has maintained and continues to protect a relatively stable status structure. The counselor may achieve what amounts to professional recognition on the job but will never be the happy victim of having professional status thrust upon him.

Lieberman, Darley, Caplow, Lasky, Mueller, Selden, and Wrenn are also referred to in McCully's work as having made considerable contributions to the idea of professionalization of school counseling. Many of these people have been concerned in their professional careers with the broader category of *student personnel services*. All seem to agree that the following list contains most of the aspects and traits characterizing an occupation as a profession.

1. The members perform a unique and definite social service;
2. Performance of the specified social service rests primarily upon intellectual techniques;
3. Society has delegated to qualified members of the occupational group exclusive authority to provide the specified social service;
4. The members possess a common body of knowledge which can be identified and can be communicated through intellectual processes of higher education;
5. Entry into qualified membership requires an extensive period of specialized training;
6. The members as a corporate group assure minimum competence for entry into the occupation by setting and enforcing standards for selection, training, and licensure or certification;
7. The members possess a broad range of autonomy in performing the specified social service;
8. The members accept broad personal responsibility for judgments made and acts performed in providing the specified social service;

9. Emphasis is placed upon service to society rather than upon economic gain in the behavior of the corporate group as well as in the performance of the specified social service by individual members;

10. Standards of professional conduct for members are made explicit by a functional code of ethics; and

11. Throughout his career the member constantly takes positive steps to up-date his competency by keeping abreast of relevant technical literature, research, and participation in meetings of the corporate group of members.[1]

STAGES IN THE DEVELOPMENT OF A PROFESSION

Stage 1. McCully (1962) further proposes six developmental stages thta are essential to the development of a profession:

1. The unique social service the school counselor performs must be identified in a manner which will differentiate it from the services properly provided by all other staff in the school setting.

2. Standards for the selection and training of school counselors must be developed and such standards must be acceptable to the corporate group of qualified school counselors as well as to those professional schools offering counselor preparation of high quality.

3. In order to make selection and training standards functional it will be necessary to develop a means of accrediting those institutions which meet such standards on at least a minimum basis.

4. In order to assure the public and prospective employers that entering school counselors possess at least minimum competence to perform their tasks, certification must be based on more valid estimates of minimum competence.

5. Qualified practitioner school counselors, severally and as a corporate group, must actively involve themselves in winning and maintaining sufficient autonomy to permit them to perform their unique service in a professional manner; they must severally assume responsibility for their individual judgments and action in the performance of their unique service, and as

[1] C. Harold McCully, 1962, "The School Counselor: Strategy for Professionalization," *Personnel and Guidance Journal*, 40(8):682–683, April. Reprinted by permission of the publisher.

a corporate group assume responsibility for safeguarding the interests of the public they serve.

6. The corporate group of qualified school counselors must possess and enforce a code of ethics governing the professional conduct of its members.[2]

Wrenn (1962) decided that *guidance worker* was too broad a term because it incorporated a vast compendium of services for which it would be impossible to prepare a professional worker adequately. Attention had shifted to the counselor as the person for whom some definitive delimiting of expectations and commitments could be made. This chapter continues to peruse the expectation and commitment placed on the counselor in the school. Wrenn gave four major tasks as defining the professional counselor in a somewhat future-orientated context in the final chapter of his *Counselor in a Changing World*. First, the counselor would continue to be influenced by psychological understandings with a broad expansion beyond individual-differences testing and the measurement level of concern and skill. In addition to these highly technical and tool subject orientations the psychological understandings were seen by Wrenn to have been more concerned with behavior dynamics of the individual and psychological dynamics in small groups. Sensitivity to the uniqueness of human behavior was especially cited as an area of the future. In our counselor education programs we currently cover much of the material referred to by Wrenn.

Wrenn's second task had to do with the environments of the individual and the counselor — the culture of both community and nation as well as international cross-cultural study. The cross-culture foundation is particularly characteristic of positions taken by the authors in other writing (Fullmer and Bernard, 1964). The professional role is that of *consultant,* as the counselor proceeds to work with teachers and parents. It is essential to understand the cultural contexts out of which people come. Many conflicts in the classroom result from the personal differences that have their roots in the cultural background of each individual person. To know this much may save hours of wandering about attempting to find a technique that will permit a teacher and a student to

[2] *Ibid.*, pp. 683–687.

work together rather than to actualize their conflicts. If the teacher can come to understand the difference between his culture and the child's culture, the problem can be solved.

The cultural context in group includes more than mere social understanding. There is an overpowering need to comprehend the economic aspects of the relationships between people and their world of work. Across cultures it is frequently possible to utilize disciplines of both sociology and anthropology in the effort to understand international and intercultural relations when inter-action occurs on a person-to-person level. For example, in Honolulu there has been a marked increase in the immigration quotas from the Philippines since July, 1968, reflected in the sharp rise in the numbers of non-English-speaking pupils in the public schools. This condition has confronted the schools with the need to understand both the local culture and the foreign culture. Teachers and counselors find a very practical application for knowledge about interpersonal relationships and their effect upon the rate of speed at which these new immigrant youngsters learn the English language and are able to proceed with the class at a given grade level.

Wrenn's third emphasis has tremendous importance in current efforts to describe the professional role of the counselor. The professional role of the counselor includes consultation with sig-nificant adults outside the school. It is realized that counselors must ultimately work with all available significant adults — teachers, parents, and other human behavior specialists — if the milieu of the child is to come under the systematic influence of the counselor. In order for the counselor to assume these responsibilities, he has to understand the curriculum, the organization of the school, and of course the way all school purposes relate to the instructional program. The professional counselor acting as a consultant will have all of the relevant information. Only a professional practitioner could be expected to have the initiative and to carry out the independent study necessary to achieve an appropriate level of knowing.

A fourth task is reported by Wrenn. If a counselor as a pro-fessional is to perform his unique services, he needs to understand the research reported in the literature. He must be aware of and evaluate its sources and apply research procedures to his own work.

At the end of his book Wrenn was able to recommend the

minimum two-year graduate counselor education program in order to assure minimum levels of preparation for the professional counselor. All of these notions have some relevance to the second stage in the development of professional counseling.

Stage 2. "Standards for the selection and training of school counselors must be developed and such standards must be acceptable to the corporate group of qualified school counselors as well as to those professional schools offering counselor preparation of high quality." Selection and training standards continue to be ambiguous and inadequately defined.

There exists a complete set of standards for the preparation of school counselors, published by the American Personnel and Guidance Association. Counselor education programs may, upon request, be evaluated in terms of these criteria to establish to what extent they meet the recommendations of the professional association.

ACES, ASCA, APGA, and APA (American Psychological Association) Division 17 have all contributed to the formulation of criteria for preparation of school counselors.

Stage 3. "In order to make selection and training standards functional it will be necessary to develop a means of accrediting those institutions which meet such standards on at least a minimum basis."[3]

This developmental task is largely unmet by most of the institutions currently training counselors. The National Commission on Accreditation in Teacher Education and Professional Standards has been the most active accrediting agency carrying some criteria for counselor education along with its efforts to evaluate and accredit teacher education programs.

Counselor education is considered graduate teacher education. The professional competence is closely tied to the quality and competence of the training program. In 1910 Abraham Flexner published his report about medical education in the United States and Canada. Following the report, the number of schools preparing medical doctors was reduced, and the quality of the remaining programs was upgraded. The result has been a continuing growth in the excellence of the profession of medicine. Probably it will be necessary for

[3] *Ibid.,* p. 685.

something similar to happen in counselor education before we can hope to see a nationwide shift in the professional quality of counselors.

Stage 4. "In order to assure the public and prospective employers that entering school counselors possess at least minimum competence to perform their tasks, certification must be based on more valid estimates of minimum competence."[4]

Our profession has been reluctant to engage in any hard-core evaluation of what competencies are necessary as well as to specify the level of competence of a given practitioner. Until these kinds of determinations are made, it may be difficult for the school counselor to achieve the professional status that is possible for him. The idea of competence is a viable criterion against which to judge quality in a professional practitioner. The "shadow boxing" that goes on, as McCully so aptly phrases it, has to do with this question of certification of counselors. Do counselors really need to be teachers first? Of course, as long as that red herring distracts the counseling profession, it will be necessary to screen out many competent counselors because they do not have (and choose not to get) the minimum qualifications required for classroom teaching.

Jersild (1955) has pointed to the possibility that the consequences of a rather simple-minded distinction between teachers and counselors have been overlooked.

Tiedeman (1961) thinks that the criteria of prior employment and specific course specification have been outmoded by new developments in the professionalization of counseling.

Stage 5.

> Qualified practitioner school counselors, severally and as a corporate group, must actively involve themselves in winning and maintaining sufficient autonomy to permit them to perform their unique service in a professional manner; they must severally assume responsibility for their individual judgments and action in the performance of their unique service, and as a corporate group assume responsibility for safeguarding the interests of the public they serve.[5]

4 *Ibid.*, p. 686.
5 *Ibid.*, p. 687.

A profession is distinguished partly by the independence of judgment exercised by its practitioners. The institution of the school is such that independent judgment must come under rather strenuous controls. The exercise of these controls can vary from institution to institution. Consequently, the amount of freedom will be prescribed.

Stage 6. "The corporate group of qualified school counselors must possess and enforce a code of ethics governing the professional conduct of its members."[6]

No group can survive for long unless it carefully polices its own operations. Group members — the community of scholars, the community of peers, and the professionals of school counseling — will require supervision in order to maintain and guarantee quality performance, professional ethics, and high regard for the welfare of the recipients of the professional service.

Counselor-Consultant as Change Agent

DISLOCATION

Change is dislocation from familiar environments to ambiguous or unfamiliar environments. The rural family moves to the city and finds the new milieu strange. The skills the father and mother bring with them are no longer productive as they were at home. Change leads to conditions in which our habitual skills do not work for us. Instead, the social system works against us because skills are not flexible. It is like not being able to produce one's own good luck. The self-fulfilling prophecy is lost or reversed.

The change agent function is to relocate the dislocated, arrange to improve learning environments, and establish opportunities for relocation. When adults in their forties change careers, consultation is more appropriate than counseling because the counselor's task is to bring together the resources necessary to create new opportunities for relocating. Counseling can be done, if needed, during consultation. Consultation takes place over a sustained period of time. Results have been demonstrated by Zeigler (1969). Creative job search techniques have been used in consulting with the unemployed and the underemployed in small groups. In task forces of six to

[6] *Ibid.*

eight the leader trains the employed members to help the new unemployed members look for job opportunities. The system includes an inventory of work skills and experiences in a résumé of all vital information useful to a potential employer.

Environments may change where one lives, not just when he moves from place to place. Skills may become obsolete because of a sudden change in business or industry. New products may replace whole industries. Industrial establishments diversify partly because the market trends pass them by on a given product; note the discontinuing of cyclamates in 1969. Knowledge is similarly vulnerable to change. New technological knowledge moves very fast toward obsolescence. Knowledge accumulates at algebraic rates that accelerate rather than just multiply. Consultation is a method of discovering together what no one person may know because of the rapid pace of change. Consulting is a way of learning. It is useful because it taps resources usually available — other people.

The school counselor is a change agent if he consults with parents, children, teachers, and other human behavior specialists. Besides using his counseling skills for all the usual problems encountered with students, he will need the consultation method to define problems that will go unnoticed unless the significant persons are brought together. In consultation, the counselor goes hunting for the newly formed environments. Prevention and development counseling are central purposes for the counselor as a change agent.

EXPANSION OF KNOWLEDGE

If one has enough relevant and authentic information, he can predict the future — at least the immediate future and, generally speaking, the ultimate direction of more distant events. If this is not the case, then guidance, counseling, and consultation represent a cruel sham. It is the job of the counselor to evaluate sources of information. Sorting the vast quantities of information is a big job, and retrieval of information is a highly specialized task.

Retrieval and evaluation of information have become monumental industries in themselves. The former can be left to machines, but the latter is bound to human values. Whereas the machine, usually a computer, may store and retrieve expanding volumes of information, it is up to people to evaluate the avalanche of available data. *Counting* things instead of *accounting* for them has led to the condition in which numbers are a criterion; i.e., the more the better; bigger and better; quantity over quality; and many others. Don't you wish everybody did? Doesn't everybody? These are statements familiar to advertising because their evaluative quality is clearly the norm or standard implied by the numbers who identify with a given product or process.

The expansion of knowledge and its rapid and appropriate retrieval constitute large problems of the twentieth century. Expansion of knowledge is another way of conceptualizing or symbolizing *change*. A further concern is expressed by Rogers (1968): How much change is a person able to absorb, and how fast? This of course includes accepting and assimilating all of the changes that will have taken place up to a given time and are indeed taking place now.

During an era characterized by expansion of knowledge, a significant shift in the purpose of education becomes apparent. The idea of education as *preparation* for living is replaced by the idea that education must in itself be an *experience* in the process of living (Rogers, 1968).

RETRIEVAL OF KNOWLEDGE

The knowledge industry expands well beyond the limits of the school as a social institution and into the world of business and industrial relations. Because the retrieval of information is a central task, it is necessary to create learning environments in the workaday world in any interpersonal arena, from a department store to a school; a learning environment is the only environment in which the retrieval process can operate. The operation is a systematic evaluation or sorting of authentic information from what is irrelevant. The human environment is the focus of all living in the world.

Listening becomes at least as important as evaluation. Listening to new information frequently alters the evaluation being employed in any given moment. In a learning environment the concept of change can actually occur as part of the process of experiencing the reality of the moment. In this case the person who is to learn a new thing has the opportunity to receive feedback from others in the group at the very time of getting new information. Further, it should be remembered that persons are usually the repositories of most new information. It must indeed exist in the mind of a person prior to being programmed into a machine. So the sequence of this may be a moot point.

PERSONS AS REPOSITORIES OF INFORMATION

A person is not controlled by a panel of buttons that may be pushed for "on" and "off." A machine responds to this kind of programming. The control factor is a central and significant concept in using the resources of other persons when they are the repositories of new information that is needed in carrying out a human enterprise. Somehow we must acquire the skill to approach other persons with a minimum of concern about whether some personal hangup may determine whether or not we shall be able to receive and/or retrieve the necessary information. This kind of skill can be taught or can be learned in a counseling-consultation framework. The consultant has to know how to retrieve information from other persons. The counselor as consultant must learn to be available when information is being retrieved by teachers, students, parents, and other significant behavior specialists. How frequently does one discover in today's world that he has been the repository of a significant bit of information and was reluctant to share it on the basis of his existing knowledge! However, when the information was shared, the enterprise suddenly regained its balance and moved toward its goal. We are pointing here to the obvious fact that one should not be just "other directed" when working with the concept of persons as repositories of information. He himself may have a considerable amount of personal information available for recall. Sharing it in a small group may enable others to solve problems.

The counselor as a consultant is no less a repository of new information of importance to the ongoing processes of the school. All specialists must be viewed as repositories of information vital to the activity in consultation. Indeed, if they were not, there would be some question as to whether consultation is a worthwhile method because individuals would have nothing to share. Since it is frequently impossible to tell in advance which items of information will have particular bearing on the integration of a specific task, *persons* rather than labeled incumbents or specialties are to be included in the group. For example, a mother or teacher's aide may have information not available to any of the behavior specialists about a particular child — in his home situation, an incident that happened on the way to school, etc.

The fact that persons are repositories of information poses a massive problem in evaluation of new information. Each person modifies within his subjective awareness certain aspects of all information that comes into his possession. The counselor-consultant is under obligation to learn to evaluate information from subjective sources, and he has several methods to draw on. One is to lay the information alongside data from a confirmed and carefully validated source of information on the same topic. This will in no way guarantee the authenticity of the new information, but it will indicate rather quickly whether there are significant deficiencies in the information. A second and equally valid method of evaluating a new subjective source is to compare the information quickly with data already gathered. This one is full of glaring potential sources of error. The third and perhaps the only really significant method of testing the information is to apply it experimentally under conditions that are sufficiently sheltered to avoid any catastrophe. Observations can be made and evaluated in terms of the degree of apparent effectiveness of the new information.

You will notice that no absolute norms were invoked against which the standard for acceptance of information from a resource could be measured. The counselor-consultant will find a wide discrepancy between the concepts of scientific endeavor and the pragmatics of actual process participation.

The Counselor-Consultant and the Teacher

A complex age brings increased emphasis upon education and choice making. Decision making in today's society faces the problem of utilizing dynamic norms or static norms. Consultation means using the small group to aid decision making, for the small group is the most available device for overcoming the limitations upon thinking imposed by static norms. Not every counselor is prepared to make a perfect blend of all these complexities. It is direction that we are concerned with rather than the product of an accomplished system (Rogers, 1968, p. 272).

Vocational development has become a lifelong process, as much for the counselor who is acquiring consulting skills in the course of his vocational development as for anyone else.

According to Calhoun (1962), the press of population may lead to the deterioration of behavior. Urbanization seems to intensify what is commonly referred to as alienation. Alienation of teacher and pupil may be the target condition used to justify the counselor-consultant function. Once again, consultation is a method the counselor uses to effect changes in the environment in which students must live and learn. Danskin, Kennedy, and Friesen (1965) have presented ideas on the ecology of students. We know from our research efforts that intelligence and socioeconomic status of the family are probably two of the most important determinants of educational success with students. We know that peer groups and reference groups influence the attitudes a youngster has toward achievement and vocational development. Although youth finds individual definition in the social encounters among peers, these groups are known to be basically the product of socioeconomic status and geographic proximity. Therefore, it would seem to be a consequence of the accident of birth whether one's reference groups and peer groups tend to support positive, negative, or other attitudes toward educational environment (Sherif and Sherif, 1964). Finally, the family is the major determining factor in the ecology of students. Herriott (1963) maintains it is more important to study the student's current educational milieu than to spend time planning a fictional future of educational and vocational choice. The goal seems to be the achievement of some control over the dynamics of behavior in the educational environment. The teacher's behavior and the counselor's behavior may be two sources available to be used in the consultation efforts to control the learning environments of students. The consultant's task is precisely oriented to this milieu.

Rogers (1968) describes the teacher of the future in terms very similar to those we would apply to the counselor-consultant. The emphasis is upon the skills and creativity necessary in the process of providing the resources of learning, as compared to traditional patterns of teaching in which the materials to be learned are the focus of attention. Here again we point to the shift in emphasis from product to process. Schools will be reshaped into much more inclusive environments for learning. The concept has changed from a geographic circumscribing area to a central or shared concern among individuals, who may be widely distributed geographically. The present model of education could not accommodate this concept in any more than a lip-service academic recognition. To breathe life into the learning environment concept one would have to go beyond the present school campus setup.

Industry is far ahead of education in utilizing new ideas about the environment for learning. The nature of what must be learned in order for an industry to maintain its life support system requires that the individual be present at the point where new knowledge is being created in order to learn it. This precludes the system now in use in schools, where information is sifted and sorted and censored into textbooks. It goes farther than using the teacher as an in-service vehicle for carrying information not available in textbooks from the special institute or workshop back into the classroom. The conference is one educational device for attempting to bypass the time lag between the discovery of new knowledge and its dissemination to students on a mass scale. With the newer media, particularly television, some of the delays in the dissemination of new information could be eliminated. It is possible actually to be present where the new information is being created. Taking full advantage of these innovations would bring our educational system into line with what industry has been doing for years, namely, training people at the point of discovery rather than with a remote and an abstracted approach to information sharing. This kind of learning environment becomes a living-in situation rather than a learning-about condition. The goal of education is considerably altered from the *preparation for* some productive role to actually *experiencing the living*.

The overriding purpose of consultation with the teacher is to hasten the arrival of the time when teachers will come together and produce the kinds of learning environments within the limits of the school that seem to be both possible and appropriate in the contemporary society. As individuals they may see themselves as powerless, realistically unable to overcome the ambiguities. But as a small group they may discover the resources and find the power to create more appropriate learning environments.

The Counselor-Consultant and the Parents

Is the generation gap fact or fiction? If we see it as fact, we may use it as an alibi relieving us of the responsibility for doing anything about it. If we treat it as fiction, we may proceed to assess the relative differences between parent and child, counselor and teacher and other significant adult. Because we cannot escape the reality that the future is delimited for any individual by what happens now, we must somehow assume that we share accountability for the future.

The myth of accountability has affected the literature on counseling to such an extent that fetishes concerned with whether one can intervene and influence the direction of another person's behavior abound. The crass denial of what is inevitably a part of any interpersonal encounter — namely, *influence* — has led us here to confront the myth. Interrupt — Intervene — and Influence (Fullmer and Bernard, 1964) was presented as a description of present reality in counseling much more than as something not yet achieved in counseling. With the concept of the three I's in counseling, it is no longer possible to avoid accountability for what the counselor does as well as what he does *not* do. Consulting with parents who are similarly aligned with children who become students in the school and counselees in the counseling office, one cannot be long impressed with behavior that denies or avoids direct confrontation with the determinants of the future of the child. We not only share accountability for the future but inherit shared responsibility for the consequences of the future. At another level of integration we actually share the consequences themselves because, as a member of this society, we must live with whatever consequences accrue to future generations.

Family group consultation grew out of the need to have some viable method of working with parents, children, and teachers conjointly. Many of the concerns appropriate to counselor contacts with individuals can be handled efficaciously in groups. The parent education potential of family group consultation is recognized as one of its more positive and useful aspects in school counseling. Family group consultation has more than a ten-year history in its initial developmental stages (Fullmer and Bernard, 1968). Rogers (1968) supports the idea that the future counselor will work more with parents as a part of his regular assignment.

Additional reasons for consulting with parents include the following: (1) The counselor needs to interpret change to both parent and child. The difference between parent and child is commonly known as the generation gap. (2) The increasing urbanization which brings people closer together geographically has resulted in the paradox of separating individuals psychologically. The small group intensive experience in interpersonal intimacy has the potential to overcome this alienating force. (3) As industry has shifted from individual to group methods of management, we will need to institute such shifts in the parent, family, teacher, counselor, school concept. Instead of having one individual in charge of many other individuals, we now have groups of individuals who organize and maintain their own social control systems and depend upon self-discipline as the social control force. It is assumed that only intimate interaction among individuals in a small group can succeed in diluting the forces of alienation.

Having parents as partners in the educational enterprise allows shared consequences and integrated concerns to become realities. The aim is for the counselor-consultant to achieve a new community of shared concern between family and school. This makes community a practical goal. In many ghetto schools today the teacher is a sort of colonial who moves in and out of the community while living in a different geographic location, contributing to the alienation of the persons involved. The neighborhood school is no longer complete when the teacher commutes from a different neighborhood. Here the counselor-consultant can create a community of common concern without attempting to control the freedom of movement of persons by insisting on a geographic definition of community. In an urban society there is no such thing as a geographic definition of community. Community must be based on a shared concern including personal contacts for a kind of mutuality that may be international in character. My friends in Nepal, Hong Kong, Djakarta, Bombay, and Rome maintain ties just as though we lived in the same geographic location. The ties are common concerns and have a purely human basis. We trust each other. The ability to maintain ties seems to be one of the major interests of young persons; they want to know how to preserve a relationship over time. When one looks at the divorce rates in contemporary American society among thirty-five- to fifty-year-old married couples, this seems a reasonable concern. What are the necessary conditions for nurturing trust among individuals?

Immediate interpersonal contacts may be lacking within a given corporation group. There is no other way to foster trust. One of the authors works in a university instructional department where the personal ties among the members are defined almost exclusively along special interest lines. Personal contacts among individuals who represent different curriculum areas are almost nonexistent; even though they are geographically contiguous, their congruency begins and ends as a space utilization factor: Where is your office? No personal ties exist to create a community of concern. No matter if you share an office (geography), the difference (change) will have bent the myth of accountability and leads to a new dimension of alienation. A major task facing the teacher, counselors, and parents is how to achieve the teaching and learning necessary to prepare people to live in the new reality. How to develop trust instead of alienation is a developmental task for more than the generation gap.

Use of the small group to bring together persons of diverse concerns who may learn to share some common concerns and thus create a new community is one way we have found productive for including parents as partners in the processes of education and counseling.

The Counselor-Consultant and the Administrators

Administration is a culturally defined system of proxy. Someone acts for others because *they* cannot be present to act for themselves. In a mass society, proxy is the source of most power to make decisions at the corporate level on any matters of consequence. The personal level of decision making may occur within the frame that is created by the corporate decisions, the consequences of which define the limits of personal choice. This concept is based upon the obsolete definition of community. Education generally persists in using this obsolete view of community and the method of administration derived therefrom, because the school units are local geographic units. Industry and business moved long ago to supersede this concept with a different idea of community, namely, *shared concerns,* regardless of geography (Rogers and Roethlisberger, 1952). Consultation with administrators in the school system is the means by which the counselor may help to initiate the newer concept of community.

The Counselor-Consultant and the Curriculum

The counselor's chief curriculum task is to bring together, so that they may consult, any group of persons concerned with any significant part of the curriculum. The curriculum is mainly people who teach subjects to students. Most teachers also have significant relationships, as persons, with the students. By working in small groups consulting on curriculum matters, the counselor may develop and multiply the human relationships. Whatever teachers help to build for themselves they will help to carry out because it is their own thing. Relationship with students has been the counselor's concern from the beginning of the guidance movement, and consultation is one way to expand the number of hands in the relationships business. The counselor can help, enhance, encourage, and avoid duplicating the ongoing personal and interpersonal relationships between teachers and students.

The counselor's involvement with the curriculum has long been regarded as desirable, yet very little more is expected of him than membership on a curriculum committee. Actually the counselor helps to make or break curriculum by the assignment of students to specific classes or sections. In this sense he shares many common concerns with other professionals responsible for the curriculum. The counselor may teach a class in guidance, vocations, personal adjustment, and how to study — this is the conventional approach (Swan, 1966).

There is now a new, largely unmapped area for the counselor-consultant to explore. It is community talent development for the extension, expansion, and multiplication of the vocational-technical and human relationships area. We live in the age of lash and backlash. The counselor-consultant has unique characteristics to prepare the way for school-community involvement by creating the happening where *access* is made possible (Fullmer, 1969a).

Many things may follow from this, but the basic industry of the future, according to McDermott (1969), will be to make sense out of change. Making sense out of change involves trying to understand what may already have changed. We believe, like Drucker (1968), that change is dislocation — due to change in a person's environment or mobility, when the person goes to live in a new geographic milieu.

Those who find themselves dislocated from previously productive avenues of living in the social system do need access to the knowledge industry represented by the curriculum and the school. The counselor-consultant may establish routes to this source.

Fullmer (1969a) first presented the idea of increasing access to the knowledge industry represented by the school curriculum in an address to the California Personnel and Guidance Association annual convention at Anaheim, California, February 1969. It is based upon the assumption that the parents of children in school may need the services of the counselor and a way of approach to the curriculum as desperately as children presumably do.

The concept of venture banking, borrowed from Drucker (1968) and applied to the human capital represented by the diverse citizenry of any school community, suggested the possibility of creating community talent centers. The counselor-consultant could produce a whole new notion of curriculum designed to meet needs of adults and students alike. The ambiguity of living in a complex world can be overcome if access to significant other persons of varied backgrounds can be established and maintained. The consultant would bring these people together at school during odd hours when the school physical facilities are available. A talent center looks like this:

> The school becomes the physical center of the enterprise. The counselor or counselors, consulting with other leaders in the community, staff it with people of differing talents. They come from the community and from the school, including the student body as a resource. The curriculum of the talent center is designed to create environments in which learning occurs at whatever levels and on whatever topics are defined as essential. The basic method is a small group model. Intensive encounter in a small group over a period of time provides environments for learning, particularly learning in the areas of socialization and development of interpersonal skills necessary to function in the real world. The small group model becomes a method for gathering and generating ideas about the needs and tasks to be developed and attacked in the talent center.
>
> The basic purpose of a talent center is to produce a living curriculum. The dynamic process of living through the learning experience while it is being created is perhaps the most striking difference the counselor-consultant can contribute in his relationship with curriculum in the school.
>
> Significantly, the discovery of talents and the access to opportunities in a complex urban society depend upon the prime mover who brings together the members of this self-help group. The radical shift is from a *service* concept to an emphasis upon *development* of a community organization for fostering human talent within the school-centered society.
>
> The counselor-consultant brings to the problem of alienation the know-how of his professional specialty. The highly useful concept

of self-help becomes productive when it is put into meaningful context. Self-help groups have produced results where established patterns of counseling have failed.[7]

Mowrer (1968) encourages the idea of using nonprofessional people in group counseling in order to effect changes of behavior.

The Counselor-Consultant and the Services to Students

A talent center can be devoted to consultation or student services. An initial suggestion is to allow students to help counselors run the talent center. Adults from the community may staff the center or assist in getting it staffed, and selection of these adults need not be restricted to the geography of the neighborhood. Students who are allowed to help counselors run the talent center learn that they may go beyond a given set of limits in order to effect better utilization of resources as well as find opportunities to establish, or even create, new resources.

Probably no greater service is rendered to students than giving them the chance to contribute significantly to the ongoing social institution of which they are a part. The school, the home, and the community are three well-defined institutional settings in which youngsters can be helped to make a meaningful contribution to the welfare both of themselves and of others. The counselor-consultant's task is to exploit all opportunities provided by the curriculum, the school, the counseling program, and the community to permit the youngster the optimum number of exposures to experience in the real world. Through student groups and community groups made up of students and adults, the counselor-consultant provides services to students at every point where involvement in a small group is possible. The counselor as counselor supplies many other services that are traditionally part of the counseling program. The counselor-consultant function creates new environments which offer the op-

[7] See the report of the rehabilitation counseling experiment, Kim Seixas, Director, Honolulu, Hawaii, "An Intensive Evaluation and Counseling Model." It was possible to get from 60 to 70 percent of the participants employed through a system of small groups and self-help. The significant change came with the last group of trainees — hard-core multiple-handicapped unemployed persons. When *they* sought and found their own employment without the usual aid from the rehabilitation counselors, the project was evaluated as a success.

portunity to learn some of the behavior needed to function in the complex society.

The counselor-consultant adds to the professional practice of counseling some aspects that are not covered in a traditional program such as liaison with state and federal employment offices, psychiatric agencies, agencies that deal with exceptional children, and police and juvenile and/or family court agencies.

Summary

Counseling-consulting is a professional practice. The emphasis in educational practice has shifted from products to the processes necessary to achieve products. Consultation is the counselor's method of achieving the capability for creating new educational products.

The process-product concept is complicated because scientific investigation requires objective description. Process is the subjective experience of living. The product emphasis is easier to investigate by using the determinism assumed in antecedent conditions such as instruction. Subjective experience, characteristic of process, does not lend itself to understanding by prior circumstances in the here and now of living.

The counselor's professional role includes consultation, carried on by people brought together by him. McCully was an early architect of school counselor professionalization, and the efforts to achieve it have continued. The American Personnel and Guidance Association publishes statements defining the most recent positions on professionalization from time to time. Consultation is the issue. The expectations and commitments of counselors include consultation as a major professional responsibility.

McCully (1962) set forth the criteria for distinguishing a profession from an occupation. He also proposed six developmental stages essential to the creating of a profession. Most of these stages have been achieved or are nearing achievement. Wrenn (1962) has been leading toward professionalization of counseling to meet increasingly complex problems in the school. He also advocated consultation with significant adults beyond the limits of the school.

The counselor-consultant is a change agent committed to relocating the dislocated. Change is dislocation of persons from a familiar to an ambiguous milieu. Knowledge has expanded to the point where no one knows the future. To prepare people to live in the unknown future is impossible. Hence the shift from school as *preparation for* to school as a *process of living* — in the here and now.

The retrieval of knowledge has become vastly important. The evaluation of new knowledge to ascertain its authenticity is now a professional-level task. Listening is a primary factor in evaluation.

The teacher and the counselor-consultant share in the process of education. Choice making and decision rendering have become small group tasks because no one person can command enough relevant data to make valid judgments in isolation. People are the repositories of most new knowledge. People program computers. People are the source for improved environments for living and learning.

The future teacher will be more like the counselor-consultant. Parents consult the counselor. Entire families may join one model called *family group consultation* (Fullmer and Bernard, 1968).

Administrators have special concern for consultation. The counselor should include them in his professional practice because there is no better way to keep them informed. Curriculum concerns come into the counselor-consultant role. Talent centers may be the way a counselor invents curriculum.

SUGGESTED ADDITIONAL READINGS

Abercrombie, M. L. Johnson, 1960. *The Anatomy of Judgment.* New York: Basic Books. *Consultation helps to translate what one knows in one context to a new and different context. The author found the problem of sufficient magnitude to prompt some unusual research effort. She discovered that medical students were unable to apply problem-solving behavior to personal problems away from the clinic. This is a case in which knowledge is unused because a person does not know how to apply it. Consultation attacks this unique problem in school and home.*

Bernard, H. W., and D. W. Fullmer, 1969. *Principles of Guidance: A Basic Text.* Scranton, Pa.: International Textbook Company. Pp. 326–344. *The chapter on the counselor as a consultant defines the functions of the newer professional role of counselors.*

Fullmer, D. W., and H. W. Bernard, 1964. *Counseling: Content and Process.* Chicago: Science Research Associates. Pp. 206–226. *Family Consultation.* Boston: Houghton Mifflin Company (Guidance Monograph Series), 1968. *Consultation with parents and families is a recent departure in professional counseling. The current interest in expanding the clientele of the counselor to include persons and groups formerly considered beyond the scope of school counseling has made this method even more important. It is a way of modifying the learning environment of the home and the community. School learning environments are also influenced by consultation.*

Lynton, R. P., 1960. *The Tide of Learning: The Aloka Experience.* London: Routledge and Kegan Paul. *The meaning and substance of process in relation to product have been perceived in ways that clearly contrast the subjective and objective realities of human behavior research. The science of human behavior calls for objective determinism. The process of living is always subjective. The empirical means to demonstrate subjective phenomena exist. The replication of subjective experience is infinitely difficult. The paradox inherent in the subjective-objective reality is more clearly defined but not eliminated.*

Wrenn, C. G., 1962. *The Counselor in a Changing World.* Washington: American Personnel and Guidance Association. Pp. 166–169. *Wrenn sets forth guidelines for the future counselor and his professional preparation. The minimum two-year graduate program and the proposal that counselors should work with colleagues and parents as much as, and perhaps more than, with students underwrite the consultation emphasis in this text.*

Chapter Six

VARIETIES OF
COUNSELING ORIENTATION

The "57 Varieties" of Heinz pickles could not go on forever. New recipes were developed to suit changing tastes. New knowledges introduced new preservatives and further knowledge condemned their use. It is likely that individual idiosyncrasies in the form of allergies gave point to the maxim "One man's meat is another man's poison."

Havemann (1969) discussed half a dozen approaches to thera-peutic counseling, then defined fourteen more in an addendum. Whatever the number of counseling orientations one might choose to identify as being distinct, that number will surely fluctuate for much the same reason that pickles come in various sizes, slices, and flavors. One would expect a particular kind of problem to be spe-cially responsive to one kind of treatment but not to another. Find-ing a suitable job might be the result of an approach which included giving various jobs a try, but sexual adjustment might deteriorate if one tried a number of partners. Confrontation and challenge might be helpful to a man whose scholarship has suddenly declined but be devastating to a girl whose problem is chronic shyness. In short, just as there are teaching styles suitable to certain teachers and situations and just as there are learning styles peculiar to certain pupils, so too there are styles of counselors, styles of counselees, and varied objectives and situations.

The concern of this chapter is to get the counselor-consultant started on the road to a knowledge of counseling orientations so that he may learn to appreciate the advantages of a varied scene. Such continuously growing knowledge will presumably help him refer a counselee — be he pupil, parent, or teacher — to the best source of help. It may lead him to recognize the strengths of various personnel and referral agencies. The study of orientations is a first step toward eliminating the neophyte's error of thinking he has found *the way* (see the case of Scientology, Chapter Seven).

The Guidance Orientation

HISTORICAL ROLE OF GUIDANCE

The origins of school guidance practices may be traced in part to Frank Parsons, who worked outside school confines in Boston. In 1908 he began to devise guidance programs for those young people who were not being served as adequately in school as our democratic ideals and traditions seemed to require. His task, he felt, was to assess the aptitudes and skills of young men so they could find secure roles in the occupational world. Unfortunately the tools of assessment were not sufficient for the job. Nor, it might be added — despite considerable improvement and expansion — are they adequate for the job today. Alfred Binet, Louis Terman, E. K. Strong, Edward L. Thorndike, and others made contributions to the testing movement, but many questions about appraising aptitudes and personality remain unanswered (Miller, 1969).

Two major obstacles block the way to accurate guidance of young people into the vocational milieu. One is the realization that growth is a continuous process and that assessment of an individual today, by means of a test score, provides only a very rough prediction of what he might become (Ebel, 1970). The other obstacle, particularly in the contemporary scene, is that jobs themselves change rapidly in an explosively developing technological complex. Even *if* the jobs were to remain the same, the identification of particular qualities needed on a job seems to be about as elusive as the identification of personal traits and abilities.

GUIDANCE SERVICES

Initially, then, guidance was vocational. Evolving concepts now tend to place more emphasis on personal guidance and development than on vocational adjustment. Barry and Wolf (1962) have asserted that vocational guidance is based on a number of myths and therefore wrote an *Epitaph for Vocational Guidance*. One myth is that vocational adjustment can be separated from personal adjustment. Most well-prepared and experienced counselors would agree that such a dichotomy is futile. It might well be hypothesized that just as vocational orientation is a part of the totality of personal adjustment, so too is the school adjustment of a pupil a part of his living in general. Hence, some professional is needed who is concerned with the coordination of school, family, and community influences on pupil development.

Downing (1968) condenses the varied statements of many authorities regarding guidance services into six categories and devotes a chapter to each:

> Pupil inventory (records and cumulative folders)
> Pupil appraisal through testing
> Counseling services
> Counseling as the integration of various services
> Educational and vocational information
> Placement and follow-up

A seventh service is included in a number of statements, namely, research and evaluation (Evaluative Criteria, 1960). The emphasis on research is a reaction against the impressionistic, subjective evaluation so prevalent in pupil personnel practices. Many professional counselors are convinced that the halo effect, the Hawthorne effect, the role of expectancy, and other thought-biasing factors have too much influence in contrast to the assessment of guidance results through testing (Gephart and Antonoplos, 1969).

The past history of guidance indicates that not all of the seven services of guidance are given attention in typical school situations. Moreover, no one suggests that any one of the guidance services deserves to be neglected. While some stress the need for assessment, others indicate that evaluation — the question of relative worth or value — is an integral part of the educational enterprise.

Probably, too, the emergence of proactive, humanistic psychology plays a part in an evolving concept of the nature of, and need for, guidance. The word *guidance* suggests that someone possessing superior wisdom knows where another ought to go. But experience indicates that a counselor cannot really solve the problems of clients for them. "They must do it themselves" (Miller, 1969, p. 157). To the extent that guidance is viewed as providing aid and counsel in the solutions arrived at by the pupil himself, the validity of the role of counselor-consultant can be appreciated. Specifically, one of the challenges to the counselor-consultant is to lead teachers, guidance workers, and counselors in their continuous study of evolving functions of guidance.

COUNSELING

Counseling is a function of guidance services which was about as neglected in the school a decade ago as the research and follow-up function is today. Too many so-called counselors had obtained their positions because they typically had good rapport with pupils and liked to work with them. Then they fortified themselves with a summer's course or two in "guidance principles" and "occupational and vocational information." A practicum in counseling procedures was so rare that in 1960 about 70 percent of school counselors had no credit in counseling practicum. The survey of other lacks (sociological and psychological theory, individual analysis) revealed such marked deficiencies that the estimate of the number of high school counselors dropped from 30,000 to 19,000 (McCully, 1969, p. 91).

Counselor educators often suggest that inadequate preparation causes those holding the positions to avoid participation in counseling. Excuses for such avoidance include lack of time, necessary for maintaining records, danger of doing damage to disturbed children, and wisdom of referring chronically emotionally disturbed children to a psychologist or psychiatrist.

Three factors have operated to greatly increase the number of counseling counselors: (1) the realization that "disturbance" just will not go away because it is ignored — or expelled; (2) the realization that there simply are not enough psychologists and psychiatrists to fill the needs; and (3) the improvement of counselor education. The conviction of Arbuckle (1962) that as long as the child is not removed from the custody of the school he should not be considered beyond the help of specialists in the school is widely shared. One problem is that counseling with those experiencing difficulty is equated with psychotherapy. Arbuckle faces the color word *psychotherapy* and derails the avoidance tendency by asserting that counseling is also very much akin to teaching, with more emphasis on what is learned than on what is *taught*. Counseling involves an experienced person's influencing the behavioral pattern of a less experienced person, and dialogue between the experienced and less experienced may be regarded as the essence of education (Bruner, 1968).

Counseling, in any of its many forms, is essentially a structured but permissive relationship between persons. Often it is a one-to-one relationship. Often, too, it involves a relationship between members of a specifically designated group. Whether individual or group, counseling entails successive encounters over a period of time. Thus it is assumed that telling and learning are synonymous and simultaneous. The content of counseling is dependent on its purpose — the counselee is seeking an understanding of himself and the dynamics of behavior that will enable him (1) to abandon some of his self-defeating behaviors and (2) to adopt more productive goals and behaviors.

Variety of Counseling Theory

Approaches to counseling technique are contingent in large part on the personality theory and psychological theory which the counselor accepts. The starting point of how one counsels is the view he takes of the nature of man.

PSYCHOANALYTIC ORIENTATION

According to some authorities, the pattern of life adopted by an individual depends on his early experiences and on instinctive predispositions. Freud postulated the theory that man was a victim of his past and of his instinctive strivings. According to this view an individual is motivated by a central force, the libido, which is expressed through the id, the ego, and the superego. The libido is the pleasure-seeking, self-gratifying tendency. The id represents animal instincts and drives such as satisfaction of hunger, sex, and comfort appetites. It is deemed necessary that these be satisfied in socially approved ways if the individual is to achieve adjustment and efficiency. The appetite is primary, and the approved manner of satisfaction must be learned — sometimes in a rather painful and frustrating fashion. If satisfaction is blocked, the result is maladjustment. The ego is the conscious or rational self. It seeks to mediate and modify, or repress, the patterns of behavior which are prompted by the id. The superego is the controlling mechanism, typically equated with conscience — the silent voice of parents or deity telling one what is right and wrong. It is the part of man that recognizes the values and customs of one's fellow beings.

The basic rationale of psychoanalytic theory is about as follows:

Early childhood experiences influence a person's psychological and social development.

A person's behavior is influenced by irrational as well as by rational factors.

Behavior has many causes and appears in many forms; it is the result of multiple causation.

A person has many levels of awareness. Sometimes he is not conscious of internal forces that are influencing his behavior.

A person maintains his psychological equilibrium by means of defense mechanisms. These are patterns of behavior which sustain the person's self-image and at the same time ostensibly recognize the requirements of society. (Defense mechanisms are so commonly used that their names — rationalization, sublimation, projection, compensation, reaction formation, etc. — have become everyday words.)

A person's development can be arrested at an immature level by inadequate rearing or some traumatic episode that occurred in his past.

The psychoanalytic approach to behavioral change, especially the approach pioneered by Freud, consisted in getting the confused person to bring his subconscious motivations and conflicts out into the open where they might be consciously examined and evaluated. This was a lengthy process involving a one-to-one relationship with a therapist (psychoanalyst) who encouraged the subject to talk about his past, to describe his recurrent dreams, and to respond to stimulus words before his conscious or rational self had time to dictate what a socially acceptable response would be. The therapist would help the subject interpret his dreams and responses in terms of such things as mother hatred, sibling rivalry, sexual lust, incestful wishes, and aggressive tendencies. Rational examination, it was hoped, would free the subject of the notion that his instinctive thoughts should be repressed, that they were abnormal and depraved. It would reveal their normality and suggest that continued denial of them would also be continuously self-defeating.

The approaches were successful, but interpretations vary as to why they were successful. Some authorities guessed that because the process involved so much time the client simply experienced spontaneous recovery — he would have gotten well without help. Others believed that communication with some other person — a one-to-one relationship — was the key factor in achieving health. Still others felt that no change took place but the individual just decided he would have to live with the upsetting persons and aspects of his environment. And, of course, many therapists and subjects believed that rational analysis of causes made it unnecessary to go on carrying the "monkey on their backs" — things that occurred in the past and now no longer exist.

A large number of persons, including some of his own students, have objected to Freud's theory and methods. They claim that he emphasized the basest and meanest aspects of man — to which Freud replied that their objections only proved their resistance to acknowledging the existence of these processes in their own lives. Menninger (1968) provides a contemporary example of a similar phenomenon in our approach to the punishment of crime. In his view, our harshness in the treatment of criminals is a disguise for admitting the same criminal tendencies, the existence of deep-seated hostilities toward others, within ourselves. Furthermore, for our own salvation as well as the recognition of the humanity of criminals, these hostilities will have to be acknowledged and dealt with. Psychoanalytic theory is alive in contemporary society in terms of mental health and public safety.

Whether psychoanalytic theory is accepted or not, some solid contributions have come from, or at least are supported by, psychoanalysis: (1) the persistent influence of childhood experiences; (2) the positive value of accepting, loving, mothering; (3) the fact of psychological trauma; (4) the importance of talk as an avenue to self-understanding and personal development; (5) the normality of sex drives and wishes; and (6), especially important to counselors, the importance of listening. There are also many concepts, including defense mechanisms, mentioned above, that are helpful to counselors: transference, empathy, repression, and catharsis, for example. An important and pervasive one is the concept of anxiety. This is an exaggerated response to a minimal condition of external threat or a state of fear arising from internal, subjective threat (King, 1965, p. 96). It is a common ingredient in many of the problem cases encountered by school counselors.

CLIENT-CENTERED COUNSELING

Carl Rogers is the leading exponent of a nonauthoritative model of counseling. It has been called nondirective counseling because the counselor is not supposed to intrude his own values or impose his goals on the counselee. The theory back of Rogers's client-centered counseling, and similar nonauthoritarian models such as existential therapy and learning-theory therapy, is that the strength and determination to change and grow can come, and must come, from within the individual. Individual freedom and responsibility are given precedence over dependence on an authority or on a father figure.

Rogers postulated that each person has evolved a self-image — as worthy or unworthy, effective or ineffective, masculine or effeminate, industrious or indolent, and the like. It is the accumulation of countless experiences and evaluations by chance acquaintances as well as by key persons in one's past. It is to be hoped that this self-perception is accurate and accords with one's own behavior as it is seen by himself as well as those about him. The healthy person can alter any misperceptions and readily admit that he fell short of some idealized action or that he has actually exceeded the level of the goals he established. These changes are effected without anxiety or guilt feelings. However, some people are not so facile and regard any behavior that does not measure up to the self-image as an indication of depravity or worthlessness. For instance, the woman who thinks of herself as a good mother finds that her compulsive cleanliness is a constant source of irritation to her high school daughter. In the face of this contradiction the mother may develop rationalizations, projections, denials, or generalized hostility in her attempt to deny the unwelcome perception. The continued denial of the reality, and of the normality, of such contradictions is a symptom of neuroticism. When one gets so miserable in the process of living a lie that he can no longer stand it, he seeks help. Often he can learn, with help, that his perception is incomplete or that it is accurate but can be lived with.

In Rogers's (1942) early work a dozen steps in the counseling process were identified:

1. The person comes for help.
2. The helping relationship is explained.
3. Establishment of a permissive climate encourages the counselee to express his feelings.
4. The counselor may identify the counselee's feelings as being negative or positive but accepts the counselee and his feelings.
5. Positive feelings begin to evolve and emerge.
6. Counselor labels and interprets these feelings.
7. The counselee begins to accept himself.
8. The counselor helps the counselee to clarify possible courses of action.
9. The counselee attempts to put some of his conclusions into action.
10. The counselor reinforces positive action by supportive behavior and verbal encouragement.
11. The counselee's behavior indicates that he has gone beyond the ambivalence level of behavior.
12. Psychological weaning begins and continues through the termination of the counseling relationships — emancipation occurs.

Rogers (1966) has proposed some hypotheses regarding the essential conditions for constructive personality change which occurs in a counseling context. (1) It is necessary for two persons — the counselor and the counselee — to be in psychological contact. Rapport, mutual positive regard, acceptance, and awareness of each other are some of the aspects of such contact. (2) It is deemed necessary that the counselee be searching for some help in order that he may resolve some of the incongruencies he is experiencing with life and his self-concept — the anxiety he feels. (3) The counselor must present himself as a congruent, genuine, real individual. Although the counselor is not the focus of the counseling relationship, it is appropriate for him to express his feelings about the counseling situation and process. (4) It stimulates personality growth if the counselor has unconditional positive regard for the counselee. No strings to acceptance are attached. The counselee's shortcomings are accepted as a part of him just as a child is accepted even when his confusions prompt him to misbehave — even when good intentions are not carried out in daily behavior. (5) The counselor possesses an empathic understanding of the counselee's problems. He is able to understand and share the counselee's feelings. His actions are in accord with the mood and content of the counselee's remarks. (6) The counselee perceives that the counselor does accept, and has empathy for, him.

A major contribution of the Rogerian approach is the technique of reflecting feelings and clarifying perplexities through careful listening. The technique of reflecting, or providing a feedback mechanism for focusing and moving the counseling sessions, is widely used. Paraphrasing the counselee's statements, or asking for further elaboration, provides time and opportunity for the counselee to resolve his own dilemmas. As much as Rogers has added to counseling techniques, it seems that the really significant contribution is his focus on the merit, worth, and strength of the individual. Not only is this high regard a part of the counselor's orientation; it must become a part of the counselee's own continuous progress in healthy personality development.

REALITY THERAPY

A favorite technique for many counselors is delving into the history of a problem. It is assumed that before one can understand and help another in a counseling situation the origins of the difficulty must be identified. This is the approach used in much of psychoanalysis — carried to the point at which things are recalled from the unconscious that the individual has repressed and forgotten.

Glasser (1966) takes quite a different point of view in what he calls reality therapy. Much of his work has been done with delinquent girls, and his conclusion is that the more a girl talks about her past — her carping mother, her incestuous father, her demanding siblings, her lack of food and clothes, her inadequate teachers — the sorrier she gets to feeling for herself. The more she talks about history, the more she can see that others are to blame for her condition. Recalling all the vicissitudes of her life seems to provide excuses for her norm-violating behavior. The counselor can listen to the story, he can understand how the girl became a delinquent, he can let her ventilate her feelings, he can empathize. But what of bringing about some constructive change in behavior?

The major contribution of history taking in a counseling situation is discovery of the point at which the individual is able to assume responsibility. He can then be praised and given recognition for some of his worthiness. But the beginning of personality development and behavior change, *from this point,* is the question for the counselee, "What can *I* do now?" The counselor's job is one of confrontation. He must seek to show the deviantly behaving individual that he does not have to act as he has acted in the past. No one forced him to steal a car, take drugs, neglect his schoolwork, show his disrespect for teachers, or deny the value of mathematics. The rules of the world do not change to suit the convenience of the individual. His actions were chosen by him and he must — because no one else can — accept responsibility for those choices.

Responsibility is a key word in reality therapy. It is easy to see the irresponsibility of lawbreakers, but depressed patients, persons who have ulcers, underachievers in school, and neurotics are also persons who have evaded responsibility. While the thread of responsibility runs through many kinds of problems, unfortunately history cannot be rewritten. What counts now is how much responsibility the individual will take for his own *now* and his own *future* — and how he will take it. Glasser also emphasizes that the concept of happiness is a stumbling block. No one promises happiness. No one promises largess without the expenditure of effort. Tranquilizers can honestly not assure happiness. Nor can the counselor pledge that there will be no difficulties in the future; he can only indicate that any course not involving responsibility is futile.

Despite the apparent toughness of reality therapy, Glasser believes that there should be a warm and accepting relationship between therapist and client. One can act friendly without overlooking faults and excusing mistakes. Reality therapy demands that there be a no-nonsense approach to problems: The subject did do this or that, it was a mistake, it was self-defeating, and there really is no valid inadequate behavior.

Glasser outlines an approach somewhat as follows: Ask the pupil what he is doing. One should not ask why he is doing it. What results does your action get? Is this the result you want? How can your behavior be changed to a more productive pattern? Rules are not changed or relaxed. The pupil chooses his course of action. No excuse is accepted for failure to follow through. When the pupil fails, he needs teachers who will encourage him to make another commitment and another try. Then he needs teachers who will stick with him through another commitment, and another, and still again, until he finally learns that he can achieve — with only the moral support of someone who believes in him. Finally, in the process of achieving he gains not only a sense of identity and self-worth but also maturity, respect from others, and love.

THE THREE-I's COUNSELING APPROACH

The long and involved processes of client-centered counseling and psychoanalysis have led to a search for more practicable models for school counseling. Fullmer and Bernard (1964), acting on the assumption that any youngster still in school deserves the counselor's help, developed a pattern which was called Interrupt — Intervene — Influence. The counselor is perceived as supplying a professional service which is unique, requires special skills, and cannot be performed by just anyone who has a good feeling for others.

Rapport between counselor and counselee is sought, but it is sought through getting to the matter of concern immediately rather than by exchanging pleasantries. The counselee may or may not wish to see the counselor. In school counseling, the youngster is less likely to be a self-referral than to be referred by someone else — teacher, parent, or family physician. On occasion, the counselor may seek the pupil and invite him to come in for a session because he has seen the youngster in some situation and gotten evidence from others that he might need help. He may have become concerned because he has gathered from chance remarks of pupils or teachers that the child could profit from counseling. However, if there is resistance after the first one or two sessions, the counselor states that his own time is valued and that should the counselee later wish to continue he will be available but for the present there seem to be better uses for that time.

Counselees are in different stages of readiness for counseling. Some can get to the heart of deep concerns within a few minutes.

Others will be frightened away if matters of chronic anxiety are approached too rapidly. Hence, both instruction and intuition are important parts of the counselor's background. At times he will use reflection, at others he will make postulations in the form of interpretations of what the counselee has said, and at still others he may confront the counselee with the latter's contradictions and inaccuracies. He is less concerned about making the counselee comfortable than with judging how much discomfort the counselee can stand. It is also assumed that dealing with the personal and intimate is difficult and therefore that escape or relief from such discussion is sought. It is also assumed that being able to stay in the area of discomfort for longer and longer periods of time is growth-producing. Since there is a resistance to change, especially on the part of those who have encountered failure and disappointment in large doses, reference is made to the *trauma of transcendence*. Trying new behaviors runs the risk of encountering new dangers or again being disappointed. By repeatedly bringing the counselee back to the area of discomfort in dialogue, the counselor diminishes the area of discomfort, and preparation is made for dealing with the matter of concern by acting rather than words.

While the counselor does not make decisions for the counselee, he becomes a dynamic force in the counselee's life. The responsibility for choice remains with the individual. He must have no one but himself to blame for future mistakes. The counselor does interrupt self-defeating behavior patterns by talking about them. He intervenes in the life process of the individual, and he influences the direction and quality of developmental processes. Reflecting, interpreting, and confronting are ways of interrupting the habitual rationalizations and other defensive patterns of action. Intervening consists in presenting some new points of view, some possibilities for alternative behaviors: "What might happen if you were to try . . . ?" Influence is exerted by what the counselor chooses to reflect, what questions he asks, or what events he picks to confront the counselee with. He influences by expressing his own feelings about wasting time, being fed a line, or being expected to endorse when the counselee knows there is nothing to endorse.

Part of the preparation for such counseling approaches is a careful and rather continuous look at oneself. That which is called intuition begins to be recognized as a tendency on the part of the counselor to be brutal or to avoid delicate issues. Some counselors prefer not to talk about mothers, or sex, or drinking, or drugs. Some like to talk with girls and others prefer to talk with boys. One learns about himself in regard to such matters by participating in interpersonal process groups. He is helped to see himself as others see him by listening to what others say about him and by watching, in a real-life situation, the impact he produces. Whether he wants to change is up to him, but the sessions teach with considerable clarity that one inevitably — by much talk, an occasional remark, or complete silence — has an effect on the group he is in. This means, also, that there is no escape from being an influence in a counseling situation.

Techniques of counseling are less important than recognition of what one is, but what one is must be recognized. Some counselors may find it easy and effective to confront. Others engage in dialogue without a predetermined goal and ask for further information on topics which typically yield results — parental relations, sibling rivalry, disinterest in school, inability to concentrate, interests, lack of friends. But when this casting-about approach is used, there is a conscious attempt to avoid concentrating on things of interest to the counselor. He keeps asking, "Is this the thing most pertinent to what the counselee is saying or trying to hide?" Still others may find it comforting to use the Rogerian method of reflecting and re-phrasing. Then too, one may find that the occasion rather than what makes the counselor or counselee comfortable will dictate re-flection, questioning, or confrontation.

COUNSELING AS A TEACHING-LEARNING TRANSACTION

Krumboltz (1966) conceptualizes counseling as a special kind of learning situation. Learning rather than therapy is the central issue. He calls this concept a revolution in counseling because it presents new answers to familiar quetsions, four of which are of uppermost concern: (1) How are the counselee's problems perceived? (2) How should goals be defined? (3) What techniques should be used? (4) How is effectiveness to be judged?

The counselee's problem is one of learning rather than a matter of being sick. Indeed, this is a problem for counselors because conventionally we think that one who is "in need of help and understanding" is sick. It is easy to think of the one in ten who needs help as being ill rather than uninformed. "What's your problem?" means to many counselors and counselees "Where do you feel ill?" Krumboltz emphasizes that a boy is a bully not because he is sick or maladjusted but because he has learned to act that way. The real issue is one of learning to answer a specific question plus learning effective ways to answer one's own questions and the next questions that occur.

Goals must be defined precisely and specifically. Self-actualization, self-understanding, realization of potential are worthy aims, but they are generalities. The problems of a particular individual are to overcome shyness with one's peers or the other sex; to choose a college; to learn how to cease irritating teachers. The desired outcome is defined in terms of individual instances, and the course of action is tailored to each individual. Emphasis remains on the learning problem. It is not, for example, simply a matter of choosing a college but one of how to gather information, evaluate the data, and project the probable outcomes of this choice and another choice. The goal is to evolve a sequence of steps in resolving this, and the next, dilemma.

There are four major approaches to the matter of techniques and procedures in the teaching-learning counseling model. One is operant conditioning. The counselor provides the reward or reinforcement by giving attention and by encouraging further talk about a specific course of action (describing plans to spend five minutes talking with one's mother, for example). Krumboltz might be suggesting a consultant role when he says that reinforcement also desirably occurs outside the counseling situation, as in dealing with modification of the competitive grading system, dealing with parents and teachers who are part of the child's perplexing milieu, etc. A second learning approach is imitative learning — the opportunity to observe models who use adaptive behavior, as revealed not only in persons but in tape recordings, motion pictures, and books — especially well-chosen biographies and autobiographies. A third approach is cognitive learning, in which the client who has reached an appropriate stage of development is given some needed information by the counselor. The learner may be helped to realize his more effective behaviors by being told of them at the time they take place. Role playing is another means of bringing about a rational appreciation of effective behavior. The fourth approach is emotional learning, which stems from conditioning and reconditioning. It is a matter of pairing the eliciting stimuli of a response with other pleasant stimuli. This model would obviously be useful in treating fears and anxieties.

The final question in this type of counseling relates to judging the result, which, says Krumboltz, is somewhat like defining goals in that what is researched must be specific. The effectiveness of counseling must be evaluated not in terms of general impressions but in terms of what kinds of situations and what kinds of persons are helped by which approaches. The need for such evaluation is emphasized by a study that in 1965 won an American Personnel and Guidance Association research award. Gonyea (1964) found a *negative* correlation between what was deemed by counselors to be a good counseling relationship and what the counselee reported as an improved pattern of behavior. Research is important not only in terms of finding effective counseling approaches but in terms of helping counselors keep an open mind toward future experimentation and progress.

BEHAVIOR THERAPY AND SYSTEMATIC DESENSITIZATION

The use of methods in counseling and therapy based on behavioral psychology gained considerable attention during the 1960's. Early in the 1950's Wolpe (1969) introduced his behavior therapy concepts heavily influenced by systematic desensitization — a technique for reducing anxiety by combining progressive relaxation and counterconditioning. The initial aim was to use systematic desensitization to eliminate irrational fears such as phobias and other inappropriate behavior. The fact that leading counseling authorities have adapted the Wolpe therapy techniques to counseling practice may cause some students concern over the issue of therapy and counseling. Fullmer (1971b) claims the differences between psychotherapy and counseling practice are largely academic because people are much the same whether they are seen in a counseling office or a psychiatric clinic. The terminology follows the physical setting more accurately than it follows the treatment nomenclature of therapy or counseling. The prestige of the authority figure making suggestions to the patient in a psychiatric clinic no doubt outweighs the prestige of a counselor in a counseling office — to all *except* the counselee. Beyond the status barrier there would appear to be no difference between therapy and counseling practice limited to the application of psychological and behavior principles or techniques. The use of behavior therapy and systematic desensitization calls for a professional practioner and one or more clients ready to enter into the interpersonal-professional contract required for establishing the treatment process.

Basic rationale of behavior theory and the therapy techniques derived therefrom is about as follows:

Human behavior is learned.

Human behavior conforms to the laws of cause and effect.

Learning is defined in a stimulus-and-response model.

Reinforcement principles can be used to strengthen or extinguish a given response.

When old responses are weakened or eliminated by new responses, the inhibition becomes reciprocal (Wolpe's Reciprocal Inhibition).

Relaxation and counterconditioning lead to systematic desensitization; thus an anxiety-producing stimulus is neutralized.

Anxieties characteristic of each person can be arranged in a hierarchy from least to most anxiety-producing.

Desensitization should proceed from the least anxiety-producing life situations (stimuli) to the more and most anxiety-producing ones.

Anxiety is the basic phenomenon in neurotic behavior.

Neurotic behavior is learned by the same process as more adaptive behavior.

Behavior is rewarded by both primary and secondary reinforcement.

Adaptive behavior should be taught so the person can discard maladaptive behaviors.

Therapy uses three main methods: assertive responses, sexual responses, and relaxation responses.

Assertive responses are any expressions made by or initiated by the individual toward others involving an overt act expressing a personal feeling, i.e., anger, love, or friendship.

Sexual responses require the patient cooperation of a sexual partner to permit the process of desensitization to happen. The contract is a three-way commitment among the therapist, patient, and sex partner.

Relaxation responses are applied to any type of anxiety because relaxation directly opposes anxiety.

Prestige suggestions are used freely in the application of all techniques.

Desensitization employs a simple concept of direct exposure to the anxiety-producing stimulus. In addition, a stimulus situation is devised to counter the effect of the anxiety-producing stimulus. The careful manipulation of the level of anxiety can effectively maintain the conditions necessary to counterconditioning. Counterconditioning describes the condition that once was anxiety-producing as no longer anxiety-producing. The process leads to a level of satiation by the exposure to increasingly larger portions of formerly anxiety-producing stimuli. For example, if a student is anxious each time he takes a test, it is possible to teach him to relax. Relaxation is practiced during exams. With extensive systematic exposure to examinations while under relaxation, the former anxiety condition is eliminated.

The paradox of relaxation and anxiety can be created by the suggestion of the counselor to substitute one for the other, which is more complex than simple exposure alone. Some things have to happen in sequence between the unconditioned stimulus and the conditioned stimulus at an optimal interval of two to four seconds. This complex process requires that the counselor command expert skills to successfully complete the systematic desensitization. The wide acceptance and application of Wolpe's methods in school counseling may require considerable retraining and restructuring for the counselor and his role in the educative process.[1]

OTHER VARIETIES OF COUNSELING THEORY

The above theories and approaches are only a small sample of the total, but they do represent the extremes of the permissive-authoritarian range and include some in between. Still another approach

[1] Krumboltz and Thoresen (1969) edited a book of contemporary readings on cases and techniques in behavioral counseling. In six parts covering more than forty articles the editors bring together much of the material on behavioral counseling. See also "Contemporary View of Behavioral Counseling," *Counseling Psychologist* Vol. 1, No. 4 (1969). The literature reflects a growing interest in this variety of counseling theory.

— chemotherapy — employs drugs such as tranquilizers and psychedelics to induce physical changes or to supplement or pave the way for the work of more conventional methods. A tranquilizer, for example, may be used by a psychiatrist to calm a patient, or counteract depression, before he institutes one of the techniques described above. Hypnotherapy consists in placing the client under hypnosis, increasing his suggestibility, and attempting to get him to lay aside his neurotic symptoms while practicing some behaviors that are likely to be more productive. Ellis (1966) has developed what is known as rational therapy. He denies that the congruence espoused by Rogers is necessary. What is vital is that the counselor understand the problem and show the client that his behaviors are illogical and unrealistic. He argues, lectures, and tries to get the client to demonstrate for himself that his mistaken beliefs can be replaced by more accurate perceptions and more productive behaviors.

The important thing about these varied approaches is that they work. No method is universally successful, and all work in many instances. All varieties seem to conclude that the essential element is a caring person — the counselor — who brings hope to someone whose attachment to others has become strained and tenuous. One counselor said, "We're not sure that hanging a person by his thumbs would not effect changes, as long as he gets attention."

Variety in the Context of Counseling

The foregoing section dealt with types of counseling in terms of the view of man that dominates the content of the counseling transaction. In this section the view of man is of minor importance and the number of persons involved in the transaction becomes the focus.

SELF-IMPROVEMENT

Some people receive their "counseling" in an indirect, individual, and impersonal manner. They read a book or an article or listen to a sermon or lecture and set their own course of making changes in personality and behavior. To deny the existence of this effective "do-it-yourself" technique would, it seems, be to deny the value of the process of education.

One does not read about it in universities and graduate schools, but many people claim their lives have been changed by study and application of Christian Science. Mary Baker Eddy's book *Science and Health* may be used as an individual project, or its reading may be supplemented by discussion in small groups.

ONE-TO-ONE COUNSELING

Representative approaches to accelerated personality growth based on a one-to-one counseling relationship have been discussed in the foregoing section.

GROUP COUNSELING

Because the greater part of one's life is spent in contact and interaction with others, counseling in groups is growing in popularity. Initially, group counseling was introduced in the hope that it might be a time saver. If a counselor could work with problems of college planning, resentment of autocratic school administration, hostility toward parents, or underachievement — or even with several different problems at once — within a group, it seemed like a good investment of time. However, group counseling was soon discovered to be much more than a time saver. The group itself was a teacher of prestigious stature. In a group one does not just talk about life. Group members live an aspect of life; concern focuses on what is going on now. They are practicing a bit of social experience but without the threat which failure in a context outside the group would entail.

Because of the importance of the group, and the group counseling context, in the total pupil personnel program, Chapters Seven, Eight, and Nine of this book deal with various aspects of groups in school milieus.

SITUATIONAL COUNSELING

Philippe Pinel has been given credit for developing, 150 years ago, a kind of rehabilitation program that has almost disappeared from the contemporary scene (Allport, 1968, p. 128). It had an institutional approach. Every responsible adult contributed to a familylike environment — a positive, sympathetic milieu of human association in which, during work and play, the disturbed person was treated as a normal person. The goal was for the patient to develop or regain his self-respect. This situational counseling approach is now experiencing a resurgence, and many mental hospitals across the nation are attempting to implement it. Where it is in effect restraint and custody are replaced by compassion, and recovery rates are high.

. . . The theory dictating milieu intervention stems from the work of the investigators [Leonard E. Gottesman, Dorothy Coons, and Wilma Donahue], from the ego psychology of Erik Erikson, and from a recent theory of milieu therapy formulated by Cumming and Cumming. Briefly stated, it assumes that ego skills develop and are strengthened when an individual faces and meets, in a protected environment, problems or crises which are part of real and meaningful social roles. In order to function, a person must have a number of ways of behaving and also the ability to select and act with an appropriate response to a situation. . . . Doors were painted bright colors, and doors that previously had been locked were opened. Furniture was rearranged, and heavy wooden furniture was replaced by more fragile, noninstitutional furniture. Long, large, dining room tables were replaced by small ones. Full length mirrors were hung, and clocks and calendars were added. Lighting was improved in the sheltered workshop room, since many of the patients had impaired eyesight.

Men were given free access to razors, and facilities were set up for women to wash and set their own hair (although visits to the beauty parlor were still available). A washer and dryer were made available to the patients, as was a modest kitchen setup. Efforts were made to have regular clothes, as opposed to hospital apparel, available. And nursing staff wore street clothes instead of uniforms to help minimize the clinical atmosphere.

The sheltered workshop had long tables for work groups. These were of such a size that each patient could talk to others in his group. Timeclocks, timecards, etc., were added. Patients were employed on industrial tasks contracted for with outside organizations. Workshop jobs included assembly of small automobile parts, sorting of chrome letters for cars, making cotton hospital swabs, and folding and wrapping bandages. In addition, high artistic craft items were made. Sold in local stores, these items carried a special tag with an oriental sign meaning longevity and the word "Gericrafter." Nothing was made for diversion or to "kill time."

Patients were paid on an hourly or piecework basis for all items manufactured, and all money realized was returned as salary to the patients except for the amounts necessary to cover costs of supplies and program expenses. All money received by the patients remained in their possession.[2]

The description of situational therapy in a custodial mental institution may seem remote from the work of educators, but parallels have been drawn between custodial institutions and schools (Keniston, 1967). The lines of distinction between a therapeutic or preventative institution and a developmental institution are not necessarily clear-cut. Reversing the course of thought, there are some who accuse the school of being conducive to the development of psychological illness such as alienation, low self-concept, repressed creativity, absence of individual identity, and intellectual dependency.

To reduce some of the criticism of the school as an unhygienic institution and to attack its defects as a coordinated and unified staff requires precisely the role of leadership envisioned for the counselor-consultant. Let us initiate some thoughts, which should be extended by the reader, by repeating certain sections of the foregoing quotation and proposing some implications.

". . . ego skills develop and are strengthened when an individual faces and meets . . ." Much greater use should be made of independent study so the pupil can form the habit of continuous, self-propelled, and governed learning. Being autonomous instead of abjectly conforming strengthens the ego concept — the feeling of worth and dependability.

". . . a number of ways of behaving and also the ability to select . . ." Prescribed curricula must be questioned; a wide variety of alternatives must be provided so there is a range for the operation of pupil choice. Because the number of teachers will not be multiplied in any one school, the concept of the school as a place for learning as contrasted to a place for teaching must be given functional consideration. A pupil, after guidance and counseling, must be permitted the indulgence of making a mistake. Autonomy granted only if its exercise results in choosing in favor of the "establishment" is not really autonomy.

[2] Clarissa Wittenberg, 1968, "Milieu Therapy and the Long-term Geriatric Mental Patient," in National Institute of Mental Health, *Mental Health Program Reports,* No. 2 (Chevy Chase, Md.: National Institute of Mental Health, U.S. Department of Health, Education, and Welfare), pp. 40, 42.

". . . doors were painted bright colors, and doors that previously had been locked . . ." Pupils might themselves join the drive to solicit funds to paint the building in which they must reside. And there is the problem of locking laboratories, drama departments, gymnasiums, playgrounds, and libraries because no custodial teachers are available for the night shift. The open school is a reality in some places. At NOVA High School, Fort Lauderdale, Florida, high schoolers ride bikes several miles instead of taking the bus so they can continue their projects in the art studio or mechanics shop or just sit around and rap.

"Long, large, dining room tables were replaced . . ." Traditional concepts of what constitutes good classroom order must be examined in terms of ego development. The day of screwed-down lines of chairs has passed, yet the idea of small groups, working at small tables, without the close supervision of a teacher, is still viewed with skepticism. While skepticism may be warranted, it should be considered in teacher in-service groups as an aspect of vital school policy.

"Full length mirrors were hung . . ." These might help adults who are bothered by mini-skirts and maxi-hairdos. Mirrors might help the pupil see himself as others see him. Other, figurative mirrors would include liberal use of photographs (a technique useful in teaching the disadvantaged whose identity is equivocal), tape recorders (as an approach to speech and reading development), and closed-circuit television.

"Men were given free access to razors . . ." Questions of freedom and autonomy are far from being answered; they have not, in many schools, even been asked. And violence is breaking out. In the summer of 1969 top school administrators, authors on "generation gap," "peer group culture," "the now generation," and high school pupils met at Harvard to discuss their mutual concern, among other things, about four-letter words, courtesy, respect, authority, legality, and how tradition kept any real communication from developing (Schrag, 1969). The counselor-consultant is one, if not the only, person who might be involved in resolving the matter of institutional preservation — and the preservation of the institution's residents. Because no surefire answers for bridging the generation gap have been found, the consulting approach might be used — before all the data are gathered.

"Workshop jobs included [a variety of tasks] and highly artistic craft items were made." High schools which do involve their students have different tasks — academic work, shop projects, crafts, and art — so that students may choose those pertinent to their self-perception and to their goals. Such involvement might give them the sense of identity that would encourage their participation in academic pursuits geared to their styles and rates of learning.

"All money received by the patients remained in their possession." There are numerous ways of handling student activity funds. However, those instances in which funds are accounted for by faculty might be challenged in teacher in-service education meetings: "Is it pupil development or monetary accountability that is the proper concern of education?"

The focus of the counselor-consultant might well be established in accordance with the concept of a developmental milieu in which all staff, pupils, funds, and facilities are directed to the considered aims of the school.

Summary

Varieties of counseling range, in terms of theory, from permissive to authoritarian. In the first instance, it is presumed that strength for growth resides within the individual; the counselor's job is to help the counselee find himself and to get him started on a productive course. In the latter instance, it is presumed that the counselor possesses the wisdom, and his job is to lead the counselee to a more productive style of living. Between the two extremes are theories which are called behavioral, reality, rational, and the like. All produce results in the practice of a sophisticated professional.

Context also varies, ranging from self-therapy, through a one-to-one relationship, to group, and the establishment of a total milieu designed to produce optimum development. The latter removes as many hazards to development as possible.

The counselor-consultant's interest in variety might be to appreciate that as far as different teachers and different counselors are concerned, the important thing is not technique. The core of learning, as well as the core of the counseling relationship, is caring and the establishment of a contingent relationship — i.e., where the experienced and the inexperienced have an effect on the actions of the other. Ultimately the caring and relationship would desirably pervade the entire school through the action initiated by a counselor-consultant.

SUGGESTED ADDITIONAL READINGS

Ard, Ben N., Jr. (ed.), 1966. *Counseling and Psychotherapy, Classics on Theories and Issues.* Palo Alto, Calif.: Science and Behavior Books. *Some of the twenty articles are of a general nature dealing with particular orientations to counseling such as client-centered, reality counseling, rational therapy, and behavioral conditioning.*

Ebel, Robert L., 1970. "The Social Consequences of Educational Testing," in B. Shertzer and S. C. Stone (eds.), *Introduction to Guidance: Selected Readings.* Boston: Houghton Mifflin Company. From *Proceedings of the 1963 Invitational Conference on Testing Problems.* Princeton, N.J.: Educational Testing Service, 1964. Pp. 130–143. *This article describes some of the criticisms that have been justly and unjustly leveled at tests. Ebel suggests some ways in which makers and users of tests may improve the situation.*

Gephart, William J., and Daniel P. Antonoplos, 1969. "The Effects of Expectancy and Other Research-Biasing Factors," *Phi Delta Kappan,* 50:579–583. *This article is not devoted to research in counseling, but some of the questions raised are quite pertinent to the research work of the counselor-consultant.*

Glasser, William, 1969. *Schools Without Failure.* New York: Harper & Row, Publishers. *This book might be called a combination of what in the foregoing chapter was described as reality counseling and situational modification and control.*

Stefflre, Buford (ed.), 1965. *Theories of Counseling.* New York: McGraw-Hill Book Company. *The various chapters in this book deal with client-centered counseling, psychoanalytic variations, and behavioral counseling but relate them to school counseling rather than regarding them primarily as therapies. Vocational and educational counseling are considered.*

Chapter Seven

THE CONCEPT OF GROUP

The group is both medium and message. Communication is one of the constant variables in all behavior. There is no such thing as *not* communicating by group members. Instead of asking, "How can communication be improved?" the task is to discover what *is being* communicated in the here and now. The concept of group is unique because it is an encounter with the sum of a person's history without being historical. Contrasted with the psychoanalytic emphasis on reliving a past, the concept of group is a focus on the living present. Groups may take many forms but the concept of group remains the same in each instance. The rationale of medium and message is that as long as behavior continues within a collection of individuals, the message continues to be expressed (Fullmer, 1971a). The group as medium is ruled by principles based upon the task or purpose the group achieves. Therefore, if one can read the language of behavior and apply the principles or rules guiding the behavior, it is possible to read the behavior (Fullmer, 1969a).

The group is a systematic linking of individuals within a given context, i.e., wife-husband, sister-brother, friend-friend, etc., in a relationship defined by the rules of the culture. Engebretson (1969) found that behavior follows relationship in each of three cultural groups. The content of the interaction had no influence on the behavior. From this study, it would seem to be important to know how the relationship is defined in order to anticipate the behavior. The concept of group has to do with the relationship and its definition rather than with the labeled description of the individual members of a given group. The connecting forces within and among a group of persons can be arranged in a taxonomy which allows for direct comparisons across what would otherwise be divergent kinds of groups. In brief, the common factor is one of *relationship definition* rather than size or task or other identifying criteria usually employed in discussion of the concept of group (Lennard and Bernstein, 1969).

Principles of Relationships

GROUP AS MEDIUM

The classification of relationships between individuals may help the student clarify what is meant by group as medium. Hall (1959) has indicated that all behavior takes place in the context of culture, each culture having its own relationship definitions built into its system of organizing human groups. Some 460 separate cultures have been identified by Mead and Heyman (1965).

Within a given culture man tends to subdivide into smaller collections of people. One collection common to all present cultures is the family, according to Mead and Heyman (1965). Although the small group or family may take a number of different forms and still be classified under the label *family,* the relationships between the significant members of a family seem to be fairly consistent across cultures. The family tends to be a biological unit and a social unit, providing for procreation as well as socialization of the young. Mead and Heyman (1965) further explain that all cultures which eliminated the family as a basic unit have ceased to exist. Group as medium is a concept about the *relationships defined* within the classification system that is linked to the cultural context. The cultural rules constitute a way of defining relationships between or among individuals in the group. This idea covers all formal rules, technical rules, and informal rules within a given culture (Hall, 1959). The medium is not necessarily hidden, but it is rarely explicit in American society because of the large proportion of behavior relationships defined by the informal rules.

Group is a medium of communication the same as television, radio, or any other instrument for interaction. We sometimes think of communication as restricted to interaction models. This is a less inclusive concept than is implied here when we speak of the group as medium. Interaction models are limited mostly to verbal exchanges wherein cognitive ideas with some emotional overtones may be transferred from one person to another. Group as a medium refers more to the total and all-at-once nature of communication at the relationships level (Watzlawick et al., 1967). The group defines relationships without benefit of interaction because of the way it links people in accord with the culture rules. Consider the governor's office, the bedroom, the principal's parking space, the coach and his team, father's chair. Most of these examples involve territory, but territory is only one of the definitive rules used in the culture (Hall, 1959).

GROUP AS MESSAGE

Message is tied inextricably to the medium carrying the message, as is indicated in the platitude that "it is not what I say but the *way* I say it." In counseling in groups, the concern is with helping persons learn how their nonverbal communication is denied or confirmed by their verbal statements. This process is fundamental in improving the quality of communication in groups. The clarification of a message that is incongruous with its medium constitutes a major source of humor in our society. The syndicated cartoon strip "Peanuts" frequently utilizes situational material reflecting the medium-message incongruity. For example, when someone says, "Tell me you love me," the verbal message is denied by the relationship message carried in the medium of the life situation — perhaps in tone of voice or some other incongruity. As Lucy laments, "He says it but somehow he doesn't say it."

COMMUNICATION

The interaction model used to study human behavior claims that it is impossible not to communicate (Watzlawick et al., 1967). If one could achieve the condition of not behaving, then it might be possible to achieve a condition of not communicating. This confirms our earlier comment that communication is going on all the time, and the counselor-consultant is responsible for always knowing what is being communicated.

A major concern with communication is: Will a counselor-consultant learn how to read the communication in the interpersonal context? For example, when he enters a classroom there is an immediate group message system in operation. The medium of the group — counselor-consultant, teacher, and pupils — has some established communication value which is instantly in the awareness of everyone in the room. This is the informal message system. Remember that in American culture the rules are not explicit because communication is predominately informal. Therefore, the awareness is tied to physiology, and response is only to violations of the rules. Since first-level sensory knowledge cannot be ignored, the counselor-consultant is encouraged to talk about how it feels to be in the room with the others. In this sense, it is impossible *not* to communicate.

BROADCASTING: PROBABILITY COMMUNICATION

Communication within a group and among groups is of paramount importance to the counselor-consultant. It is indeed a two-way street. Group members must have a way of reporting back (feedback) what they have received, what they understand, and how they intend to respond. The probability of achieving meaningful communication by general broadcasts of items of information becomes a factor in every ongoing human organization. The communication may be formalized in a written memo, a verbal commentary over an intercom, or an announcement at a general assembly. These types of communication are necessary to punctuate the ongoing life of the group, but there is always the probability that such communication does not reach a given individual. Frequently probability communication or broadcasting is carried out to highlight the change from one activity to another in the life of the group. General-interest feedback may be included in the all-points broadcast category of communicating, whereas in small groups the communication is almost always a person-to-person interaction rather than a general announcement (Cohen, 1953).

The counselor-consultant is responsible for conveying information to many different groups, a task he can achieve by any one of several broadcast techniques. The nitty-gritty communication within group is crucial to the productive life of the group. The person who makes general announcements to everyone else in a group may disqualify himself from group membership, while the charismatic leader may capture the group with his overwhelming attractiveness. These are similar possibilities in within-group broadcasting. Since a group is a way of communicating, the need for broadcasting is usually more disorganizing than enabling, for it shows that the person or condition is in some stage of ambiguity, and ambiguity is disorganizing in individual or group.

FORMAL, INFORMAL, AND TECHNICAL MESSAGE SYSTEMS

Hall (1959) divides the culture into three general systems. *Formal, informal,* and *technical* may be applied to learning time, interpersonal relationships, or any other categorical behavior in the culture.

Formal systems are taught by exhortation, admonition, and precept. The formal system accommodates no variation, no exception, and no substitution. A mother says, "Do it this way," and her child responds with "Why, Mommy?" "Because this is the way it is done." The significant content in the communication is that no exception is allowed. In American culture the formal rules are few but they are precise and nonnegotiable. Formal communication systems are further identified by tone of voice, which is always firm and uncompromising, leaving no room for ambivalence.

The informal message system may be characterized as a grapevine or folklore or a shared story. Whichever it is, it is the model for imitation. Unlike the formal or technical system, the informal system lacks admonition, precept, or even conscious awareness of the rules governing informal system behavior, though if the rules are broken, there is instantaneous awareness. Perhaps this factor makes it more difficult to explain how to recognize the informal system. The example of sex education comes to mind. One of the reasons American school systems have difficulty in conducting sex education in a technical and formal way is simply that most sex knowledge in American society is part of the informal social system.

Sex education programs are attempting to make technical what has been traditionally treated as informal. The reaction of those who oppose the program is aimed at the inexplicit taboo instead of at any explicit rule violation. The reason is plain enough. Hall (1959) explains that Americans treat sex knowledge and sexuality as an informal system of rules, biological but not verbal (explicit).

The counselor-consultant understands there is no way *verbally* to explain sex for those who react. Technical explanations are interpreted as a violation. Even state legislatures are pressured into responding because no one can seem to explain what the cultural concern in sex-sexuality education is all about. The informal system need for a model to imitate has led Dundes (1969) to remark that the computerized folklore about man and machines has come to the point that, when asked a question, a machine may say, "I would like to tell you a story about that." Whenever the counselor-consultant resorts to a story to explain the relationship, he is dealing with the informal system, which has infinite variation potential.

The informal message system in group is extremely important, but almost taboo so far as direct intervention is concerned. It is very difficult to get a group to handle its informal communication system directly. However, one can usually observe the formation of a way of talking in a group, which somehow gets established depending on how the leader sets up the demonstration model and uses the *formula* for interaction. The way of talking or formula leads to a way of thinking which, in turn, accommodates the rules operating in the group. An informal message system must be experienced directly if one is to analyze it. The private code of symbols and meanings evolved in a group is unique to a given group at a given time. These symbols and meanings are also part of the formula. The shared system of beliefs may be included as a part of a formula, whether it is made explicit or left in the informal system. An example of the latter is the frequently repeated report by someone fresh from a group experience who says, "You should have been there; it was wonderful!" The person is unable to explain more because of the informal nature of the experience. Again, nature is equated with culture in formal social systems.

Technical systems, unlike either formal or informal systems, become almost exclusively one-way (Watzlawick et al., 1967). The knowledge or communication flow is from expert to neophyte. The technical system is less dependent upon creative and intellectual aptitude and more dependent upon conformity and the following of direction. The size of the group has a direct bearing upon how technical the communication must become. Instruction involving large numbers requires the presentation of information to be more technical, and it is frequently in written or outline form. This large group technical preciseness is then explained by some kind of analysis, put together in simple and coherent terms. The technical system requires that the individual handling the transmission of the communication prevent his own bias or involvement from modifying the content. Contamination of communication will result in chaos because the options will be open instead of prescribed.

The counselor-consultant might use the example of the behavior modification reinforcement schedules employed in teaching the three R's as a contrast to the informal system for small group counseling with no agenda and no specific items listed in the content of the curriculum.

Another example that students might like to try to classify with the above information is the social system of inmates of a prison. There are several systems in any institutional structure. The formal system of the prison might be indicated by the flow chart from the warden to the lowliest subordinate. But any warden knows that he operates his prison with the informal consent of the inmate social system (Gaddis, 1955). Anything that upsets the continuity and dependability of the ongoing system may trigger a riot. The riot is an attempt to force the formal system to reconstitute itself so that it can again be regarded as predictable. The new systems of rehabilitation employed in correctional institutions may be unpredictable for the inmate social system.

Groups in Action

SOCIAL LITERACY

Social literacy is one way to measure the level of socialization achieved by an individual, and the concept of group is concerned with the level of socialization. The term *socialization* is sometimes used to indicate the degree of maturity. However, in group work we have found it more profitable to think about competence and incompetence as dimensions of socialization rather than to employ the concept of maturity (Fullmer, 1969b). The competent individual is able to define relationships for himself without being dependent upon other persons in a way that requires them to duplicate or mirror his request for confirmation. He is able to decide that his world is a safe place for him to be, and he can therefore proceed with his task without further ritual.

Social literacy is determined by the person's ability to read the cues that are coming to him from internal sources in relation to the cues he is aware of from the external culture (Watzlawick et al., 1967). There is some similarity between the taxonomy we will use here and the one used in reference to communication in the immediately preceding section. The socially literate person is able to read the formal social system in all of his actions. This ability is equated to the concept of group as medium. It is assumed that if one can read the context of the social system as a medium, he can also read the message system as a language of meaningful symbols. The matching of knowledge and behavior is one way to measure the level of social literacy. If an immigrant from a foreign culture had no information concerning the formal structure of the social system in the new country, his behavior would not match the social system and would therefore be conspicuous. This example of easily recognized differentness is one way to identify behavior that would fit the formal statements in this text.

According to the concept of group, any collection of persons within a given social system or culture will exhibit a similar social system for living in that group. They will also share the same formal system governing activities away from the group and out in the society (Sherif and Sherif, 1964). Therefore, it is possible to help someone who does not know the formal system to acquaint himself with it in a safe practice arena: the *group*. Because we assume that all young people and children are less practiced in group behavior, we sometimes commit the error of assuming they do not know the formal social system. But by the time a child reaches age nine or ten he is fully cognizant of the formal social system in the culture in which he is growing up. His exposures to the models of the culture, however, may have left him without adequate socialization in the informal social system, and the group is also useful in helping him become more socially literate at that level (Fullmer and Bernard, 1968).

The Informal Social System

One of the major issues facing the counselor-consultant in today's school concerns the notion that in order to teach the informal social system to children, teachers, and parents it is necessary to reduce it to a technical level. Once the informal social system has been put in technical terms, this information can presumably be transferred from one person to another by means of some method of instruction or a combination of several methods. However, the individual will not be able to apply his new knowledge until he has spent significant amounts of time with appropriate *models* who are utilizing the knowledge. Because informal social system knowledge can be learned only from imitating models, having technical instruction about it leads to the formation of a *formal* social system.

An example is the formation of a new group. Initially the group has a wide range of information and relatively loose rules for interaction. As time passes, the process becomes more and more technical until in the later stages of the group life the system becomes extremely formal. Even small variations in the way the formal social system is conformed to become items of concern to group members. A violation is corrected in the same way a mother admonishes her child when the formal system is being taught: "We do not do that" — and no explanation is given (Hall, 1959).

Social Action

Social literacy is usually reflected in the level of social action engaged in by the group or individuals. The successful operation of a human organization is likely to depend upon the social literacy that has been mastered by the members. The socially illiterate person is unable to function in a way that will contribute significantly to the group's social action.

Social action within the group attempted by any individual member will reflect quickly the level of his social literacy. If he is skilled in making his behavior generate the kinds of responses he hopes for, he is considered more socially literate than if his solicited responses are discrepant from his aspiration.

Social Power

French (1956) identifies five kinds of power. They reside in (1) the nice guy, (2) the specialist or authority, (3) control of the rewards, (4) control of punishment, (5) the legitimate right to prescribe behavior. There is a sixth category in the 1970's: the power of the dropout — the nonpower power posture.

French's social power constructs are particularly useful in observing the behavior in groups. It is possible to look at the systems of group counseling in terms of the selections of social power employed by the intervention system. We might even find persons and systems denying the use of power as here defined. French offered his original theory as a way of looking at opinion change. The concept of group implies the need for opinion change on the part of some individuals within each group.

CULTURE AS HUMAN ORGANIZATION

When individuals organize themselves into a group, this group is in fact a complete human organization. Whether the group meets the ideal of the culture depends upon the proficiency of its membership.

The group is a way of being in the world. The relationships within the group confirm, deny, or somehow define the individual's relationship between himself and his environment. If his environment is basically people, then group is a direct learning experience for him which is at the same time a part of his process of being in the world.

IDENTITY OF THE INDIVIDUAL

The individual gains his identity in his relationship to significant others. Relationships are defined in groups, and the relationship definition either confirms or denies the self-concept of the individual. Disconfirmation occurs usually in the smaller arenas of subgroup interaction and is leavened by the proliferation of positive feedback of positive reinforcement and supportive forces provided in the group. However, disconfirmation may be disproportionately high in any initial meetings of a new group.

Confirmation of the self-concept of the individual is one of the many significant events in group. The process of making self-conscious the identity confirmation experience is a major consequence of the group encounter.

An Application of the Concept of Group

A group develops a formula through which it permits its members to interact. The formula defines the rules by which individuals talk to one another and/or about themselves. It is designed to define relationships in order to influence individual behavior. There are systems like dianetics, invented by L. Ron Hubbard in 1951, in which an entire language is provided for guiding the interaction. The unique thing about dianetics, later known as scientology, is that relationship is defined with the group only so long as the interaction formula is being used. In group, the formula becomes the vehicle through which the individual defines his relationship with other persons. His behavior is a response to the relationship as it is defined at any given time in the group.

The following transcript has been edited to protect the identity of the individuals and the group. It is included to show how one seventeen-year-old girl reports her experience of nine months with the scientology group. We are interested in your seeing how the *formula* for interaction is used to define relationships for the girl. With the new relationships she (Mary) can now behave in new ways. The ways of behaving led to new relationships. The new pattern had come from the formula for interacting.

Mary's Report

C. Do you think that you have been able to change your attitude and your self-perception?

M. Oh, yes. I've changed a lot, especially in the past year or nine months.

C. What are some of the things that have happened?

M. Well, I used to be withdrawn. I hardly talked with anyone. I remember on all my grade school report cards the teachers would write comments like "Mary won't play with the children; she plays by herself in a corner of the playground and won't participate in group activities." Now, I can get up in front of a group and talk to them. I can do what I want to do because I'm no longer afraid of people. Before, I was so frightened by people that I wouldn't telephone a stranger. I don't know, I was very withdrawn then. Now, I can talk to anybody.

C. What has brought about this change?

M. Well, have you heard of the "blank" "blank" group?

C. No, I haven't.

M. Well, it is a group where each person talks first to one other individual and eventually to a whole group of other persons.

It is sort of like, well — you help me and then I help others help themselves.

C. That sounds familiar, but can you tell me first *how* you go about it?

M. Oh. Well, there's a group, ah, L. Ron Hubbard originated it, and I guess he's back in Washington, D.C., but they have these processes, and through these different processes you have an auditor, a person who processes you and you are a preclear, and they run, ah, different commands on you. They have you do different commands and this, ah, removes a lot of Engrams, you know, things in the past that have inhibited your actions, and it removes a lot of charge off of various things that happen to you, and gets you so that you can take things or leave them and make a better person out of you, generally.

[*Note*: At this point in the series of interviews the counselor, who had never heard of scientology, was given the complete nomenclature including detailed definitions for each label.]

C. How did you become a member of this group?

M. My parents knew people in the group. They came and talked with me and I've been going twice a week since then. I've gone mostly to classes with one other person. I have had regular processing too.

C. What's the difference?

M. Well, co-audit is where two people who really don't know too much about it get together and trade off and process each other. Regular processing is where a certified public auditor processes you — a person who has gone back to Washington, Arizona, or L.A. and has learned everything there is to know about in co-auditing. The person guides the auditor in the session and tells him what to run — what processes to run. He tells him when to start and when to stop. The other auditor does this himself. He knows he's able to decide what the pre-clinics run on him. I'm learning now to be an auditor.

C. Then you feel that Scientology is largely responsible for your change of attitude.

M. I'm quite sure of this.

C. How big a role do you think you yourself have played in this?

M. In which?

C. In changing your own values.

M. Oh! Well, I did it all myself. I mean, you can't be, you can't make any gains in Scientology unless you do it yourself. I mean, the auditor is just there to guide you along the right path. They take the charge off first, and then they slowly work until it's clear. It raises your IQ; it changes your personality completely.

C. You mentioned some of the factors that inhibited your behavior. What were some of these things that you found?

M. Well, mother, my real mother, we ran that for quite a while and it's still not flat. But I can take it or leave it now. I almost hated her. I didn't consider her as a being; I considered her a fink and that's changed a lot. Then usually they run main people in your life that, I don't know, who have done things against you or you've done things against them. This takes a lot of charge off and changes your whole attitude. Then if you've had any major accident or injuries — anything like that — those always leave Engrams so they always run those off. But I haven't.

C. Why, ah, was your mother the biggest charge?

M. Well, ah, this may sound strange but I've had a lot to do with her in past lives. Ah, now this you don't have to believe. But you are your body but in your body is you and this is called a Thetan in Scientology. This Thetan gets bodies as it goes along. As a body dies it picks up a new one and my Thetan has been around her Thetan quite a bit and I guess, I mean they always get related to each other in a lifetime. Anyway, I've done to her some things in past life and she's done some things to me and you have to run those off too.

C. Are you sorry for any of the things that you've done to or towards your mother?

M. Well, that's something we're still working on. I am sometimes. I mean not now. I know it's wrong, but I'm not quite sorry yet — see it's not quite flat.

C. Then, knowing that it's wrong but realizing that you shouldn't do ...

M. Well, I haven't quite taken all the responsibility for that I should. I can't quite take all the responsibilities for it. I can take some responsibility for things I've done to her.

C. Understanding a little of Scientology, now that you've told me, what are some of the things we can do for you here at the counseling center that Scientology can't answer for you?

M. Well, they don't know about colleges.

The interview terminated with another appointment the next week. Subsequent interviews went into the details of Mary's experience in the group. The reason for including this part of the transcript is to show how the formula concept works in a group.

There are some antecedent conditions to be met before a person will join a group. This was done with Mary through her parents and through a status leader from the group who actually came to Mary. The invitation was accepted. Mary began to participate, and she began with a young man her own age. They were given the formula for talking with each other. The nomenclature was known (somewhat) to the young man, but he was only *slightly* more experienced in the formula than was Mary. The power used to modify Mary's opinions of herself was what French (1956) would label legitimate power. Mary believed that the *leader* and the *process* had the right to prescribe her behavior. The prescription was: You do it yourself. The paradoxical intent described by Frankl will help the reader understand the impact of "you do it yourself" (Patterson, 1966).

The belief system is basic to any group. Each participant must believe that the group and the task are legitimate. It must be believable, but it does not need to be devoid of mysticism or yet unexplained phenomena. The *formula* carries the person on into the ambiguous and unknown. The belief is that all will be explained or, as Mary says, become clear.

The following excerpt from the tape of a subsequent interview illustrates this point.

C. Can you explain more about how you acquired this ability in such a short time?

[*Note:* Mary is most pleasant in explaining to the counselor every detail she has learned. She is even able to cover those points on which she is not clear—no pun intended. Mary explains about her Thetan and how she has gone back in time some fifty trillion years. Mary: "You live many times because Thetans never die."

It wasn't unusual for each Thetan to have five or six bodies at a time. They (Thetans) began operating out of control, so that is how automatic withhold came into being.]

C. What is the lifetime of a Thetan?

M. Lifetime? Why, it is infinity. Yeah, some go insane. That is what ghosts are. You probably don't believe in ghosts.

C. How do you get back in time?

M. Well, we have an E-meter, which is similar to a lie detector. The preclear holds two cans and the auditor checks it.

C. Tell me more, please?

M. We can get down to the exact second something happened all that long ago.

C. Can you tell me, Mary, where is all of this taking you? Will you eventually become clear?

M. Oh, yes, I would like to have done it this summer, but there wasn't enough time.

C. What happens after that, after you're clear? Do you need to continue the processes to remain clear?

M. No.

C. Then will you continue with the group, or will you be free to go?

M. Well, usually people who go that far become interested in the work and go into it as a business or just to help others.

C. Do these services cost you money?

M. Oh. Yes. Five to ten dollars for two sessions per week. You pay according to the degrees the auditor has.[1]

Self-determination seems to be central to the process. However, the process is a prescription. Mary is not concerned with this because she believes the leader's power is legitimate.

Self-respect has been achieved. The formula gave Mary the means to demonstrate to herself that she could do some things, accept others as future challenges, and receive positive feedback from other members of the group. These ingredients must be present in every group.

The formula (nomenclature and process) has been used to establish the parameters of the group. These rules become guidelines and

[1] Daniel W. Fullmer, 1971, *Counseling: Group Theory and System* (Scranton, Pa.: International Textbook Company), pp. 117–134.

permit the new relationships to evolve. Once the new relationships exist, the behavior changes to respond to the new expectations. Mary's case represents this phenomenon. It matters not whether anyone else believes the things Mary has acquired with the formula and its social system. The vehicle to propel her from a withdrawn person to an outgoing and active personality was self-evident.

No evaluation or interpretation of scientology is intended here. The example is useful because it comes directly out of a counseling experience. The element of group is central as a concept. Because the nomenclature is unique, the material lends itself to demonstrating the point of this chapter.

Summary

The concept of group is a representation of the structure basic to human organization. It holds for all groups in a given culture. Whether family, peer, or contrived task group, the group is the vehicle for being in the world in some meaningful relationship with others.

Relationships are defined and expressed according to the rules, guidelines, and parameters used in the culture. Behavior is expressed to confirm or deny a relationship. The group is the medium for communicating relationships. The group is also a message, the content of which is defined by relationships. If the message and relationship are in conflict, the behavior will be distorted and probably confusing. The identity of the individual is linked to relationships and behavior in a group or groups. The formula for expression determines the process of a given group.

A group is a social system. The culture provides the parameters for behavior and for groups, being literally a defined way of being or living in the world. According to Hall (1959), there are three forms of the social system: the formal, the informal, and the technical.

An example was provided to demonstrate the way a verbal formula is used to establish and define relationships. Once the relationships are determined, the behavior is expressed in response to the expectations an individual perceives. The person's perception is influenced by his view of the world in relation to his perception of self. Selective perceptions are vital forces and are directly influenced by his view of the world in relation to his perception of self. Selective perceptions as vital forces are directly influenced by group.

SUGGESTED ADDITIONAL READINGS

Armor, D. J., 1969. *The American School Counselor: A Case Study in the Sociology of Professions.* New York: Russell Sage Foundation. *This is a Harvard doctoral thesis (1966) based on sociological study of secondary school counselors. Personal-professional characteristics and functions of counselors were studied in relation to their influence on the students. The concept of counselor function Armor used is outdated, however. The value is in getting a look at our profession from another (sociological) point of view.*

Fullmer, D. W., 1971. *Counseling: Group Theory and System.* Scranton, Pa.: International Textbook Company. *The treatment of the concept of group as an information system is dealt with in depth. A theory of how behavior is formed is included in Chapter 3.*

Hansen, D. E. (ed.), 1969. *Explorations in Sociology and Counseling.* Boston: Houghton Mifflin Company. *Sociology is one of the important disciplines for counselors. This volume helps counselors see the way we are perceived by some sociologists. The theme of the authors holds that the social context of interpersonal relationships is as important as are the individual differences in determining behavior.*

Keniston, Kenneth, 1960. *The Uncommitted, Alienated Youth in American Society.* New York: Dell Publishing Company (paper). *The research and writing make this book especially important to the counselor-consultant. The material on mother-father influence on the development of boys and the adolescent transition hazards makes for provocative discussion because the issues are not totally without controversy.*

Mahler, Clarence A., 1969. *Group Counseling in the Schools.* Boston: Houghton Mifflin Company. *The student is encouraged to read the material on leader-group behavior. The two-way influence of counselor and group is an important concept.*

Mayer, G. R., R. M. Rolien, and A. D. Whitely, 1969. "Group Counseling with Children: A Cognitive-Behavioral Approach," *Journal of Counseling Psychology,* 16(2):142–149. *Social learning theory and cognitive dissonance theory were used to create dissonance in a group counseling setting. The efficacy of dissonance in relation to behavioral outcomes is discussed.*

Chapter Eight

SMALL GROUPS IN SCHOOL

Since ways to satisfy needs are learned in groups, there seems to be good and sufficient reason for considering the implications of small groups in school. According to Gibb (1968), the differences between group processes and education have diminished because education as preparation is rapidly declining and education as direct experience is growing in relative importance (Farson, 1968). The processes in group closely parallel the prime tasks in the real world. Goals are set by the individual in relationship with other individuals in a group. Besides bringing goals into the living arena of the individual, the task loses its dogmatic and abstract nature as imposed by tradition and other former systems. Group members set their own goals, form the control systems, and establish their own norms in an open way (Lennard and Bernstein, 1969). Feelings and other noncognitive elements are confronted. Privacy and trust emerge as parts of the conscious goal structure. Decisions made in an interdependent mode have the advantage of consensus. The enhancement is obvious. As in the real world, other persons are part of the solution instead of part of the problem. Farson (1968) suggests that the greatest single resource for people problems — for example with alcohol, drugs, delinquency, and poverty — is the problem population itself, which seems to defy being "cured" by outsiders.

Group Activities of Counselors

EXPANDING RESPONSIBILITIES

The counseling and guidance movement has spent its energies in trying to bring services to others. In the decade of the sixties it became apparent that, because of rapidly changing environmental conditions within our social system, parents, teachers, and other significant adults were in need of services comparable to but not identical with those provided in schools to students. Community involvement of counselors is seen as a new dimension in the 1970's (Lipsman, 1969). The epitome of involvement is the self-help group — a problem population helping itself. Here an individual manages his own motivation, and self-determination is therefore tied into this life condition. There is perhaps no greater corruption of self-determination than a well-intentioned case of management of another person's motivation.

The concept of involvement has directed attention to the impact of various human groups on the management of needs within the school counseling program. The counselor-consultant is a key professional person in relation to creating the kinds of groups that will provide for the development of appropriate needs within the framework of the school. Appropriate needs are those which fit the culture social system. Students whose needs differ significantly from them will somehow protest or be bypassed in the arenas of encounter within the culture.

The economic aspects of need satisfaction have been largely ignored. The counselor-consultant has a stake in the school's concern for perception of needs in students because one form of being disadvantaged is not to need the school. Students who drop out are only one example of the kinds of consequences underlying the concerns discussed in this chapter. Involvement is important because we assume that if an individual is motivated he will join with other persons in groups and in this way learn the needs appropriate to the social system and its welfare. This assumption may be without substance if no one attempts to structure and systematically to guide the development of groups particularly in the stages represented in elementary and secondary school student bodies. A newer concept is that the counselor's concern extends beyond the boundaries of the school into the community. Involvement is part of the expression of this concern.

TEACHER, PARENT, STUDENT INVOLVEMENT

Involvement takes on importance when an individual can see how his behavior connects him in a significant way — that is, it makes a difference — to a life event or to another individual. The idea that "I count" seems to be notably absent in the perceptions of alienated people. Alienation may be one of the symptoms that could be regarded as the opposite of involvement. It can be viewed also as a form of negative involvement. Basically, one who feels that he is important and that his action counts for something with someone has the necessary elements for productive behavior and meaningful involvement. The alienated individual does not feel that he is important or that he counts for anything to anyone.

The counselor-consultant is accountable for a vital part in the involvement of teachers, parents, and students in the significant enterprise of learning, teaching, counseling, and consulting. The small group is the model and the method for accomplishing this task. Counseling and/or consultation may happen in a small group, which is formed for one or more sessions depending upon the purpose to be served. Short-term groups may deal with crises and other immediate decision making. Longer-term groups may deal with decisions, policies, instruction (in-service), counseling, consulting, therapy, or similar matters. The small group is a way of giving expression to a person's involvement. It may be convened within the school, in the classroom, or away from school in the community. Successful patterns of operation include almost any conceivable arrangement if it serves the purposes and produces the positive consequences of involvement.

SIGNIFICANCE OF THE INDIVIDUAL

The small group is one way to validate and confirm the importance of the individual in relation to other persons. It was not invented by anyone; it seemed to be part of the cultural structure that somehow became disorganized in the urban press of population. The rediscovery of the small group as a method for creating the intense and intimate interpersonal encounter is probably the most significant development in the recent history of the counseling and guidance movement. As a learning-teaching device the small group led to a completely new structure in the supervision of counselor education and counseling practice.

The ultimate development of the small group in counseling practice seems to have found its form in the counselor-consultant function. The individual becomes the crucial factor because the group provides an arena in which his importance is accentuated, confirmed, and validated in his own terms. The group is a practice arena in which real life is simulated under safe conditions. Self-determination is perhaps one of the strongest motivating factors in human behavior. Creating an environment in which self-determination is in fact experienced may be one of the more potent contributions of a small group.

The small group provides a practice arena in which verbal behavior may be learned; the individual can experiment with it. Nonverbal behavior and noncontextual behavior become subjects of study for members of small groups. The counselor-consultant may utilize the symbolic behavior in a group to help individuals learn the ways they use to express their meanings in the world. The counselor-consultant concept is closely tied to the idea of the small group.

Purposes of the Small Group

SMALL GROUP IN THE COUNSELOR'S WORK

The small group can be defended as a legitimate part of the counselor-consultant function in the school to the extent that it contributes to the instructional goals of the school. Gibb (1968) thinks that if the "natural" groups in home and school were healthy, there would be no need for therapy, counseling, or consulting groups. The tasks that the school has and is responsible for developing should form the parameters of the small group program in a school. Each group should have its own unique purpose, serving the individual and connecting with the total program of instruction. The purpose should be clearly stated in behavioral terms affecting individuals who are members of the group as well as other persons who are somehow related to the group's function.

Talent development through participation in small groups is the central purpose in the concept of group and the major concern in small groups in school. The counselor-consultant has the responsibility for bringing together persons whose talents are shared in order that students may develop an awareness, a need, and indeed the talent itself.

The extrinsic reward system employed in the educational institution frequently results in managed motivation. The small group has the potential to replicate all the significant life events ranging from authority to conformity. If the small group is managed too, "forget it." The coercive forces will permit manipulation of the extrinsic rewards and attempt to manage the intrinsic and internal rewards. Motivation managed in this way is doomed to failure.

Examples of Purposes

Small groups may be utilized in schools for the following purposes.

Orientation and Information. New students and transfer students may be helped by upper-division or advanced and experienced students in small groups to become oriented and to become aware of certain indispensable information. Orientation and information sessions are necessary for the older students whenever new programs are introduced into the school. The orientation and information program may be a productive means of handling career data and vocational development.

Social Control. Social control is a central issue in every classroom in every school. The rules for behavior may be compared to the parameters of the social system or the culture; they are the framework in which behavior is acted out. The counselor-consultant will receive frequent requests from teachers who have social control problems in their classrooms. He will be faced with deciding how to establish programs that will change behavior. He will be concerned with conformity and norms for behavior. The issues facing institutions, adults, and students are all part of the social control concerns of the counselor-consultant.

The small group may be one way to meet this purpose. Information flow in a social system is improved by the encounter in a small group. Facts and directions can be written and distributed in announcements or memos. The informal social system is enhanced by having a group for members to model.

Recruitment. Recruiting goes on at all levels in our society. It consists in getting others to participate in pursuit of a certain goal or in the adoption of a circumscribed mode of behavior. The counselor-consultant is involved with recruitment at a number of significant decision points in the life of students. When students come to school there is usually some recruitment process going on between them and their parents. Parents frequently want the child to be an extension of their own ego. The well-known "generation gap" may be portrayed as the difference between the parents' ego-extension ideal for the child and the child's self-concept in relation to his future career development. As the rate of change accelerates, the gap widens.

The counselor-consultant may bring together parents, teachers, and children in a small group in order to assess the amount and kind of recruitment being used by each significant adult. The small group is used to combat some of the major hazards in contemporary society. Those in the protest group or on the drug scene may recruit on the basis of the in-thing or some other commercial issue much as advertising operates in our society.

In the closing years of the 1960's, peace groups, militant groups, and various other movements were examples of recruitment forces faced by youngsters in schools.

Recruitment in any form deals with group formation, which is probably a central concern of this chapter. How to form a group and launch, maintain, and terminate a group is a skill the counselor-consultant needs to command in order to function appropriately in small groups in school.

Formation of a Group

STEPS IN GROUP FORMATION

The counselor-consultant may wish to modify the sequence of the steps mentioned below, which are arranged partially sequentially and partially for convenience. Further, the steps indicate the action to be taken and the decisions to be made subsequent to the formulation of purposes and goals for the group. That is, the counselor-consultant's reasons for forming a small group are assumed to have already been activated.

Step 1. Recruitment. Screening and selection of members for a group are particularly important because the behavior they will exhibit in the group is significant to the purposes the group will serve. Sherif and Sherif (1964) found that persons join groups because they assume that the goals espoused by the group are goals they want to achieve. The characteristics of the group are characteristics the individual wishes to acquire. On the basis of this research report one might assume that if reference groups help individuals define the characteristics they wish to achieve, such purpose might be served by small groups convened by the counselor-consultant.

Selection of members may be made on one dimension, e.g., sex, grade level, or acting-out behavior; the group would be designed for a specific purpose. If, because of the age level, socialization becomes the major concern, mixing the sexes may be called for. Mahler (1969) suggests that junior high school youngsters should be handled by segregated sex groups if the problem is social control. Senior high school and older persons should probably be handled in mixed sex groups.

Our best guess about the membership of a given small group is that one should pay close attention to the characteristics of members in relation to the specific goals of the group. A word about purpose, goals, and membership is in order. The reason for using groups at all needs to be clear in the thinking of the counselor-consultant. If the small group is to serve as another method to reach the goals of education missed by regular instruction — if it is just an alternative to the school's system for managing individual motivations through external rewards: grades, approval, affection — he will be wasting his time learning to use groups. The small group is doomed if the goal is motive management. The aim of group is to avoid the error of managing motives with the attendant consequences of dropout, apathy, or rebellion. The purpose of group is served when self-determination is achieved by each member.

In professional practice the kinds of groups that permit only volunteer membership are different from those that include involuntary membership. For example, in working with any given family or group of families one often discovers that a number of the members of the family are reluctant participants in the group. There is a generally shared myth in the literature of counseling that only volunteer membership in group activity is desirable for counseling-consulting. This assumption is not supported by our experience with families and delinquent adolescent groups. We have worked with a number of families in which the family or juvenile court has made the attending of family counseling sessions a condition of probation. The achievement of goals or the rate of success seems to be about equal in groups that are reluctant or required to attend and those that come on a voluntary basis. A brief comment on this apparent similarity might be in order.

The idea that resistance to the impact of group interaction is reserved to nonvoluntary membership in group may rest on the fallacy that voluntary agreements (or deference) to the implication of membership in a group somehow automatically establishes a better opportunity for pervasive behavior change. We question this concept on the basis that deference is sometimes as powerful a defense as directly expressed hostility. In fact, it is more subtle and more hidden-agenda oriented — and therefore more difficult to use as a delay in the here and now of group. Hostility, on the other hand, can be directly confronted and is easily defined and identified as a reality. Thus dealing with hostility in an open situation is as productive a learning experience as any other, more positive experience might be. The assumption that if I give my permission to be here I have also given my permission to have my behavior changed may be unfounded, therefore. Conversely, required attendance often gives way to a climate of self-determination. However, if motivation is managed, the behavior will show resistance.

Recruitment will always be tempered by the social structure and policies of the institution. The counselor-consultant, having gained considerable skill in the interpersonal process, may be able to recruit people to assume membership and to attend sessions simply through his own charisma. There is some hope that a stronger purpose than personal attractiveness will draw group membership.

Step 2. Determining the Quota. How many members will the group have? The size of a group has tremendous influence upon the activities it engages in. The small group of families has to be left flexible in order to accommodate one, two, or three extra members. The group may be as small as a single family, and the family may have only two or three members. The counselor is not counted as a member of the group. In working with families counselors typically work in teams of two or more, so there is frequently an increase in the number of persons present in each of the group sessions. There should probably not be more than three or four counselors, an excellent number for training and practicum purposes if the counselor-consultant is cooperating with a university counselor education program. It is all right for these people to sit in.

A small group cannot be larger than ten or twelve people altogether because the nature of the process changes when more bodies are added. A larger group reduces the possibility of the leader's influencing decisions made within the group. A self-help group should have twelve to eighteen members.

When the counselor-consultant is considering the use of small groups, he must avoid feeling that the same experiences have to be given to all members of the school. There will not be enough time or enough counselor-consultants to create enough small groups to allow each member of the student body and the faculty to participate.

Step 3. The Frequency of Meetings. There are a number of questions that will determine the frequency of meetings:

  a. How many meetings will the group hold? How long will the life of the group continue?
  b. How often will sessions be held?
  c. How long does the group meet in each session?

The counselor-consultant may wish arbitrarily to decide the number of meetings, the frequency with which they will convene, and how long the life-span will be. In addition, he will need to determine ahead of time the length of each meeting, the endurance or duration of the group, and the number of obstacles it will attempt to meet.

The number of meetings and the life-span of a group, including the length of meetings, are affected by the membership. If parents are included, we have found that up to twelve meetings may be necessary to accomplish the goals. We do not recommend going beyond twelve sessions of about an hour and a half each (Fullmer and Bernard, 1968). If the meetings are designed to be held with teachers exclusively, one to five sessions should be sufficient for the counselor-consultant to achieve his goals. Counselor-consultant meetings with students exclusively will require one to ten sessions to accomplish most school-type small group goals. If a group needs to meet more than ten times it probably should be reconstituted and the membership divided among other groups in order to avoid the formation of in-groups or elites.

Another type of group has to do with the community at large. The idea of one or two or even no sessions that convene the entire membership of a community group is a different subject. The possibility of seeing individuals in the community singly and collectively, bringing their ideas together without committing their time to a single geographic meeting place, may be a useful idea for many counselor-consultants. The counselor-consultant should not attempt to gather a community group on a continuous schedule of meetings for a number of reasons, not the least of which is the matter of time and energy committed to the school program in total by community leaders. This type of thing should not be confused with talent centers or community counseling centers operated by counselor-consultants as part of the regular program beyond the perimeter of the school campus (Fullmer, 1969a).

Step 4. The Territory for the Meeting. Every group needs an environment for meetings that creates the kind of setting appropriate to the group's goals. Territory is basic to identity in our culture. Sitting in a circle may be a viable model for many types of groups but it should not be considered the only possible configuration. The equipment in the room that is used by the group is extremely important as far as small groups in the school are concerned. If the counselor-consultant must use a classroom and the furniture provided in it, he should attempt only certain kinds of tasks. If the territory is more of a lounge or family-living-room-type setting, the activities of the group are limited in a different way. If the territory is simply a vacant space with some cushions for sitting around on the floor, this signals yet another type of activity group.

Step 5. The Instruction of Members. The grooming of members for group participation is vital. People join groups, whether voluntarily or reluctantly, with the notion that they may be able to contribute something. It is particularly important for school-age youngsters to have some cognizance of their potential contribution to the group. Preparation of the members for participation, a primary concern of the counselor-consultant, becomes even more crucial in groups that plan only a few encounters or sessions.

Step 6. Inauguration. The counselor-consultant must decide whether the participation will be voluntary and free or involuntary and required. In family groups and groups involving teachers and other behavior specialists, some members may well be involuntary in their attendance. Ideally, the membership should be clearly voluntary or involuntary in any given small group (Schein, 1969).

Step 7. Public or Private Group. The public group is open to persons who want to join after it has begun meeting. The private group remains closed to additional membership once the group has begun its meetings. In family group consultation we allow for both models to be used. Some groups remain closed and private while others remain open and semipublic.

Step 8. Termination. There are specific steps to be taken in the process of termination. A group should not be allowed to approach a windup session without having come to some resolution of its separation anxiety. Every group that has been meeting for a period of seven, eight, ten, or more times will develop a kind of cohesiveness that remains significant to its members after the group ceases to meet regularly. It is not unusual for certain individuals in the group to have increased anxiety levels as they approach the termination and separation time. The counselor-consultant can easily manage this issue by allowing the people to talk about their anxieties and helping them understand their reasons for not wanting the group to terminate.

At this point the counselor-consultant can use the original specification of number of meetings to good advantage, reminding the participants of the contract to remain only for the prescribed number of sessions. It is difficult suddenly to invent a good reason for terminating what has developed into a good experience. It is extremely important to set the limit on the number of meetings for any group at the beginning because members of the group are quite likely to use the original contract to petition for continuing the sessions.

Examples of Small Groups

Small groups in school counseling may include students, parents, teachers, administrators, human behavior specialists, and community agency persons. The exclusive or integrated membership may vary in accordance with the counselor's goals for each group. The consultation process uses a group setting for much of the productive consulting because it is more efficient in the sharing of ideas. The one-to-one encounter for consultation is reserved for particular purposes that can best be achieved this way. Sometimes physical and mechanical conditions in the schedule dictate the time and place for consulting. It may not be possible to consult with more than one other person at a time.

Family consultation groups (Fullmer and Bernard, 1968) have been employed for over a decade. The goal is to help the family members modify their relationships within the family unit. The counselor-consultant may use this method whenever a student's general behavior patterns need changing.

The specific goals for behavior modification have become increasingly important in small group work. As the doctrinaire lines fade, it is possible to begin to combine the behaviorist learning theory principles with the activities in counseling groups. Family group consultation has been particularly adaptive to employing the behavior principles (Williams, 1964), i.e., reinforcement, extinction, generalization, desensitization, and discrimination. We have found that "modeling" has desirable outcomes when systematically applied.

Varenhorst (1969) presents a rationale for behavioral group counseling. Besides verbal conditioning it was found that modeling was effective. The techniques applied in groups have been developed for individual counseling. The increase in number of members in a group is seen as an additional positive reinforcing agent. Behavioral group counseling is organized around tasks or activities in order to specify the goal and be able to evaluate the results. The counselor is active in the process of the group; a plan is made by the counselor and implemented by him. The methods and activities are varied and include role rehearsal, reinforcement, verbal modeling, and simulated games — the Life Career Game (Varenhorst, 1969) is one example.

The counselor-consultant and small groups of teachers may select any of several patterns for meeting together. Information exchange groups may be set up as workshops, institutes, or conferences. When only one or two teachers are in need of information, the counselor-consultant can meet them individually or together. Usually in consultation the reason for using a group is to generate a new solution for a continuing problem; the group, being a collection of resource persons, generates innovation.

Student groups are quite different. The consultation process may be part of the strategy for bringing diverse types into membership in one group. An example is family group consultation. Age, status, role, sex, and interests are ignored in deference to a common linkup with family. To such a group may be added the teacher(s), other human behavior specialists, and community agency personnel. The method is appropriate for a wide range of tasks.

Mahler (1969) gives a concise list of purposes for counseling groups in schools. These are the purposes to be achieved in groups convened for consulting work, too.

1. Exploring the meanings of being a person.
2. Increasing confidence in self-perceptions and perceptions of others.
3. Listening to one's self and others.
4. Feeling and thinking congruently.
5. Increasing effective social behavior.
6. Evaluating new values and experimenting with present values.
7. Exploring and controlling feelings in a safe emotional climate.
8. Being responsible and accountable for one's own behavior.
9. Defining one's relationships with significant others.[1]

The use of relationship as a condition for further interaction and participation is another way to influence behavior in others. The counselor-consultant may be the only resource person in a school who is able to convene a new group and establish a new condition in the life of someone else. The principal cannot because he must remain the principal, a relationship condition of authority. The counselor

[1] Clarence A. Mahler, 1969, *Group Counseling in the Schools* (Boston: Houghton Mifflin Company), pp. 15–16.

is in a unique role when he consults. He may be the master facilitator when he is a consultant. In this sense he has become the prototype of the teacher of the future. See Chapter Fourteen for more discussion of this important new development in American education.

Summary

Small groups form the method of the counselor-consultant. In the small group the problem of managing other persons' motivations is brought under some control. It might be said that managing people without violating the privacy and trust of the individual is the special mission of the small group.

Interdependence and consensus form the guidelines for helping a problem population find its own solutions to its own problems. Family consultation and teacher-student consultation are arenas in which the counselor can employ his knowledge and skills to form small groups. Small groups have the potential to create an environment for problem solving.

Membership in groups has to be founded on some relevant purpose. The volunteer is no less recruited than is the reluctant participant. The quality of participation may be quite varied, depending on willing or reluctant membership.

The quota of members in a small group cannot exceed ten or twelve. It may be as small as two or three.

The frequency of meetings influences the nature of the group. A marathon is capable of pursuing different goals from those of a group scheduled to meet five or ten times for two hours each week. The counselor-consultant makes the decisions about the type of group and the frequency of meetings.

The group must have a place to meet. Territory determines some important variables in group action, especially relationship. Indeed, it usually influences all other aspects of group behavior. The counselor-consultant gives instruction to group members to prepare them for the small group interaction. He will start and stop the group and determine whether it is to be public or private.

SUGGESTED ADDITIONAL READINGS

ERIC Counseling and Personnel Services Information Center. *Integrated Personnel Services Index,* Vol. 1, No. 1, June, 1969, University of Michigan, 611 Church Street, Ann Arbor, Michigan, 48104. IPSI *is new to the literature and is designed to be a clearinghouse and source of information on information. The listings go beyond periodicals and books to include items otherwise unavailable except to local audiences. The counselor-consultant may contribute to the listings as well as subscribe.*

Fullmer, D. W., 1969. "Future of Supervision," *Educational Perspectives,* 8(3):29–32. *This statement is an attempt to show how supervision in counselor education is a small group model for possible adaptation in teacher education. The small group is the nucleus of the supervision concept as a learning environment.*

Gazda, G. M., and M. J. Larsen, 1968. "A Comprehensive Appraisal of Group and Multiple Counseling Research," *Journal of Research and Development in Education,* 1(7):57–132, Winter. *The article includes a comprehensive table abstracting the group and multiple counseling research up to the time it was compiled in 1967. It is a good reference statement in addition to summarizing the pertinent research findings reported in the literature.*

Krumboltz, J. D., and C. E. Thoresen (eds.), 1969. *Behavioral Counseling.* New York: Holt, Rinehart and Winston. *This collection of the contributions of the literature in the area of behaviorist learning principles applied to counseling is one of the more recent and comprehensive collections. There is a range of articles dealing with counseling, therapy, and instruction.*

Muro, J. J., and S. L. Freeman, 1968. *Readings in Group Counseling.* Scranton, Pa.: International Textbook Company. *The small group is a subject that requires exposure to many points of view. This book brings together material designed to expand the awareness of students of group counseling to those ideas found to be of value by practitioners of group counseling.*

Chapter Nine

BASIC ENCOUNTER GROUPS

One of the most significant developments in the 1960's was the rapid development of what has been called basic encounter groups. The movement grew out of an innovative surge involving many leaders in the field including Bach, Stoller, Wolpin, Waller, Wickland, Rogers, and others (Gazda, 1968).

During the 1940's the National Training Laboratories (NTL) became established at Bethel, Maine, where Leland Bradford, Ronald Lippitt, and Kenneth Benne succeeded in translating the ideas and theories of Kurt Lewin into an action model to modify the social organization of human groups. The T-group or training group became accepted by industry and business as a means to change the organization through training that improved the human relations skills of normal people (Birnbaum, 1969).

During the 1950's and early 1960's a shift toward personal development began to expand the use of group methods for more than just organizational change. The *encounter group* was differentiated by its para-therapeutic focus upon feelings and motivations of each group member. The parallel of group therapy is what shifts the focus away from training aimed at organizational change.

The behavioral scientists including psychiatrists began using T-group and sensitivity methods during the 1950's (Birnbaum, 1969), but schools were reluctant to move until the 1960's. There remains considerable controversy about the appropriateness of training groups or encounter groups in the school organization. Because the school organization is hierarchical, the authority centers may continue to resist. However, encounter groups that deal with individual development will probably be admitted to practice (Birnbaum, 1969).

Concept and Features of Basic Encounter

ORIGINS OF BASIC ENCOUNTER

Encounter groups grew out of almost twenty years of history of the T-group, originated by the founders of the National Training Laboratories. T-groups usually lasted two weeks, with a living-in situation, in which a group would be concerned exclusively with its own relating and interacting. A leader to guide the development of the process tends to facilitate interaction. Although there were many variations within the basic T-group model, the major aim was to guide the individual toward encountering his usual mode of behavior in interaction with other persons. The impact of this training was meant especially to improve the communication among individuals who had to work closely together in team relationships, management, and research types of industry and business. The focus was upon the human organization, whereas in sensitivity and encounter groups the emphasis is upon improving the efficacy of the individual's behavior.

One of the better descriptions of the T-group and its underlying dynamics is given by Lynton in *The Tide of Learning* (1960). In this in-depth experience cross-cultural representatives came together for a two-week period called the "Aloka experience."

The essence of the T-group and its dynamics with accompanying innovations of group models was to permeate industry and to influence the business community (Rogers, 1968). Educational institutions have been slow to participate actively in the more innovative practices of group encounter. Only in recent years have institutions of higher learning supported the use of encounter groups, sensitivity training, marathon therapy, and other venture-type groups. At the present writing there are still only a few universities with officially developed training programs for preparation of leaders of the intensive small group experience (Birnbaum, 1969).

This reluctance has led to the rapid commercialization of basic encounter group training. As is true of most areas in which educational institutions neglect to supply training or access to service lest academic safeguards be endangered, commercial interests move in to capitalize on opportunities in the vacuum thus created. There is some indication that in the near future, perhaps before the end of the seventies, the basic encounter group concept will have been sufficiently researched and demonstrated to have accomplished its potentially revolutionary innovativeness — that of replacing the major commercialization with free-lance self-help groups. Several prototypes of self-help groups such as venture groups (Fullmer, 1969b; Mowrer, 1968) have been developed during the 1960's.

Mowrer (1968) claims that the professional therapist is not necessary to create the healing experiences and to reestablish self-respect for the individual. The whole concept of professional intervention between the individual and the restoration of his health or self-respect has come down from an earlier time when some basic beliefs that may be erroneous were introjected into the American cultural thinking system. The culture believes that confession is somehow a dangerous thing. Mowrer ties this back to the movement of the early Christians when a system of restoring self-respect and returning to full membership in the community existed as common practice. However, when Christianity became a state religion, a significant change was instituted. The status of a state religion required a shortcut to reinstatement for each wayward citizen; thus an essential process in the system for restoration of self-respect and full membership in the community was eliminated. The process used by the early Christians was a self-help model like the model used in small groups for basic encounter experiences.

INTIMACY IN BASIC ENCOUNTER

Short-term intimacy is an element in the several forms of the basic encounter group. The central idea is to allow the individual the direct experience of intimacy. There is one caution concerning a short-term intimacy: It may be a force for alienation and disappointment. The person who seeks repeated encounters with short-term intimacy may in effect be alienating himself from the maintaining of a long-term intimate relationship. Disappointment may arise from the short-term sequencing of encounters with other individuals (Whorf, 1956)—with its cycle of separation, encounter with new individuals, separation again, and so on, ad infinitum.

Long-term intimacy builds trust, security, and fulfillment. Our kind of mobile, affluent society has evolved to the point where the individual may fulfill all of his basic security needs without having any significant intimate relationships with another human being. The net result is isolation, loneliness, and alienation (Washington, 1968). This condition is highlighted in urban centers where people have been geographically and psychologically dislocated (changed) by having moved from rural to urban surroundings or from an environment of low-density to one of high-density population (Drucker, 1968).

The capacity for long-term intimacy is perhaps one of the crucial developmental skills necessary for survival in a mobile, changing society. Some models of the basic encounter group innovated in the past ten or fifteen years will support and develop long-term intimacy skills. Others, however, tend to capitalize on short-term intimacy which may result in alienation rather than health.

Trust and Human Relations

The keystone in human relationships is trust. Mankind never has been especially noted for maintaining high levels of trust in interpersonal relationships, though they seem to be possible among small communities of people who share a common destiny over a long period of time. The level and quality of trust vary with the nature of the relationship. The more personal the relationship, the more refined testing behavior[1] becomes — before trusting is established. The more impersonal the relationship, the greater the trust without resort to testing behavior (Dundes, 1969). An example exists in suburban neighborhoods in American cities (Cole, 1958) The neighbors live close to each other, perhaps even next door, without knowing each other's name. In fact, very little is really known concerning the persons living in the immediate area. However, there is a high level of trust because no apparent need exists to test the trust relationship by finding out any details of a personal sort. Trusting behavior is tested by time with another person, and

---

[1] Testing behavior here is used to denote the trial and error use of behavior acts in a here-and-now event of life.

trust at all levels is rare. Trust seems to be defined in terms of certain conditions: "I trust you as long as I can see you." "I will trust you if I find that you believe the way I do." Is this latter statement trusting or a result of common cultural conditioning? The condition is what is specified. The trust is promised only if —. A popular notion in counseling is that I can trust you as much as I can trust me. That is the way, but where is the control? There is no guarantee, only the hope of trust. The paradox is familiar. There is no trust until I trust you or you trust me. The risk is a constant because anyone who trusts is vulnerable. How vulnerable can you be? I can be as vulnerable as the limits of the group permit.

In the basic encounter group, it is often noted that individuals do not trust other members of the group. This arena creates a kind of instant awareness of the amount of trust an individual has toward others. The intense experience in interpersonal interaction and intimacy must be preceded by a level of trust essential to maintaining the behavior characteristics of deep interpersonal involvement. People can learn to invest in interpersonal involvement at an intimate level relatively quickly in a small group. The small encounter group has a limited arena in which interaction takes place and an even narrower gauge on transactions within and among individuals in the group. This situation tends to allow for a fairly high level of intensive intimate relationship, with almost complete trusting. However, it is a question whether behavior in the small encounter group will really transfer to the larger society, where features of interpersonal interaction are less likely to be controlled. The encounter group, being a limited life arena, may be safe, but the real world may not be. It would seem somewhat naïve to expect bland transfer from the controlled arena to the open society, where the safeguards inherent in the group would be missing or ambiguous.

The theory of trust concerns itself with whether trust changes in quality as transaction changes in quality. No constructive behavior seems possible without minimum levels of trust between individuals significant to the transaction. Basic encounter groups attempt to foster the skill to develop trust in an interpersonal relationship by strengthening the security of the individual in terms of his lifestyle. For example, the suburbanite can go on trusting his neighbor as long as they transact only ritual and impersonal obligations. As in the city, freedom of movement must be maintained. You are free to go.

By being radically honest we can trust not only ourselves but others, particularly significant others in our life situation. This form of honesty or trust has been rediscovered in the innovative recent developments in basic encounter groups. The dynamics of how trust actually operates and the role of the group in relation to the individual represent a drastic shift in the emphasis of interpersonal, interaction treatment models, especially since about 1965.

ACCEPTANCE OF SELF AND OTHERS

Acceptance is defined as unconditional relationship with regard to a person's being and his right to be equal and complete in his own way (Huckins, 1966). This definition of acceptance inevitably leads to the paradox which will not allow separation of acceptance of self from acceptance of others, very much as in the concept of trust. The basic encounter group leads to confrontation in the matter of self-acceptance and acceptance of others. Whether or not one uses Huckins's definition, based on some major authorities in the field of counseling, it is possible to understand that acceptance is a condition and not a process. If the condition is the consequence of the acceptance a person has of himself, then the task facing basic encounter groups has to do with developing the capacity for self-acceptance. A curious paradox comes into the process of basic encounter groups at this point. The person who has a low regard for self and is reluctant to accept his self at face value must first experience unconditional acceptance by others. This self-system is something each individual develops from his repertory of interpersonal encounters. The encounter group is basic to restructuring the individual's concept of himself particularly in regard to self-acceptance. The individual's self-definition is anchored in the concepts he has accumulated over the years as his interpretation of the responses of significant others. His self-concept is a consequence of the way others have defined him. The basic encounter group operates on the assumption that because the individual is a product of his interacting with others he cannot change or become something else without continuing interpersonal contacts, and the latter may be structured and controlled in the basic encounter group.

The individual's psychological set predisposes him to structure

interpersonal situations so that his relationship with others is determined by his sense of adequacy or competence, which resulted from
the way he was accepted by others. The self-fulfilling prophecy
of what one expects in terms of how he is valued positively or
negatively by others, welcomed or rejected, may be linked to his past
experience. The self-fulfilling prophecy is simply that the way one
expects to find and experience people is probably the way he interprets most of the feedback he receives (Watzlawick et al., 1967).
In basic encounter groups it is possible actually to confront this
experience, to have it validated by the experiences and observations
of others in the group, and to confirm one's own ability to read
accurately the feedback coming from others. Accuracy is defined
as relative agreement with the perceptions of others in a given group.
The discrepancies inherent in this process constitute part of the
dynamic learning condition created in a basic encounter group.

The level of competence an individual actually commands is
revealed by the way he is threatened when interrogated by others.
A high level of frustration tolerance, with thresholds that do not
become easily swamped, is characteristic of the person whose self-
acceptance is high (Adams, 1957). The converse is an individual
with low self-acceptance; the threat can be anxiety-producing under
much less strenuous conditions. The more threatened an individual becomes, the more defensive he is likely to be, and a
defensive position is not a very productive growth-producing arena.
One who is able to change and modify his behavior and remain
open through stress-producing encounters in the group is more
likely to be able to function in new ways (Irish, 1966). A person
who feels overwhelmingly insecure and threatened, unaccepted and
otherwise handicapped, probably should be referred to a therapy
group. To be most productive for its membership, the basic encounter group requires a high level of tolerance for stress.

Value and Hazards of Self-Disclosure

It is true that one cannot *not* self-disclose (Mowrer, 1968). This
concept in basic encounter groups has permitted the confrontation
of personal feelings, self-perceptions, basic identities, and meaning.
There is perhaps no substitute for a thoroughgoing and unreserved
self-disclosure if one has any intention of discovering his true self.
Because it is not possible to self-disclose at depth levels without

bringing to the surface strong emotion, the experience is of such a nature that a small group is needed to weather the emotional storm that will come with a change in the emotional climate.

Perhaps the metaphor of the seasons is appropriate if one can equate emotions with changing from cold to warm and warm to cold. One must live through his Indian summer to encounter the coldness of winter if he is ever to feel the breath of spring. Looking forward to a bright summer may be the only prize one can expect from such an experience in self-disclosure. The alternative to self-disclosure in a group is some tenuous organization of a bundle of conflicting emotions. The group can help one to sort out his feelings into rationality and fantasy to achieve a competent balance.

Self-disclosure is not something that an individual can do by himself. A group is required to validate and confirm his perceptions of himself and whether or not they match those of other persons who see him from an entirely different perspective while sharing in the same life event (Watzlawick et al., 1967). The identity construct and all the masks necessary to bolster the concept that one carries of himself have to be examined in relation to the reality experienced by others (Scheflen, 1961). The phony, the pseudo, and the real are all clear and present identities in each person. The basic encounter group uses self-disclosure as the avenue to a look-see at this particular dimension of his existence.

The individual through self-disclosure is able to confront his fantasies and his realities in looking at what the existential concept of meaning might be (Heine, 1953).

SELF-RESPECT

Self-respect is a product of the process of group (Mowrer, 1968). Probably the most difficult concept to accomplish in group is the realization that self-respect cannot be given anyone but must in fact be encountered by the individual from his own experience. Self-respect in many ways characterizes the confirmation of competence. Competence may be developed, and the experience of confronting it may be the prerogative of the group. The individual becomes a recipient of what could not be won alone by any one of us. Mowrer (1968, p. 135) explains the group process by which self-respect returns to a person through his own efforts coupled with the life of a group. The balance between charity, respect, and courage is very delicate. Self-respect does not seem to be a virtue that can be achieved without external demands.

SELF-DETERMINATION

The only motivation that seems to be of any consequence in the behavior of the human being in the higher order of activity beyond the basic animal drives is the idea that he is actually in charge of his life at the moment, whether he is a small child playing with a flashlight, a skier on the slopes, a surfer riding a curling wave, or a motorcyclist breezing along the highway. The mountain climber must share something of this concept as he steps to the top of the mountain.

Self-determination is characterized in the behavior of the human being. The response to a question of purpose in the behavior, such as "Why did you climb that mountain?" is "Because it is there." Why did we go to the moon? Because it is there!

FIRSTHAND KNOWING

Firsthand knowing is the only defense against secondhand anxiety. The process is the product, in group. In a society of secondhand and thirdhand information we are likely to become dependent upon the bureaucratic party-line type of information (Dundes, 1969); like the convict in the prison, we have almost no firsthand information. Therefore, our test of validity for information rests on an assessment of its source. The authority from which the information comes is taken as the measure of its authenticity. Firsthand knowing is the product of being involved in direct interaction, as one is in the basic encounter group. Indeed, one of the more important aspects of the basic encounter group may be its provision of a learning environment in which firsthand knowing is possible. Perhaps at this level the game ends and reality begins. Most interaction engaged in by most persons in our mass society avoids direct encounter with the process of evaluating information. We usually accept or reject the source of information without needing to examine our own process. In the bureaucracy, this shortcut gains us efficiency. In daily living and person-to-person encounter, it brings isolation and impersonal communication. The counselor-consultant can use firsthand knowing as a leadership skill (Berne, 1961).

Processes of Basic Encounter

THE BASIC ENCOUNTER

Basic encounter can range from the philosophical Buber concept of I-Thou (Buber, 1958) to the simple metaphor of the hole and the doughnut or the sublime boy-and-girl demonstration of theory and practice. In each, the paradox is completed only if one steps outside the confines of the concept to look at the whole.

Buber's "I-Thou" proposes that without the other person the self probably does not exist. It is an abstraction which interaction with another person makes concrete. If I, indeed, do not exist except as in some defined relationship to you, it is perhaps possible to understand the level of abstraction involved in this paradox.

The hole in the doughnut is an entirely different paradigm. The hole is said to have reported to the doughnut, "Without you I would be nothing." The fact that the doughnut circumscribes the hole, which ceases to exist at the point where the doughnut ceases to define its limits, is particularly useful in the basic encounter concept. Basic encounter groups put individuals into a life condition in which the limits are prescribed by the membership of the group and the rules chosen to guide its interaction. The rules and guidelines are the main parts of the formula (Fullmer, 1969b).

The theory-and-practice concept is represented by the boy who goes to see his girl and gets half the distance each subsequent hour he travels toward her home. The question of whether he gets there can be answered in two ways. In theory, of course, he always has half the remaining distance to go, but in practice he is close enough for all practical purposes.

The ridiculous, the sublime, and the paradoxical all form a part of the complex human basic encounter concept. The basic encounter incorporates the ideas of losing or saving face, which is the Oriental ethic, and the Western ethic of guilt. The resolution of guilt is usually a pardoning process by which self-respect is restored as a consequence of group commitment, interaction, and involvement. Losing or saving face does not depend upon group interaction but is completely and solely the responsibility of the individual. It is an interesting contrast to put these two ethics together in the basic encounter group and observe the behavior that may be attributed to each. It may be said that a group for basic encounter is the new arena defined to permit one to save face and to be absolved of guilt. The goal is to practice new behavior. The aim of the basic encounter group is to *form new behavior* (Fullmer, 1971b). The practice and evaluation of new behavior is particularly important in our kind of society, which provides almost no arenas beyond the family where one can practice — at least without risking vulnerability and the exploitation of the mass society.

Helping an individual become self-determining may be the greatest contribution of the basic encounter group. This phenomenon is missing in the literature of the behaviorists on theory and practice with human behavior.

The positive feedback system of the basic encounter group provides for the need that is resident in everyone's life. The person who cannot get the feedback he needs by himself must trust in someone else, and this kind of trust can be freely expressed in few arenas in our society; the family, the basic encounter group, and the intimate peer group are three of them. The basic encounter group enables one to "see" how he comes across to others without the risk of social-personal-emotional disaster. *Feedback* is a computer term useful in the present context. The self-correcting quality of feedback is evident in the above description as safely employed in basic encounter methods.

METHODOLOGY IN GROUP ENCOUNTER

Up to this point we have talked about the various forces manipulated in the basic encounter group that change behavior patterns of individual members. The group focuses upon the impact one person's behavior has in conjunction with the behavior of significant other persons. The interaction is observed. The theoretical frame of reference is an interaction model in contrast to an intrapsychic model.

In this section we will look at some of the methodology by which individuals are brought into the basic encounter. The intensive interpersonal relationship is the product of a special confrontation arranged within the safety of a group. This takes a wide variety of forms and employs a range of techniques. The emphasis is on the here-and-now action. What is happening? (In the intrapsychic model interpretation is central in the method.)

The reader is reminded of the context in which all behavior

occurs. We have tried carefully to develop the rationale, beginning with the cultural context of behavior and moving toward the individual, small group, and family paradigms. In these contexts behavior is in process. Interpretation is lower in priority than is a description of what is happening.

We will describe some of the paradigms used for manipulation of the behavior arena so that certain confrontations become possible. The context will prescribe the rules governing the confrontation as well as the safeguards for controlling the intensity of the emotional encounter accompanying the experience.

Some short-term groups used for basic encounter are marathon, sensitivity and awareness, body tactile, sense relaxation, and microlabs (Gunther, 1968; Birnbaum, 1969). There are a number of longer-term intensive encounter groups, including the standard T-group, the venture group, the Synanon game, psychodrama, and the standard nonbehaviorist-oriented counseling group (Fullmer, 1971b). Still other intensive encounter groups are the friendship groups of therapeutic social groups, which are a type of continuous self-help therapy (Mowrer, 1968).

It is not our intention to review all the methods utilized in all the different groups. We offer representative models that might be utilized within the educational structure as part of the counselor-consultant's role with students, teachers, administrators, human behavior specialists, parents, and significant other community leaders. The counselor-consultant should in no way be expected to conduct deeply therapeutic ongoing groups. However, it is presumed that he will have accumulated direct experience in a number of group models and will be prepared to apply it in the work of consultation within the school setting. This function is described by some (Farson, 1968; Rogers, 1968) as the teacher role of the future — that of facilitator (see Chapter Fourteen).

The Venture Variety. The venture group is probably the easiest of all to use for schoolwork; it can readily accommodate consultation. It meets for two to three hours at a session, and the sessions may number from a minimum of eight to a recommended maximum of twenty. The leader is permitted to expose his feelings and engage in the group interaction as a participant in addition to being the leader. Leadership is always shared with a minimum of two persons convening the group so as to correct for the bias of participation. Whereas the individual who is allowed to participate and is also designated leader sometimes utilizes his power to exploit the group in his own behalf, coleadership (or two conveners) is a significant departure for creating a facilitator-learning environment.

The venture group meets once a week for eight to twenty weeks, conveners and members numbering up to a total of twelve. The rules for interaction are standard encounter group guidelines. They include speaking in the first person with all statements containing the basic self-reference. The self-reference is in terms of self-generated or response-generated feelings, ideas, and fantasy. Each other person in the group is encouraged to speak of his self-oriented experience in terms of what is happening within the group on a here-and-now basis. *Here-and-now* refers to those events which take place in sequence within the happening of the group. No historical reminiscence is permitted except as an occasional digression to reduce the intensity of the emotional encounter. This is a function of group leadership and must be learned under supervision in a laboratory of human behavior. We would not advise that anyone unfamiliar with these methods attempt to apply any of them without first having undergone direct supervision in the experience of group. It is recommended that students who are learning these ideas for the first time do not experiment alone but with an experienced leader who can help them manage the level of intensity of emotional experience most appropriate to their level of maturity and personality organization.

The topics of venture group interaction depend upon the contributions of the members. The counselor-consultant would use this method with colleagues, teachers, other behavior specialists, administrators, and parents. Students may be involved in venture groups providing there is clearance from parents and the school officials to carry on such groups. Leaders should be the students themselves, trained and supervised by the counselor-consultant. In addition there should be sufficient safeguards provided to control any explosive development that might emerge from the interaction. Of all basic encounter group techniques, venture group is probably the safest self-help model and requires minimum supervision in order to function successfully over long periods of time with the least difficulty (Fullmer, 1969b).

In lieu of a protocol of a venture group we offer an interaction paradigm. The guidelines for interaction go about like this:

> I see me. You see you. I see you seeing me. You see you seeing me. Each person reports his perception of how he sees himself and how he sees himself seeing someone else. Validation is possible at the point of comparison between the "I see me seeing you" and the "you see you seeing me" level of abstraction. Granted, it is possible to agree to a pseudo representation in each case. An exceptional amount of growth is possible if the person can move to the next level of abstraction, namely, "I see me seeing you *seeing me*." Confirmation at this level will be about as far as the more mature group will be able to progress.

The Marathon Variety. The marathon form of the basic encounter group is an innovation of the 1960's. Stoller (1968) has described the operation of a marathon group. It is a continuous-session, intensive group encounter going on for anywhere from twenty-four to seventy-two hours. Some variations run for shorter periods under the title of marathon but they are not considered marathon in the present report. The idea is that a group of persons make a contract to spend a given number of hours in continuous session. The essence of the marathon is the contract and the guidelines, which do not permit the individual to depart from the group physically during the session, except to take care of body function needs. The marathon group differs from other groups in several significant ways. However, the interaction formula remains very nearly the same as for venture groups.

The marathon group method is organized in a setting that includes all of the necessary facilities for preparing food and having a place to sleep, and for rest rooms, showers, etc. The setting must be a living-in situation, either austere or plush. Homes or motels are particularly adaptable to marathon use. The facilities should be large enough to accommodate a group of from ten to fifteen persons.

The marathon is designed to establish intimacy. Intimacy is increased with geographic proximity and a long enough period of time to allow for personal interaction to progress to a point where individuals begin to think of themselves as part of a unit, but separate entities. A definite beginning and ending time should be announced in the printed matter that is part of the contract each person signs, but there are many variations in scheduling between the beginning and ending hours. For instance, the members may convene for blocks of time, adjourn for blocks of time, and have periods interspersed for sleep and informal chitchat. Or the group may be in continuous session, with individuals withdrawing periodically to take care of vegetative needs. However, the schedule is set up and becomes part of the style of the leader's preference for running the group. It is more than a matter of the changing dynamics of what happens in the group. We are here concerned with the fact that variation in pattern is possible without destroying the utilitarian aspect of the group.

Food should be served by nonparticipants in order to insure the continuous interaction of all members. Involvement is the goal, and all the time should be used to achieve it. If participants prepare the food, then *all* persons join in to make this a cooperative task.

The contract is definitive and made known to each participant prior to the convening of the group. In order to have a successful marathon group experience, it is necessary to have complete and candid agreement concerning each individual's participation in the group.

Rules and guidelines are provided to insure the interaction formula success and the general safety of the group. The culture is redefined within the rules and guidelines set forth by the leader before the group is convened. The goal is to achieve authentic encounter between individuals within the group. Authentic encounter with one's self is a goal of high priority in most basic encounter groups; it may or may not be achieved in any given marathon group experience. Individuals may be members of one group, allow some time to pass, then enter a second group and perhaps even a third and fourth. There does not seem to be any reason for limiting the number of groups one might sequentially encounter. At some point participation in marathon may become significantly less productive. Usually individuals who attend more than two or three marathon groups become leaders or assistants to leaders in subsequent marathon groups.

The only way to learn how to conduct a marathon group at present is to participate extensively in the method. One is encouraged to seek admission to marathon group experiences over a period of time, perhaps one or two years, before becoming an independent leader and organizer of marathons. The reason for this precaution is the same as for other counseling-consulting and encounter group experiences. When an individual meets an intensive encounter, emotional stress may increase to a point beyond which he is capable of maintaining his personality organization. Therefore, it is always necessary to have backstops to protect anyone who will be in danger of personality disorganization because of the experience in intensive group encounter. The necessary safeguards are provided by having at least one experienced professional leader available to the group either as a participant or as a consultant.

The key notion in the interaction in marathon is that one must immediately respond to the impact others are having on one's self. Having insight into or understanding of someone else's motives is considerably less valuable than having insight into one's own experience. The authentic encounter then is defined as a matter of both self-encounter and encountering another person.

Marathon restricts the use of language, particularly jargon. The attempt is to use simple, straightforward verbal expressions that describe one's present condition rather than interpret it in terms of a dogmatic system of psychology.

The leader is responsible for all arrangements and the creation of conditions which allow the group to convene, operate, and terminate. These are all specific processes to be learned before one attempts marathon experience. The leader conducts the interpretation of rules and the application of the formulas for interaction. Once this teaching has been accomplished, the leadership role changes to that of convener and facilitator. The leader may wish to arrange for one or more follow-up sessions after marathon encounter termination. Follow-up sessions are necessary if one is to assess degree of permanence achieved in the behavior changes observed in the encounter group sessions.

Summary

The basic encounter group is a recent innovation created mostly out of small group participation in the 1960's. The T-group model, which has been available for nearly thirty years, was one of the original points of departure.

Mowrer (1968) has shown that the small group phenomenon was rediscovered in the second half of the twentieth century. The antecedents of this method and why it is a productive model for reconstituting self-respect in the individual were described in Mowrer's research on the early Christians.

Intimacy, trust, acceptance, self-disclosure, self-respect, self-determination, and firsthand knowing are the important concepts in the basic encounter group and how it helps the individual's growth and development.

Counselor-consultants need to learn to use encounter group methods and adapt them to their work in the school. These methods are particularly appropriate to working with teachers, parents, and students in groups over short periods of time, with intensive involvement possible. The nature of the basic encounter group makes its use possible where adult attitudes must be changed in order to allow for the child's growth and development in a less obstructed way. The adaptation of innovations and adoption of new ways of behaving are essential in these times of accelerated modification of traditional patterns. Changing times, changing values, and changing methods in the school program have brought to the counselor-consultant the task of passing the innovations across established barriers in the culture, namely, adults and children. The professionals have no less formidable barriers between their own specializations. Teachers, human behavior specialists and counselors all face these barriers.

Basic encounter group offers one way of utilizing people in a problem population in a resolution of their own problems through self-help and guided group interaction.

SUGGESTED ADDITIONAL READINGS

Ashley, W. R., 1956. *An Introduction to Cybernetics.* London: Chapman and Hall. *Cybernetics has introduced much of the language used to describe communication principles in human organizations. The idea may hamper the development of a metalanguage for more precise description of the phenomena in human communication. The student may wish to know more than his language will reveal to him.*

Berne, E., 1961. *Transactional Analysis in Psychotherapy.* New York: Grove Press. *This book and Berne's best seller,* The Games People Play, *make up one of the more complete descriptions of behavior patterns within the context of cultural rules. There is the light side, but the serious side is the realm of our study of group. The encounter and what is transacted become the reality in living.*

Bradford, L. P., J. R. Gibb, and K. D. Benne, 1964. *T-Group Theory and Laboratory Method.* New York: John Wiley & Sons. *The history and development of T-group is important to understanding of the encounter group movement. The use of T-group by industry and business led to earlier adoption of the newer group training forms and methods. Educational institutions seemed to resist the developments in group encounter.*

Mowrer, O. H., 1968. "Loss and Recovery of Community," in G. M. Gazda (ed.), *Innovations to Group Psychotherapy.* Springfield, Ill.: Charles C Thomas, Publisher. Pp. 130–189. *The essence and power in a group therapy encounter are explained as encounter through self-disclosure. The ancient practice of the early Christians seems to have been rediscovered in the 1960's.*

Ohlsen, M. M., 1969. *Group Counseling.* New York: Holt, Rinehart & Winston. *The author presents ideas for initiating and maintaining groups. The practical applications of group encounter models help to explain how groups are formed and managed without managing the motives of individual members.*

Chapter Ten

COMMUNICATION:
A BASIC PROBLEM

Communication is such a basic problem that, at least in a way, it is essential to the process of becoming human. Communication may indeed be as necessary as food or water to human life itself. For example, babies, despite being well fed, warm, and dry, will wither physically and display no interest in life if they are not talked to and shown they are valued by being cuddled. They lack appetite if someone does not communicate to them that they are loved, esteemed, or at least acknowledged. If the message of *being someone* is not conveyed (communicated) to the individual during infancy and childhood he develops a personality with flat affect. He can know neither joy nor sorrow, challenge nor defeat, love nor hate. Communication is essential to one's being physically healthy, emotionally labile, and intellectually alert. In short, communication is basic to becoming human.

In the human species speech is the major, but not sole, medium of communication. Hence, to a remarkable degree one forms his self-concept through speech. "Speech *is* everything we call specifically human, because without speech there can be no true ego . . . the self system is primarily a linguistic, symbolic device whereby one relates to others" (Becker, 1962, pp. 28, 90). If this statement be true, it is not surprising to find that communication is a basic problem — and tool — of the counselor. It is important to communicate with young people, as Salinger suggests in his book *Catcher in the Rye:* "Well, if you really want to listen." For a counselor-consultant, communication is vital to getting parents and teachers, specialists and administrators to work together.

Many volumes, technical articles, and conferences have been devoted to communication. In this chapter and the following one, we only introduce the problem as it relates to the counseling process.

The Generation Gap

DIFFERENCES BETWEEN THE GENERATIONS

Some people do not believe there is a generation gap (Bealer et al., 1969). Differences between the generations are simply phases of the process of growing up, they say, and ultimately and typically the younger generation will move into adult society bringing with them some new ideas but, in the main, building upon the accumulated wisdom of previous experience. The alleged gap decreases if lines of communication are kept open and patience is exercised with the steady processes of growth. Cultural continuity, which is dependent on communication, is facilitated if we know the characteristics of, and take advantage of, communication.

There is a growing body of behavioral scientists who perceive the generation gap as being real, wide, and crucial. Because of the critical nature of the gap, establishing communication becomes much more than a matter of uttering clichés about listening and about mutual positive regard. A beginning can be made by understanding some of the salient differences between the generations that have been noted — or nominated.

THE IMPACT OF TELEVISION

For one thing, but not necessarily number one, the current generation is like no other because it is the first which, since infancy and through its entire course of life, has been exposed to television. The usual thing noted about television is that it shows violence as an approved and normal phenomenon. It seems to suggest that popularity and success are facilitated, if not guaranteed, by use of the right cigarette, deodorant, mouthwash, automobile, or vitamin.

The good old Judeo-Christian ethic of working for that to which one aspires is replaced by NOW. This instantaneous feature of television means also that the world has changed from that which adults think they know. What happens today in Vietnam, or Israel, or Africa, or the Northwest Passage is instantly available. Life becomes an instant replay!

As though these differences, and others like them, were not enough, Hayakawa (1968) indicates that television is all input and no output as far as the child viewer is concerned. The child can ask no questions, suggest no doubts, express no opinions. His alternative is to "turn it off," which he sometimes does, physically. Often he turns it off psychologically, then uses the same technique for dealing with adults who are not in the box.

In terms of its one-way communication, television may have considerable impact on the teaching process. By the time the average individual reaches the age of twenty-one he has spent as much time watching TV as he has in school. It has been suggested that the typical classroom — where the teacher does 90 percent of the talking — is doomed to failure because most teachers cannot match the drama, vivacity, vividness, color, and conviction of the professional actor. TV may be used advantageously if it provides the stimulus for implementing genuine dialogue in classrooms.

STRUGGLE FOR EXISTENCE

Another generational difference, at least as far as life in the United States and most of western Europe is concerned, is that the struggle for survival is over. With less manpower, both relatively and absolutely (Billard, 1970), the United States can produce not just enough food but, despite disease and disaster, an oversupply of food. Unemployment insurance, social security, aid to dependent children, installment buying, Medicare, welfare, and continuous inflation which wipes out savings and incentive for "saving for a rainy day" have virtually eliminated the struggle for survival. The parental generation worked for and planned for the future; the younger generation says NOW. The communication rift is as hard to understand as it is for an American male to understand that buying a bride for twenty cows can be normal behavior. The contrasts between now and the future and between a bride for cows and a bride for love are illustrative of the contrast between the older generation's struggle for survival and the younger generation's search for fulfillment.

ACCELERATED MATURATION

Many things — passage of the struggle for survival, communication (especially TV), and improved diet and medical care with an attendant acceleration of physical maturation — have contributed to a superficial sophistication of the younger generation. They readily perceive the discrepancy between the ideals and the accomplishments of the older generation. They see adult hypocrisy in such things as starvation and inadequate nutrition, the pursuit of undeclared war, racial discrimination and prejudice, and criminal punishment meted out in terms of financial resources. And there are adults who agree that the charge of hypocrisy is soundly based (Wyzanski, 1969). A complex phenomenon cannot usually be resolved by a simple explanation, but it does seem that a factor in this discrepancy between ideals and accomplishments and in the charge of hypocrisy is partly a generational difference between things and people. Too often a program is judged in terms of its costs rather than in terms of its impact on human welfare. Heilbroner (1970) states that it is easy to rank national priorities for the 1970's. The military outranks civilian needs, private interests outrank public interests, and the welfare of the affluent outranks the needs of the poor. Both hypocrisy and the predominance of materialism over humanitarianism are exemplified in such priorities. Whether national priorities accurately represent adult attitudes or not, the fact remains that such is the perception of some young persons. The perception must be taken into account in attempting to bridge the communication gap.

AUTHORITY VS. AUTHORITARIANISM

The question of "Who's boss?" is an unresolved one. To a considerable extent the younger generation has been brought up by permissive parents, encouraged by Dr. Spock. A theory of individual autonomy in the schools, abetted by a misinterpretation of progressive education, has left both children and adults bewildered by the need for and the lack of structure. The danger of inhibiting creative potential is counterbalanced by another danger — that of frustrating the child's safety needs by lack of order, rules, regulations, and routines. Not enough people have seen the inseparableness of freedom from responsibility (McCully, 1969, pp. 13, 90, and *passim*), and particularly the younger generation. Certainly, for many, the matter of freedom and responsibility constitutes a generational difference which complicates communication. Some of this bewilderment, superficial sophistication, and disdain for authority is summed up in the following:

> . . . The average suburban teen-ager is often pictured as either consumed with self pity or alienated into withdrawal from society. He is said to know it all, to be intelligent and amoral, well-mannered yet merciless, cynical in a young-old way, and oh so sophisticated. Some suburban youngsters are in flight from their own lives; others are deeply worried about what the future holds for them; and some are in revolt against their parents' suburban values. . . . Yet many of today's middle-class suburban youngsters exhibit disturbing character qualities — sexual libertarianism, vehement rejection of adult authority, and a widespread disposition to experiment with drugs.
>
> Our nation's suburbias are evidently becoming so segregated that children can grow up without genuine contact with others of different racial, religious, or social backgrounds. The result is a growing provincialism in spite of ease of travel and communication. Suburbia's children are living and learning in a land of distorted values and faulty perceptions. They have only the slightest notion of others; they judge them on the basis of suburban standards (such as "cleanliness" and "niceness"), generalize about groups on the basis of the few they might have known, and think in stereotypes.[1]

The shift from parental authoritarianism and the communication which flowed from, or was blocked by, "Because I said so" needed to take place. But there is a difference between authority and authoritarianism. It may take both verbal and nonverbal communication to establish the inevitable truth that parents and teachers by definition and by biological and social fact are not peers. Cottle (1969b) asserts that there is neither the phenomenon of nor the possibility for an *even* exchange between the generations. The

---

[1] James A. Meyer, 1969, "Suburbia: A Wasteland of Disadvantaged Youth and Negligent Schools?" *Phi Delta Kappan,* 50:575. Reprinted by permission of the publisher.

younger generation needs someone with strength to fall back on in time of stress. In "good" custodial institutions, where the distinction between authority and autocracy is drawn, the youngsters often say, "I like it here. They care."

ROLE VS. GOAL

A good deal of the above is summarized, and some wisdom is added to the notion of generation gap, by Glasser (1970). He asserts that, without their being mutually exclusive, the older generation is primarily goal oriented while the younger generation is primarily role oriented. This is quite similar to what Erikson (1964a, pp. 81 ff.) calls youth's identity crisis. Many psychologists have referred to the individual's need to be a cause, to be recognized as making a difference.

A Portland high school girl, having presented to the school board her case for greater autonomy of adolescents, was patiently told why her requests could not be granted. After reiterating her case several times, with what seemed to be more valid arguments on her side than on the part of the board, she seemed to concede defeat but said, "I guess I got what I came after." She may have meant finding out that you can't beat the establishment, but the authors hope she meant, "I got time. I was a factor. My case was listened to [if not heard]." She had found a role.

Adults see goals clearly: the need for getting a diploma or degree, for saving part of what one earns, for becoming a competent worker or performer. And in the pursuit of goals they achieve an identity — a role. For adults it is difficult to perceive that goals are unimportant, or at least incidental to having a role. For the young, one must be with it, one must be a part of the group. The peer group is a standard for adolescents. There are at least two reasons why the contrasting orientation toward life has become prominent. One is population structure. With about half the population of the United States under the age of 27.7 years (200 million Americans, 1967, p. 7), the adolescent and youth group includes about one-quarter of the total population. And it is this group that to a considerable extent has no productive role. The goal of academic superiority is not big enough to go around. The other factor is that the goal of work is on uncertain ground. We are told repeatedly that ever smaller proportions of the population produce and will produce increasingly large amounts of goods and services. It is therefore not relevant for the young to be deeply concerned about work as a goal.

There are probably other factors in the generation gap: Some speak of the deterioration of moral tone as manifested in increased numbers of teen-age premarital pregnancies and the widespread use of drugs. Some point to the frustration war places on the young — especially when they are not allowed the dignity of a vote. Whatever the causes, it does appear that there is a generation gap which is unlike any previous ones. The young are quite different from their elders. Words alone will not bridge the gap; but words backed by feelings, empathy, the attempt to understand, trying to gain the perspective of the other may render the gap negotiable.

Social Isolation and Alienation

SOCIAL ISOLATION

One of the cruelest punishments devised by man is solitary confinement. When one is cut off from his fellows, feelings of frustration, hostility, and defeat in unpredictable combinations and degrees are likely to be aroused. To a marked extent the work of the counselor-consultant revolves about the phenomenon of isolation. The young, cut off from meaningful participation in adult society because there are no jobs for them and because they believe the lack of a vote makes them powerless, feel isolated. Teachers, shut up in a room of individuals with immature minds and short-term objectives, feel isolated; the feeling is compounded in schools where the administration is authoritarian — where teachers have no effective voice in how school affairs are conducted. The isolation of adults from adults in the school setting is illustrated in the frequency with which certain remarks are heard from teachers: "We could . . . if only the parents . . ." "We could . . . if only the administration would listen." "The only time we see the supervisor is when . . ."

It would be difficult to estimate how much of this isolation is real and how much of it is imagined — or consciously or subconsciously contrived. Certainly, some of the social distance could be reduced if one person would take the first step. It is here suggested that an important function of the counselor-consultant is literally to take the adults who constitute school personnel by the hand and introduce them to young people.

Social distance seems to be increased by the press of population numbers. When America was a rural nation, the neighbors may have lived a mile away but there was concern if one did not see smoke rising from the chimney of another's house when it should. One knew when his neighbors were going to town, when a letter was received from an absent son or daughter. One knew when there was hardship and lent a hand. In city apartments neighbors may live next door — with only one wall separating them — for a year and not know each other's names. Absences, sickness, family are simply not matters of mutual concern. Perhaps because there is also a neighbor to the right, two live across the hall, one is on the floor above and another on the floor below. No one feels responsible for taking the first step toward acquaintance.

The isolation which exists in the crowd is illustrated in a case cited by Darley and Latane (1968). Kitty Genovese was attacked by a maniac in Kew Gardens, and though she screamed for help and fought off her assailant for more than half an hour before she was murdered, not one of the thirty-eight witnesses would help or even bothered to call the police. In a somewhat similar case a switchboard operator was raped in her office. She escaped, ran naked into the Bronx streets bleeding, and was again attacked by the rapist with no one in the crowd of forty, who watched in fascination, interfering. It is almost unbelievable, but it would be still more unbelievable if one person in the country or wilderness area stood by without interfering on such occasions.

IDENTITY AND ALIENATION

This apparent digression into crowd behavior is made because a degree of the same impersonality seems to exist in school personnel and school pupils. What is everyone's concern is nobody's responsibility. And this apparent lack of concern is compounded for youth by their exclusion from adult society. The consequence is that the great problem of youth is that of identity; their primary developmental task takes the form of a search for identity (Erikson, 1964a, p. 94). When the search proves futile, the result is a feeling of alienation — and it is not in a foreign land but in home port.

Hickerson (1966, pp. 31 ff.) points out a number of beliefs

teachers have about children that contribute to this feeling of alienation. One belief is that an intelligence test determines the capacity to do schoolwork. Hickerson asserts that motivation is more important. Another belief is that children should use decent language as opposed to vulgar language and that language should be grammatically correct. Children should have "clean" sex, drinking, and other behavior habits — whereas, of course, some have the habits they have seen in adults. Children should talk about, rather than fight over, their problems, yet look at how their language is criticized. Children should understand the relationship of effort to future success, but work is denied to youth, Negroes, Indians, Mexicans, etc.; and academic successes and rewards are restricted to those who come with a head start and whose behavior becomes self-reinforcing.

There are few — students or teachers — who do not appreciate the implications of such school factors in the evolution of alienation. Furthermore, the threat of alienation will not be eliminated by the counselor-consultant's taking a few steps toward implementing communication. It is realistic to hope that some borderline cases of alienation can be averted, and some of the school-generated factors of alienation can be modified, by the initiation of dialogue.

Pepi and Sumi were fraternal twins nearly thirteen years of age when we first encountered their family in family group consultation. They were the only children in a family with a father and a mother, each of whom worked at a responsible supervisory-level job. Pepi and Sumi had been adopted at age two. For more than ten years they had lived the usual way twins live in a middle-class family. They went to school. They had separate rooms. A grandmother lived next door. Each child was moderately successful in school achievement.

The presenting problem was reasonably believable. The chief complaint rested with the control of the twins' stealing. Pepi and Sumi were real hoods who would steal almost anything from food to cigarettes. We were never able to determine the exact date the behavior began. We do know the date it ceased.

Both parents held jobs away from the home. The children would return home from school several hours before the parents arrived. When we began family group consultation, the house was kept locked, and the twins were not permitted to be at home until the parents were present. Everything within the home was kept locked: the refrigerator, food lockers, bedrooms, dresser drawers, closets, and all storage areas. It was reported that each twin would go to almost any extreme to "break in" the house or its contents. The grandmother would also lock out the twins, especially if she were away and they might be in her home unsupervised.

One consistent thing kept being repeated in each account of behavior violations: Almost every violation committed by either twin was done in such a way that he was caught. This seemed strange until the problem behavior was resolved.

Each child was overweight, carelessly groomed, and usually apathetic in appearance. The alienation seemed complete. The treatment plan required almost six months to carry out. The first two months were spent collecting data on the "terrible two." There seemed to be no good reason for their behavior. The parents held steadfast in their belief that they were good parents with only the welfare of the children at stake. We later came to believe these initially controversial statements because the parents persisted in coming to counseling even when no change in behavior was in evidence. We staffed the case, met in conference with the consulting psychiatrist, the psychologist, and all of the several counselors involved. The psychiatrist claimed the parents were normal persons who were probably telling it the way it was. The twins were without any pathology and did not show any thought disorder. Testing and the psychological write-up gave no clues to account for the behavior reported by the parents. We decided to try a new strategy. A new summer program was to begin in a week. The children would be asked to participate with us in the program. If they accepted the invitation, they would be spending each day with one or more of the counselors in the program. The twins did accept. A month later we had another case staffing. The mystery had shifted but had not vanished. We had learned that the twins would not steal from us.

The parents were confronted with the apparent discrepancy in the behavior of the youngsters with us and with them. Why would the twins steal only from their parents?

The mystery continued for several sessions. Finally, in a meeting about six months after family group consultation began, a group member who was a parent in a different family confronted the father with his extremely strict attitude toward Sumi's behavior. In the reply was the answer to the question "Why do the children steal from their parents?" The father explained his strict attitude toward Sumi as his way of showing love. If he had not loved her so much, he would not have cared how she behaved. Through a veil of tears the two formerly alienated persons found a common identity and a new way to communicate their feelings to each other. Pepi was very close to Sumi in their sibling peer group relationship. Whatever was happening to one was apparently also happening to the other. The stealing ceased and counseling was terminated.

Almost a year later the father called the counselor to report an incident. The parents had gone away from home to have a brief holiday, leaving the twins behind. They were called home suddenly because the twins had been picked up by the police for shoplifting. The father said it was all resolved. He knew why the children had done it. Now they were about to make a second attempt at a vacation — and the children were going with them.*

Communication: Teachers-Counselors

TEACHER-TEACHER COMMUNICATION

It would be unsafe to generalize about the quality of teacher-teacher communication. Obviously in some schools and with some teachers there is a great need for improvement. Pupils experience disadvantage because insights about them are not shared by teachers and because pupil behavior — especially misbehavior — is projected on former or other current teachers. In other schools the lines of communication are open, and the counselor-consultant needs only to provide, administratively, the time to exchange ideas and information.

In view of the differences between the younger and older generations, cited above, a gigantic change in educational procedures is needed. Indeed, the shortcomings of present education are such that some persons go so far as to recommend the elimination of schools. They say we need to find a way of educating the young which involves them *now* in political and social affairs. The concept of a school isolated from other social institutions is abhorrent (Goodman, 1962, p. 56).

Less drastic ideas for the improvement of schools than their elimination have been recommended. Seemingly excellent plans

---

* Names used are not the real names of the twins. Follow-up after four years confirmed that identity is more conducive to adaptive behavior than is alienation.

have been proposed, but their implementation takes place at a snail's pace. The rationalization is that the new ideas have not been tried extensively enough to warrant their being put into effect. If this is not a defense mechanism used to escape the discomfort of change, at least it deserves to be talked about. The real reason for slow change is probably that the change is sought through conventions, one-shot teacher institutes, or disparate training of various teachers in various summertime courses in different institutions. There is no pervasive theme to the retraining. In order to implement innovative ideas more rapidly, it will be necessary to involve the entire school staff of an ongoing program in the process of change. When change is the responsibility of teacher education institutions, not enough people are involved soon enough.

An effective approach to teacher-teacher communication is via team teaching. Too often team teaching is merely a matter of teachers' combining classes and then teaching in tandem. But in genuine teaming which involves cooperative planning, cooperative teaching, and cooperative evaluation there are some marked advantages.[2] One teacher reported as follows:

> I volunteered to team-teach as an experiment and I found that it makes my work harder. When I could close the door on myself and my pupils I could become impatient. I raised my voice — well, I screamed. I could blame the pupils for inadequate work. With another teacher present this changed. I found that, with another adult there, there were fewer occasions for displeasure. I didn't shout because I knew an adult would see that I was, at least partially, to blame. And anyway she and I knew who had responsibility for correcting inadequacies.
>
> In the good old days there were times when I did not make careful plans. Those days are gone. I'll not flounder around with poor preparations. My teammates do not have to criticize. They stimulate my own self-criticism and, in discussions which are not of a critical nature, they also stimulate new ideas.
>
> Team teaching is not easy. It's hard work. And it's rewarding. Given my choice, I would not go back to the one-teacher class.

[2] Team teaching provides a structure in which curricular materials and human resources can be used most advantageously. It encourages cooperative planning, decision making, and educational assessment. It capitalizes on the opportunities made available in nongraded organizations, flexible scheduling, and independent study (Beggs and Buffie, eds., 1967, p. 60).

This teacher's words illustrate that communication is more than a matter of words. Provision needs to be made for teachers to get together. Team teaching is not simply an approach to communication but a result of the communication which must also precede its successful use. It has been observed that teachers often take three years to prepare for the novel roles called for in innovative programs (Anastasiow, 1969).

The facilitation of teacher-teacher communication is a problem which has been thought about very little — and still less has been done. It is something like motherhood: It is such a natural function that suggesting that communication can be taught is an insult to one's sophistication. However, continuously accumulating evidence indicates that school effectiveness is dependent upon just such open communication.

COMMUNICATION AND OVERALL SCHOOL EFFECTIVENESS

The following is a paraphrased and condensed account of what happened in one school district.

> Superintendent Kimple was hired in 1962 by the school board of South Brunswick, New Jersey. The board wanted experimentation, change, and improvement. The principals of nine schools had no authority, teachers were "scared of everybody including themselves," and all decisions were made in the central office. One of Kimple's first moves was to send all the principals to a summer session at the National Training Laboratories in Bethel, Maine. There they learned some more about people, feelings, and how they "came across" to others. The program emphasized the study of problems and the study of self. One of the participants said that most of them saw two persons — the one shown to others and the one that hides behind the facade. They saw things they really did not want to see. Perhaps it might be better to say they were willing to experience the temporary trauma of transcendence for the sake of greater self-realization.
>
> By 1967 part of the NTL program was brought to South Brunswick so teachers and students could be involved in it. Teachers are expected to be experts in subject matter and pupil development on a somewhat equal basis. Each is expected to spend half his time helping pupils with learning and personal habits — aimed at initiating and sustaining independent study. . . .
>
> Letter grades have almost vanished. Teachers enjoy their

work more. Standardized achievement tests show yearly increasing superiority over national norms. The atmosphere has moved from one of mistrust to one in which teachers trust enough to permit video tapes to be used to evaluate teaching. Students are listened to and are less "up-tight" than they used to be. There is some criticism, by parents and students, but families from neighboring districts are bringing their children, wanting to know how much out-of-district tuition would cost in order to get their children in the varied programs.[3]

Teacher-Counselor Communication

As with so many other problems of human relationships, the case of communication begins with first person singular. Many teachers have disdain for, if not active distrust of, counselors. And many counselors blame the inadequacies of their programs on teacher resistance, active opposition, or indifference. A typical question asked by teachers is "Why do counselors think they are wise enough to judge the wisdom of a teacher's decision?" Of course, counselors generally *don't*; but *some* may think they have such omniscience.

We have been interested in what is called "source of certainty" in the counselor's work. This certainty is sought in the list of forty jobs the employment counselor has in his desk drawer. It is sought in the test scores the counselor has in the cumulative folders. It is sought in the sophistication of the facilitator in a group sensitivity session. It is any structure or systems "map" to show the way to move toward a goal that would otherwise be clouded in ambiguity. Ambiguity in any human organization is disorganizing to the uncertain person while structure is organizing. Sources of certainty tend to be depended upon even though some creative risk taking might be more productive. The counselor-consultant seeks to develop toleration for ambiguity, and its stimulus to innovation, by making dialogue feasible.

Kushel (1967) reports that discord and misunderstanding are realities in teacher-counselor relationships. His approach to the reduction of misunderstanding is for one of the parties (the counselor) to issue an invitation to the other for a discussion. An elaboration of the discussion approach is the presentation of case studies and

---

[3] Material from Charles H. Harrison, 1970, "South Brunswick, N.J.: Schools Put a Town on the Map," *Saturday Review*, 53(8):66–68, 90, February 21. By permission of the publisher.

participation in role playing. The important point is not who initiates communication, or what the techniques are for processing it, but the fact that it takes place. Schools in which communication occurs between all personnel, pupils, and community members are the ones with distinguishable superiority (Harrison, 1970).

Although the impression that discord exists between teachers and counselors is widespread, there is at least sporadic evidence that such is not universally the case. An investigation conducted by Sherman and Shapiro (1969) began with the assumption that teachers and counselors did not get along well, but the evidence gathered from 22 schools and 418 teachers by means of the Teacher-Counselor Communications Inventory denied the popular belief. The majority of teachers perceived counselors as having friendly and cooperative attitudes. The investigators deemed it significant that personal rather than professional characteristics were ranked highest by teachers. A number of ways were mentioned in which counselors could be helpful to teachers; the four that ranked highest were (1) helping with pupils referred, (2) providing information which promoted pupil understanding, (3) helping with students, and (4) identifying students who had special problems. The two lowest-ranked ways of assisting were (1) backing teachers in contacts with administrators and (2) helping with personal problems. The latter is not surprising because some authorities regard helping teachers with personal problems as outside the counselors' range of function (Faust, 1968, p. 130; Stefflre, 1966).

The study by Sherman and Shapiro (1969) also specified some barriers to teacher-counselor communication. An examination of these affords the counselor-consultant clues about where the task of improving communication might begin. The investigators considered the major blocks to communication to be lack of information about the counselor's role and heavy schedules for all school personnel. The three highest-ranked barriers mentioned by teachers were that either the counselor or the teacher was too busy and they had conflicting schedules. It was also noted that counselors were seldom available and that counselors were inconveniently located. Lack of confidentiality is a dilemma. Here it is cited as a block to communications. Teachers observe too that help from counselors is hindered because counselors will not tell them what went on in counseling sessions.

The most important aspect of the Sherman and Shapiro study, in this context, is how communication was achieved when it was achieved. The two highest-ranked methods of communication were teachers' visits to the guidance office and casual meetings around the school. This finding should give the counselor-consultant serious pause. It would seem to be a justification for implementing the counselor-consultant role because neither the work of the teacher nor the work of the counselor can have maximum influence on the pupil unless their efforts converge. The convergence would seem to be most likely when the counselor visits the classroom. This point is listed in the Sherman-Shapiro study but it is sixth on the list and mentioned by only 17 percent of the respondents. The important thing is that a counselor's visit to the classroom can be an occasion which is appreciated. When counselors work with teachers and pupils in the classroom, teachers quickly come to see the complementary value of teamwork in which one focuses on adjustment and the other focuses on teaching-learning transactions (Bernard and Huckins, 1967).

> Teachers do wish to participate in guidance activities. They see themselves as engaged in a wide variety of guidance activities on behalf of their own students. They seek greater involvement by the counselor in helping their students.
>
> Much griping and complaining are evident in urban school environments. It is suggested that these are functions of the environment and are not necessarily indications of personal ill-will. Under such conditions the counselor is often the butt of gripes. This does not mean that teachers feel personal enmity toward the counselor, as this study has clearly shown. It is time for counselors to stop worrying about being loved, feel a sense of professional competence, and get on with the job to be done.[4]

Supervisor-Teacher Communication

VARIETIES OF MANAGEMENT

In typical conversations of teachers about principals and department supervisors there are likely to be some sweeping generalizations about the "nosiness," "curtness," "know-it-all" quality, or cooperativeness or helpfulness of their attitudes. The temptation to

---

[4] Robert Sherman and Ida Shapiro, 1969, "Teacher-Counselor Communication," *The School Counselor*, 17:62. Reprinted by permission of the publisher.

categorize, which tends to block communication, is an ever present danger. Gibb (1965) has noted that the behavior of administrators, department chairmen, supervisors, and teachers and parents, when placed in positions of responsibility, falls between the two extremes of defensive and participative management. Gibb's analysis is of special interest because he not only notes the extremes but also suggests some causes of that behavior and its probable outcomes.

A high level of fear and doubt and a low level of trust in others is characteristic of defensive management. In contrast, participative management is indicated by low fear and high trust. Some things administrators do that are conducive to the building of distrust are keeping close time checks, requiring frequent reports, making frequent inspection tours, issuing orders without explanation, insisting on tight rules, withholding information, and insisting that subordinates stay in "channels" in communication whereas supervisors can go out of "channels" when contacting others. These techniques arise from fear, ambiguity, and distrust and, of course, tend to sustain — if not magnify — them. For this reason the defensive management approach is self-sustaining and self-confirming.

There are administrators of another stripe. They have confidence in themselves and know that with the help and cooperation of others they can do the job. Their assumption is that those on their team or staff are capable, responsible, and trustworthy. Such administrators, despite teachers' griping about authority figures, are probably more frequently encountered than are the defensive ones. Leadership positions are probably most often achieved by virtue of competence. Hence, the leaders have confidence in themselves, have little fear of "the competition," and can trust others. Trust stimulates the best productive efforts on the part of the "troops," and the cycle of success tends to be perpetuated. The pooling of wisdom, when the leader does not feel a compulsion to parade his prowess, also enhances the team endeavor. There is always a risk in trusting others, but it appears in the eyes of the confident and competent person to be minimal. At any rate, the outcome is worth the occasional price extracted.

Elements of the contrasting milieus described above were observed by one of the authors (Bernard) in a staff meeting of a junior high school. A recently passed state law required that teachers be visited periodically for the purpose of instructional improvement. It was evident that some of the teachers regarded such supervisory visits as being evaluation. Despite the fact that they graded their own pupils in various ways, there was considerable antipathy to the thought of their being similarly evaluated. The more experienced teachers thought that new teachers needed the evaluation more than those who had taught for some time. The new teachers felt that they would be experimental and innovative because they were seeking ways to be most effective — they did not need further instruction (a la student teaching) to complicate their search. They thought that the older teacher, who might be getting into a nonproductive rut, was the one who needed supervisory evaluation. Some of both the old and the new teachers said they wanted evaluation of their work but showed their skepticism of its merit by stating strong preferences in how and by whom the evaluation was done.

Fortunately, for balance in the group, some teachers, both new and experienced, said, "If there's some way my work can be improved, let's have at it."

TEACHER-ADMINISTRATOR COMMUNICATION

There is no technical approach that will automatically facilitate communication. The barrier exists in preexisting orientations. It is improbable that either teacher or supervisor could explain satisfactorily to the other the dynamics involved if doubt existed and self-acceptance were lacking. The projection of blame, or the inference that one was being blamed, would tend to obscure the perception of mutual effort. At this point a third party — the counselor-consultant — might render service. Somewhat like the marriage counselor in a court of domestic relations, he, simply by being present, makes a difference in how one reports his feelings and how attentively one listens while his counterpart speaks.

Regardless of what attitude the principal has toward guidance and counseling, the effectiveness of counseling throughout the school will depend heavily on the counselor's relationship with the principal. The latter's attitude may range from fear of and reluctance to accept guidance services to acceptance of the service and wanting it for his personal use (Faust, 1968, p. 72). Because of this range of feeling there is no assurance that the principal will readily choose to be a participant in an interpersonal process group in which feelings, perceptions, and attitudes are expressed. To the extent that the counselor-consultant fails to get the principal to participate, his success will be limited but not totally denied. Getting teachers to see how their defensive behaviors affect pupils can still be a major achievement in terms of releasing pupil potential. For what comfort it may afford, and for what incentive to persistence in the pursuit of administrator participation, let it be observed that change inevitably involves conflict (Kemp, 1969). The price of flexibility and growth is, almost inevitably, some discomfort. The price of rigidity and sticking to the present is also discomfort, but it is delayed, more persistent, and eroding rather than rewarding.

It is not so much the function of the counselor-consultant to resolve the question of how teacher-administrator relationships should be conducted as it is his function to focus on dynamics. The co-operative participation of all staff members can best be served by examination, analysis, description, and interpretation of "what's happening now."

Teacher-Pupil Communication

THE NEED FOR COMMUNICATION

Earlier it was stated, in effect, that the mother talking earnestly and lovingly to her babe in arms is teaching him his first lessons in humanity. Unfortunately, tradition, which mistakenly assumes that telling is equivalent to learning, makes the teacher's role as talker predominant when the child enters school. Recently some doubts have begun to be aroused and expanded regarding the wisdom of the teacher's being the major initiator of communication. Ginott (1965, p. 25) asserts that children do not always ask the questions they really want answered. They ask questions, for instance, about others which really are intended to uncover what might happen to the questioner himself in a similar situation. The adult communication expert listens for those feelings rather than focusing primarily on verbal contact.

A panel of the President's Science Advisory Committee, reporting to the U.S. Commissioner of Education, emphasized several ideas. Prominent among these, and expressed in various ways, is that the pupil should take a more active part in learning and that there should be a reduction of the teaching-as-tutelage method. For example, discovery offers the opportunity for pupils to ask questions rather than to rely on teachers' questions which pupils did not understand or perceive to be important. It was felt that there should be better balance between presentation and discovery. Furthermore, when material was presented it should "involve" (see Glossary) the student.

> . . . One particularly promising lead came out of the conference's study of various new curricula in mathematics, science, and the social studies. It has to do with the effectiveness of "contingent relationships" between a learner and a tutor, i.e., situations where the learner has some control over the pacing of the information he is getting and over the nature of the information he gets next. The ideal form of such a relation is probably the dialogue between a learner and a wise and informed tutor. But it is encouraging to see the extent to which improvement in performance can be achieved by organizing class discussion into a generalized form of dialogue, using texts and documents as resources to be tapped when needed.[5]

Flanders (1965), investigating communication in the classroom and its effect on behavior and academic achievement, studied several hundred teachers in Minnesota and, to add an international flavor, New Zealand. He found that most of the teacher's influence was verbal; it was the teacher who was talking 70 percent of the time. He categorized teachers into those who were predominately direct and those who were predominately indirect. Direct teachers used verbal statements that tended to restrict freedom by focusing on the problem and interjecting teacher authority. They lectured, gave directions, criticized, and exerted authority. Indirect influence consisted of verbal statements that expanded a student's freedom by encouraging his verbal participation and his initiative. This meant asking questions, accepting and clarifying the ideas or feelings of students, and praising and encouraging them. Achievement on standardized tests turned out to be greater with the indirect teachers. It had been expected that results would vary with different learning styles of the pupils, but no such differences were found. All pupils learned better when their role was participatory.

> . . . Some critics of the public schools have advocated that teachers "get tough," tell students what to do, and demand high standards. Our data show that higher standards can be achieved

[5] *Innovation and Experiment in Education*, 1964, A Progress Report of the Panel on Educational Research and Development to the U.S. Commissioner of Education (Washington: The President's Science Advisory Committee), p. 13.

not by telling students what to do in some sort of misguided "get tough" policy, but by asking questions and then using student ideas, perceptions, and reactions to build toward greater student self-direction, responsibility, and understanding. If "getting tough" means helping students face the consequences against living with the consequences of the teacher's ideas and opinions, then indirect teachers are much tougher.[6]

At least some of the protest coming from high school pupils stems from the fact that they feel they are allowed no autonomy in their own affairs, no voice in their own destiny. At a 1969 meeting in Cambridge, sponsored by the Harvard Advanced Administrative Institute, school superintendents, spokesmen for youth, school board members, *and* high school students met and found that communication was virtually impossible. Each was trying to *tell the other what he should do* to remedy the generation gap and to calm turmoil in the schools. Schrag (1969), reporting on these meetings, suggests that the old rhetoric used by adults is becoming unpersuasive. Fewer students are listening even a little bit, and more are not listening at all.

Bruner (1968) emphatically asserts that sound educational theory must have roots in political, economic, and social reality. Any education that does not justify itself in these terms must be considered trivial. Hence, education of the young must bring them into contact with these phases of life, and preferably in company with an adult. Add to this, in a world of rapid change, the necessity of developing a problem-solving attitude. Complexity will be resolved through research, and the young person who asks questions is the potential researcher. The most crucial way, says Bruner, for the human group to assist intellectual and educational growth is through dialogue between the more and the less experienced. Thought processes are to some extent internalized dialogue. He summarizes these ideas by stating that the major factor in successful education might very well be the courtesy of conversation.

THE ANTECEDENTS OF PUPIL-TEACHER COMMUNICATION

One way to approach better pupil-teacher communication would be to emphasize techniques. This is done here and there throughout

---

[6] Ned A. Flanders, 1965, *Teacher Influence, Pupil Attitudes, and Achievement* (Washington: Office of Education, U.S. Department of Health, Education, and Welfare), pp. 116–117.

the present book. Here the problem is approached through emphasis on the persons primarily responsible.

A major aspect of teacher-pupil dialogue is the teacher's attitude toward self. If he is confident of his own knowledge and regards it as incomplete but growing, he can tolerate and welcome opposing viewpoints. If he has learned his own worth as a person, he finds it unnecessary to be defensive and he can then respect pupil individuality. If he has been autonomous in his childhood home and has no fear of authority, he does not need to compensate through exercising authority on pupils. In short, the absence of defensive posturing and of need to compensate for real or imagined inadequacies provides him with personality characteristics which make dialogue between the experienced and the novitiate possible. And if one's background has not made these things probable, it is still realistic to regard them as possibilities. Through psychiatric or counseling aid, or through participation in interpersonal process groups, one can look at himself and decide what changes he can and will make (Jersild and Lazar, 1962). It is not necessary to carry on one's back the monkey of inadequate self-concepts acquired in childhood all his life.

The other approach to improved teacher-pupil communication derives from the first part of this chapter. Unless there is open and facile communication between teachers, administrators, specialists, and supervisors, the classroom atmosphere between pupils and teachers is not conducive to communication. What the counselor-consultant does to improve communication between adults in the school milieu may do more to improve teacher-pupil communication than will direct emphasis. That is, when the teacher has experienced the process of improving communication with his peers, he is left with freedom to develop his own idiosyncratic approach to communication with pupils. If there is direct tutelage of teacher-pupil communication, the process is more likely to be technique than a manifestation of individuality.

Summary

Contrary to the opinion of some, there is real reason to believe in a generation gap. Young people are different today from the elder generation for many reasons, including television, accelerated maturation, waning of the struggle for existence, equivocal role of authority, and youth's primary concern of role before goal.

Rapid change and the generation gap make the achievement of identity somewhat more difficult than it has previously been. Rapid population increase and concentration of people in the cities, although brought about because man prefers things that way, make for social isolation and alienation. Communication is a tangible and manipulable approach to the reduction of alienation.

Effective communication within a school begins with teacher-teacher communication. Direct training helps, but cooperative endeavor in such things as teacher in-service education, educational innovation, and especially team teaching are even more effective. Communication between teachers and administrators may or may not be a basically difficult problem. Sometimes the problem is attitudinal rather than a proved reality. Teachers so readily anticipate the negative that they render its occurrence more probable. But there are management techniques that inhibit communication too. Defensive management inhibits while participative management promotes communication. Counselor-consultants, teachers, and administrators who appreciate the dynamics which lie back of the abundance or scarcity of communication have taken one step toward improvement.

Removal of the generation gap *and* more effective education depend in some measure, perhaps largely, on teacher-pupil communication. The direct approach, through direct training in group procedures, may be effective, but it is probably less effective than emphasis on improved communication between all adults who are involved in the successful functioning of a school.

SUGGESTED ADDITIONAL READINGS

Cottle, Thomas J., 1969. "Parent and Child — The Hazards of Equality," *Saturday Review,* 52(5):16–19+, February 1. *It is proposed that parents and children are not equal, and children are confused when parents do not act the part of guides and superiors. The article is recommended here for what inferences may be drawn for teacher-pupil relationships.*

Friedenberg, Edgar Z., 1969. "The Generation Gap," *Annals of the American Academy of Political and Social Science*, 382:32–42. *A critic of the schools and a defender of youth outlines some of the cultural factors which are involved in the sharp conflict between the younger and older generations.*

Halleck, Seymour L., 1971. "Why They'd Rather Do Their Own Things," in H. W. Bernard and W. C. Huckins (eds.), *Readings in Human Development*, 2d ed. (Boston: Allyn & Bacon. From *Think*, 34:3–7, September–October, 1968). *The hypocrisy of adults, the discrepancy between professed and practiced morality, and failure to achieve humanitarian ideals are offered as some of the reasons for the generation gap.*

Harrison, Charles H., 1970. "South Brunswick, N.J.: Schools Put a Town on the Map," *Saturday Review*, 53(8):66–68+, February 21. *Beginning with his sending nine principals to the National Training Laboratories at Bethel, Maine (for sensitivity training), Superintendent Kimple got teachers, administrators, pupils, and parents talking about effective schools. Parents from surrounding communities want their children to attend South Brunswick schools, where achievement is high.*

Sherman, Robert, and Ida Shapiro, 1969. "Teacher-Counselor Communication," *The School Counselor*, 17:55–62. *Contrary to their expectations, these investigators found that generally teachers reported counselors to be helpful and communicative. In terms of those items on their questionnaire which indicated lesser degrees of satisfaction, the authors suggest some improvements.*

Wyzanski, Charles E., Jr., 1969. "A Federal Judge Digs the Young," in H. W. Bernard (ed.), *Readings in Adolescent Development*. Scranton, Pa.: International Textbook Company. From *Saturday Review*, 51(29):14–16+, July 20, 1968. *Rapid change, racial prejudice, adult hypocrisy, inability to communicate, and instability of values are factors which need to be understood if we are to understand today's adolescents.*

Chapter Eleven

THE DYNAMICS
OF COMMUNICATION

Chapter Ten discussed the need for clear communication for the sake of developing humanness and for institutional efficiency. The problem of communication is dealt with further in this chapter but with emphasis on the dynamics, or processes, of communication.

Girls walk differently from boys in our culture. No one tells either the boy or the girl how to walk (except later on girls may be taught to walk in a stylized manner to present clothes in a style show). It is learned so subtly that it is taken for granted that no instruction is needed. Similarly communication is learned so spontaneously that only a few scholars have taken the trouble to examine its dynamics. Boys and girls learn the language and grammar of local speech and use it freely without being aware of its structure and form. Only when they attempt to learn a foreign language do they pay attention to declensions, number, voice, and the like. An anthropologist learns to be alert to nonverbal clues in order to understand the culture he is investigating, but these same nonverbal clues may be overlooked by persons to whom they are native.

If we knew the dynamics of our own communication system, we should probably be unable to condense it in one chapter. Here we will describe some of its gross features, hoping that the counselor-consultant will seek to improve his own perceptions of important clues to understanding that are typically overlooked.

Communication Requires a Connection

ONE-WAY COMMUNICATION

Communication means to give, or to give and receive, information. It means that there is a connection. Where morale is high, when goals are clear and commonly accepted, when the leader is truly charismatic — then communication can be pretty much one-way. A platoon leader briefing his men for a dangerous mission can lay out the strategy and tactics and communication is effective. One does not expect that there will be much give-and-take in discourse when a coach is briefing his team for a crucial game.

Watzlawick, Beavin, and Jackson (1967, p. 48) emphasize the fact that it is impossible not to communicate. There may be no feedback to the coach's admonitions, but there is response. Indeed, in some situations no words are spoken by anyone, yet silence may carry a message of disdain or of deep sympathy. A child may indicate his response to attempted communication by failing to hear — he turns off his parents or teachers. Adults can, and do, do the same thing to their companions and colleagues.

Because, in regard to communication, things are not what they seem to be, it is necessary to analyze the various modes of communication. Trying to judge the personality or feelings of the participants in a communication milieu from the words spoken is, in the authors' estimation, in about the same category as trying to assess personality from an individual's drawings or paintings. Some people think they can do this; others are extremely skeptical. As is the case with other phenomena in both the physical and social realms, things are changing so fast and knowledge is accumulating so rapidly that we are not sure whether communication is just being recognized as a concern of counselors, whether it is a well-developed appreciation, or whether it is in quite rudimentary stages. Hence, the following observations are stated as propositions which merit attention rather than as principles that must be translated into action.

PROPOSITIONS REGARDING COMMUNICATION

Huckins (1971) has formulated six propositions representing current knowledge and theory about communication.

1. There is no such thing as noncommunication when two or more persons are in each other's presence. By one's mere existence and presence he proffers a message. An infant makes a difference at a bridge party, in the home, or at the hospital clinic. He easily steals the scene from an accomplished and attractive flirt. Is it because he offers no threat to others? Can others thus offer a bit of themselves without danger of trauma — psychic or physical? Whatever the answer, the point is that one makes a difference; something is communicated.

Being quiet in school, at a concert, in the presence of another can be a coercive or a confirming action. The client-centered counseling espoused by Rogers has been called nondirection, but there are those who point out that silence can be very directive. "It really doesn't matter," says the teacher to the principal as she clamps her jaw firmly shut and sits rigidly in the staff meeting. But she and everyone else knows that "it" does make a big difference. Silence may be a matter of comfort and rapport — as when husband and wife or young sweethearts watch a seething sea. Maslow (1954, p. 255) suggests that self-actualized people who are in love need not use words to express their appreciation of peak moments.

The more typical use of silence is to show resentment or anger, to pretend not to hear. Hence, withholding feedback is compelling more often than it is complying. It indicates disdain and contempt for another. He is so insignificant, so much a nothing, that the silent person does not deem it worthwhile to become involved. In part, of course, this reaction of silence is based on what others in the situation expect.

There is no cure-all for the threat of silence to communication — when it is a threat rather than a matter of implicitly felt accord. Noninvolvement may be nothing more than indifference, but when used in a coercive manner it cannot be ignored while hope for concerted group action is maintained. The usual technique for dealing with the nonparticipant — the boy who will not play if he can't be first baseman — is exclusion. The Quakers may have suggested a more pertinent approach in their tolerance for the deviate. The deviate is respected and accepted. He is, in fact, needed to confirm the stability and strength of the group (Lowry and Rankin, 1969, p. 511). The silent adolescent or teacher or parent is not necessarily seeking exclusion; he could just get up and leave or not have come in the first place. His silence needs to be discussed by others in a respectful tone in the hope that some of the conjectures will at least merit a verbal endorsement or disavowal from Mr. Silent. The discussion provides a means of inclusion and a recognition that one does make a difference.

2. The meaning derived from communication is mainly dependent upon the receiver or interpreter. Words are uttered or written by one person with a clear conception of the message he wishes to convey. What the other hears is frequently quite another matter. The receiver has a background of experience or a relationship with the initiator of the message which may belie the words uttered. Thus, an adolescent has been arguing loudly and persistently about whether she may drive seventy-five miles to an overnight beach park. Mother, after having stuck with "No" for some time, finally says, "I give up. Go ahead and go." Upon which daughter says, "You really don't care what happens to me." In this relationship mothers have the role of decision maker, director, crutch, and haven of safety, and abandonment of this role, which was imposed by daughter, is a disappointment. But mothers can't win because they are unable to perceive the expectation placed upon them by off-spring. Another mother might have maintained to the end, "You can't go." To which daughter would have replied in some such words as "You are unreasonable and old-fashioned. None of the other kids have such suspicious and untrusting parents."

Much of the disharmony within a school stems from the assignment of roles to one another. "Principals are not interested in innovation. They just want teachers who will keep still and not rock the boat." There are teachers who believe that physical force has a salutary influence on a disobedient child. "One dare not yank him out of line when he persists in poking others with a pencil because parents would complain to the board." Parents might; but they also might sigh in relief with the pencil poker's learning that others have rights. The gratuitously assigned parental role, however, governs the situation, even though the parent has said, "We will back the teacher in her disciplinary actions."

The message that is received, rather than the one sent, is the one which determines the respondent action (Thayer, 1968, p. 39). Failure to recognize the role of the receiver causes considerable confusion. The initiator may become bewildered, angry, or suspicious if he thinks that his suggestions were logical, pertinent, and kindly disposed. Congenial and meaningful communication is made difficult by the assumption that the message is contained in the words. Interaction with other persons may be facilitated by the realization that perverse and obstinate colleagues are perhaps that way because they did not hear what was said rather than because they desired to block progress. When communicants know what they are looking for by way of clarification, the matter becomes one of "What did you hear me say?" Too often the assumption is that the initiator did not make himself clear so he repeats or restates the words; but the message continues to reside in the receiver.

3.   Much of the content of a communication is controlled by nonverbal rather than verbal symbols. The attractive young lady in a restaurant observing who is at each table and noting the appearance of each new entrant does not confirm her words "I'm listening." And she does not hear her host invite her out a second time. The bright young miss who maintains some degree of eye contact with her host, smiles at the anecdotes, and cocks her head occasionally, conveys a message that is much more credible than "Is that so?" The counselor who leans back, puts his feet on the wastebasket, gazes out the window, and says, "What's your problem?" may not (depending somewhat on the status of Proposition No. 2) elicit confidence. On the other hand, if he leans forward in his chair, keeps his hands apart, and focuses on the counselee, he invites the confidence which is not even verbally requested. And what is the counselor to believe when the counselee says, "Understand now — I love my mother," while her eyes and posture indicate quite another thing every time the word *mother* is spoken?

Those treasured fireside chats of husband and wife will be curtailed as the husband dutifully mutters, "Is that right?" or "Huh?" as he cranes his head to read from the newspaper who won the second game. He is in fact, giving a double message — one of interest by keeping his hands off the paper and another of disinterest by so obviously restraining the impulse to reach for it. One of the skills of the counselor is reading the messages which are given nonverbally (Shostrom, 1967, p. 48).

"Every little movement has a meaning all its own" are the words from a song of yesteryear. No doubt the nonverbal indicators have been present for years, but Ruesch and Kees (1961) state that only recently has there been appreciation of the principles of gestures, stance, movement, and physical setting as important aspects of the communication transaction. Foot-tapping, finger-drumming, hair-twisting, tooth-grinding, and so on give messages counter to the verbal assurance "It's O.K." However, the movements are no more an indication of *what* is wrong than is a temperature of 101.6°.

The effect of uttering verbal content which is contrary to non-verbal clues is psychological discomfort for the perceiver. He does not know which message should merit the response. Because of this dilemma, its concomitant discomfort, and the tendency for people to avoid discomfort by withdrawal, the utterers of the conflicting message find it difficult to establish close social relations with others — in fact, many become social isolates. The explanation is clear (the nonverbal message is clear) — clear in the expression of disavowal and disapproval but *not* clear in terms of specifically what is disavowed and disapproved.

Those who would avoid the clarifying impact of interpersonal process groups seem not to realize that discomfort in an equivocal situation is unavoidable. The choice is between the temporary discomfort of participation in a growth process and avoidance of the issue but continuance of the discomfort.

4. Communication is a major process through which people discover and define their identity. Verbally and nonverbally a mother communicates to her infant that he is cute, lovable, valued, and worthy; or that he is ugly, despicable, dirty, and unwanted. Between these extremes, at some unstable point, may be varying degrees of equivocation and ambivalence. But equivocation or rejection is psychologically intolerable as far as the establishment of a healthy sense of identity is concerned. The choices are between (a) confirmation and validation, (b) rejection and minimizing of the person, and (c) ignoring and disconfirming individuality (Watzlawick, Beavin, and Jackson, 1967, pp. 84 ff.).

The establishment of a sense of identity is regarded by some authorities as one of the more pressing developmental tasks of today's adolescents (Erikson, 1964b; Friedenberg, 1970; Mead, 1970). There is a conviction on the part of some authorities (Glasser, 1970; Moore, 1969) that this striving for identity has never been so intense as it is today for the NOW generation. The threats of nuclear annihilation, population explosion, environmental pollution, and catastrophic rates of change have left young people in an unprecedented state of anonymity. These threats cannot be removed by legislation, by the building of new institutions, or by denying their existence. The remaining alternative is to learn to deal with them. A start, but only a start, is to treat purposefully with the communications aspect of identity.

The process of talking with a child gives him a start on the establishment of identity. *Immediately* he is worthy of time and attention. He is valuable enough to be talked with as a person. Even the misbehaving child at home or school seems to recognize this. It is often better to be admonished and scolded, or even punished, than to be ignored. If teachers are to accept the postulation that today's youngsters *are different* from any preceding generation because of television, because of the population explosion, because of technological change, they may well begin with an appreciation of the thesis that when teachers talk 70 percent of the time (Flanders, 1965) they can hardly argue that they are engaging in a communication process which confirms identity.

The nonverbal aspects of communication also play their part in the confirmation of identity. The advice to young people that men teachers should never touch a girl, that even a hand on the shoulder may be misinterpreted, and that to black pupils physical touching is an act of aggression may need to come in for some reassessment. There is enough success in "touching behavior" — even at the high school level — in relation to rapport and identity that, at the minimum, experiments and testing of the traditional "hands off" proscription should be described and discussed in school faculty meetings.

O can accept (confirm) P's definition of self. As far as we can see, this confirmation of P's view of himself by O is probably the greatest single factor ensuring mental development and stability that has so far emerged from our study of communication. Surprising as it may seem, without this self-confirming effect human communication would hardly have evolved beyond the very limited boundaries of the interchanges indispensable for protection and survival; there would be no reason for communication for the mere sake of communication. Yet everyday experience leaves no doubt that a large portion of our communications are devoted precisely to this purpose. The vast gamut of emotion that individuals feel for each other — from love to hate — would probably hardly exist, and we would live in a world devoid of anything except the most utilitarian endeavors, a world devoid of beauty, poetry, play, and humor. It seems that, quite apart from the mere exchange of information, man *has* to communicate with others for the sake of his own awareness of self, and experimental verification of this intuitive assumption is increasingly being supplied by research on sensory deprivation, showing that man is unable to maintain his emotional stability for prolonged periods in communication with himself only.[1]

5.   Communication is the principal process by which the aspects of behavior devoted to manipulation of others are accomplished. "Sticks and stones will break my bones but names will never hurt me." This childish assertion is a case of whistling in the dark. The name-calling does hurt and may be more permanently traumatic than the broken bone. Some teachers have been concerned for a long time about the effects of labeling in school — gifted, slow learner, remedial cases, problem child — because the categorization is seen to influence behavior. The report by Rosenthal and Jacobsen (1968) on the salutary effect on pupils of teachers' having been told that those particular pupils were about to blossom intellectually has been criticized as a statistically unsound research study. The critic (Thorndike, 1969), however, suggests that the report may be an effective addition to educational propaganda. The report and the criticism both illustrate the proposition that communication is designed to manipulate the behavior of others. Rosenthal and Jacobson suggest the need for faith in children, or for expecting much of them. Thorndike suggests that the self-fulfilling prophecy may be quite pertinent but it has not yet achieved the status of a cure-all for the ailments of education.

Manipulation does not need to mean exploitation. Communication is a major means of gaining access to a group, of achieving inclusion as a member. As the wishes of others are learned, one is

[1] Paul Watzlawick, Janet H. Beavin, and Don D. Jackson, 1967, *Pragmatics of Human Communication* (New York: W. W. Norton & Company), pp. 84–85. Reprinted by permission of W. W. Norton & Company and Faber and Faber, Ltd.

"manipulated" to modify his behaviors so he can belong. The first-grader (as well as the college student) gets his clues on how to behave from the verbal messages of his teacher or instructor. He gets feedback on the acceptability of his behavior from both verbal and nonverbal communication. Communications, especially words, set the tone for action and provide a trial run (through discussion) for the proposed or anticipated action. Much of the effectiveness of counseling depends on the fact that if one can test a plan or theory beforehand in verbal symbols it becomes somewhat less necessary to act out the postulated behaviors.

The basic patterns of manipulative communication are learned early in life. The child discovers that there are ways to get what he wishes and to compel others' actions by responding in given ways (Beier, 1967, pp. 20 ff.). These become styles of life. Thus some people are fundamentally agreers, some are arguers, some lend nonverbal (active) support and some support verbally, and some gain notice and influence others' behavior by criticism and dissension. We could call this communication a matter of games, as does Berne (1964) except that it is much more serious than the implication usually given to "games."

"Manipulating others" has an unwelcome connotation. It is contrary to the ideals of independence, autonomy, and individual responsibility. The existence of pressure groups and pressure politics is recognized, but as something which others attempt to do to us. Less objectionable are the concepts of education, teaching, child rearing, and acculturation. However, the longer we permit ourselves the delusion that we are not manipulative toward others, the less control we will have over the effects of communicative manipulation (Shostrom, 1967). Unwelcome as the admission might be, the competent professional must admit his personal responsibility in manipulative transactions.

6. Persons tend to be unaware of many of the implications of the process and content of communication activities. The basis for this proposition lies, at least in part, in the second proposition cited above: Meaning in communication depends mainly on the receiver. Both the initiator and the receiver tend to make implicit assumptions about the other which modify what is transmitted and what is received. These assumptions are often embedded so deeply

in cultural expectations that we are unaware of them until the unwritten rules are broken. Hall (1959, p. 71) points out that, although Americans have no great difficulty with whether to call their new associates by their first or last names, they cannot state the generalizations by which their name references are governed.

The fact that we are unaware of much of the dynamics of communication does not mean that we must remain so. An effective approach to a clearer perception of what transpires is to talk with someone who is outside the emotionally familiar milieu. The outsider is more capable of viewing with objectivity the actions and assertions as they occur. His need to understand makes it necessary to gain clues to comprehension which will supplement the purely linguistic ones (Thayer, 1968, p. 337). Rather than getting help from a person who has had experience outside the dominant culture, one can much more probably increase his awareness by verbalizing about and analyzing with his colleagues the discrepancy between intent and meaning. This process is strikingly similar to the kind of transaction which takes place in counseling or psychotherapy. In both instances, with outsider or colleague, the concern is to raise to the level of consciousness the things one does habitually or automatically so that improved control over actions can be exerted.

Facades and Barriers

THE FUNCTION OF FACADES

A facade is a front presented — in communication terminology a false front intended to cause an observer to focus on positive attributes rather than correctly to read animosities, fears, or anxieties which exist. As long as people associate with others, it is likely that those below the level of self-actualization will need facades to protect their vulnerability. The protection is not simply a matter of defense mechanisms employed by poorly adjusted persons. Many facades serve a useful cultural purpose and have been built up over centuries of experience. The polite language and posturings of diplomats in international relations are an example. Inwardly, but not entirely secretly, the diplomats fear or hate one another. They know, however, that abandonment of the facades of courtesy and respect would immediately sever chances of communication and the hoped-for understanding. The facade of the brave little boy who stands up to the big bully may get him into trouble but it may weaken the facade of boldness assumed by the bully. The facade of the teacher who resigns herself to some unwanted administrative restriction may aggravate a persistent problem or may cause the principal to soften the command because of the teacher's apparent cooperativeness.

Facades are not always interpreted as facades. Sometimes the soft inner core predisposed to conciliation remains better hidden than is feasible. In such cases the facade becomes a barrier to communication. Whether the facade is successful or acts as a barrier, it merits attention in the matter of clear communication. It may be less a matter of removing the symptom which is called facade than a matter of changing the nature of the relationship and reducing the need for using it.

In summary, facades deserve to be recognized. But the actual work involved in getting behind them is as important as is the actual unveiling. Sometimes it is beneficial to maintain the facade; for example, when honesty prevailed in a sensitivity group the hopeful wife would not continue the marriage after the honest partner admitted promiscuity.

BARRIERS TO COMMUNICATION

Facades are only one class of many barriers to communication. Parry (1968, p. 84) lists several, some of them parallel to the propositions described in the preceding section.

1. Communication is limited by the receiver's capacity. The obvious example is deafness of the person being addressed. It is also clear that use of a language unknown to the listener will prevent communication, except in the form of facial expressions and other nonverbal clues. Listener's background of experience and information conditions the clarity of communication. Paucity of background might, however, be compensated for by additional or varied explanations (demonstrations, display of realia, graphic materials, etc.) by the presenter.

Intelligence of the receiver influences the amount of communication. In the event of language differences, dialects, or limited background, the more intelligent person can extrapolate from the words and clues he does understand and then, with the bits that are picked up later, can check the accuracy of his perceptions. Thus, a counselor tries to understand the specifics of a situation which the counselee finds it difficult to describe accurately and in detail. The counselor makes guesses and checks them against later revelations or by direct — but not leading — questions.

A function of training in communication is to increase the capacity of the connection, as the diameter of a water pipe or the circumference of a wire which conducts electricity is increased. The human simply says, "He talked too fast." "There was no time for it to sink in." The counselor-consultant, in approaching a conflict within the school or seeking to implement innovation, can see from the foregoing that going slowly — giving feedback on small gains, using those who are ready as helpers — may be an asset in situations involving limitations on the part of the receiver. T-i-m-e is as important in the consulting, or the counseling, process as is love in the raising of a child.

2. Distractions limit the amount that can be heard and comprehended. Noise is an obvious distraction. In a room with many people talking it is not easy to hear what any one person is saying. The hard-of-hearing person notes this fact with special recognition. The differential loss of ability to hear certain sounds makes it difficult to hear the pitches used for speaking even a single word, and the whole becomes an irritating buzz. Oddly enough, young people raised in the television and continuous radio era have used the background sound provided by these media as a device for tuning out other noise distractions. They can study better, they say, if street noises and voices from adjoining rooms are screened out by background music. Parry (1968, p. 89) may give the clue for understanding this phenomenon in his comment that it is easier to tune out distractions which are unlike the stimulus being attended. Thus, it is harder than usual to tune out an adjacent conversation when it parallels that in which one is engaged.

Environmental stress, such as is imposed by conditions of extreme humidity, temperature, vibration, noise, or glare, has a degree of barrier effect, though research has not revealed its exact nature. Concentration may be maintained up to a certain point and possibly even improved up to a lesser point. The effect of environmental stress may be to make a situation more tiring; thus concentration is maintained for abbreviated periods. Empathic teachers and speakers note this phenomenon and curtail their presentations under conditions of environmental stress.

Parry (1968, p. 88) includes internal stresses such as sleeplessness, ill health, fatigue, and unfamiliarity with the communicative medium in the environmental stress category. However, he says that they could as readily be grouped with the limited-capacity-of-receiver category.

3. An unstated assumption may act as a barrier to communication. The unstated-assumption barrier may be illustrated by the speaker's use of a proper name. The Smith or Jane to whom he refers in his presentation may not be the Smith or Jane who comes to the listener's mind (Parry, 1968, p. 91). This is a failure of cognition rather than one of feeling or emotional bias. William Glasser's book titled *Schools Without Failure* (1969) has led some readers to assume that all children should be successful at something. Glasser does not believe that success is always possible, or even consistently salutary. He is emphasizing that a child should not be forced to stay in a situation in which academic failure is inevitable. The science of semantics is an attempt to reduce the error of such unstated assumptions. It sometimes becomes necessary to grope for words which mean almost, but not quite, the same thing in order to make one's meaning clear.

Often confusion over meaning is bypassed. The receiver thinks he has missed something when the presentation continues on what seems to be a tangent. Instead of calling attention to the fact that "I don't get the point," he covers up because he thinks others will regard him as stupid — and, of course, those who assume that the receiver has the same background as the presenter *will* take this view. The fact that the one who misunderstands had a different background is easy to overlook, as is seen in the readiness with which we speak of the "culturally disadvantaged."

Effective speakers are typically those who are sensitive to the response of the audience. They have an awareness of when they are being redundant and when there is need for reiteration. A writer faces a more difficult task because what to one reader is repetitious writing is to another an expansion which clarifies by means of restatement and emphasis on the more salient points. In regard to such dilemmas, Parry (1968, p. 95) makes the point that communication need not aim at full understanding. There is a case to be made for leaving something to the wit and imagination of the receiver. The assumption that the receiver has no background is as hazardous as the assumption that he has the same background as the presenter.

4. There is a personal aspect of communication which constitutes an incompatible schema for the presenter and the receiver. Behavioristic psychology has influenced teachers to believe that presentation leads directly to learning. Hence the compulsion to cover the assignment or the syllabus. Gestalt psychology, however, calls to attention the fact that the total situation, background as well as figure, is what results in perception. In Snyderian terms, you have to read the white and the black. Humanistic psychology lends support to the Gestalt orientation by emphasizing that one is proactive (the human looks forward, dreams dreams, postulates theses, formulates goals) as well as reactive (he responds to past and present stimuli). The need for recognition of different schemata is well illustrated in the generation gap.

> A problem of particular interest concerns the values and attitudes of different generations. The organic changes that occur throughout life predispose us to think that young and old will view many things differently. Such differences may be exaggerated or underestimated, but nobody has thought it sensible to suggest that they do not exist. What is hard is to determine how far these perennial shiftings are overlaid by changes in the climate of opinion. This theme should prove a challenge to the social psychologist; indeed, at least one research bearing on it has been conducted in this country. This was Kelvin's (1963) attempt to find out through the readers of *New Society* the views of different age-groups on the factors that had made England a great nation in the past and those that were likely to make for greatness in the future. Admittedly the sample was biased in that it was drawn mainly from readers of one journal, but this did not lead to any obvious uniformity of view. One of the things suggested was that the 20–40 groups (roughly those born between 1923 and 1943) tended to an extreme radicalism in the main areas (defense, immigration laws, education, sex), whereas the under 20s and the 40s–60s to some extent shared a more traditional approach. What this valuable

piece of work could not unravel was how far such a pattern might have been discerned among the generations of any period and how far it is the product of our recent history.[2]

There is accumulating evidence to support the idea that oldsters should not expect the younger generation to mature and finally to decide to "join" the existing culture. Those things which have contributed to producing children of a different kind — continuous exposure to television, the reduction of the threat of starvation, the population explosion, the discrepancy between adult behavior and verbally expressed ideals, the reduction of work opportunities, etc. — suggest that the revolution in culture requires the oldsters to share the youthful ideals rather than vice versa. An example of the incompatibilities of the generations is provided by Heilbroner (1970), who asserts that the priorities of today are as follows: Military needs take precedence over civilian needs; private interests rank above public interests; and the comfort of the affluent assumes priority over the needs of the poor. The younger generation's disgust with this ordering renders the process of communication one of staggering challenge — unsurpassed, the authors believe, in the educator's work. The challenge is not impossible to meet. We do not have the answers, but it may be that communication provides access to at least tentative answers to bringing the schemata of youth and adults closer together.

5. Unconscious and partly conscious factors cause the recipient to play an active role in the interpretation of that which is communicated. Unconscious factors may be either facilitators or inhibitors of communication. For instance, the child in a foster home who receives a letter from his mother saying, "Dear Ronnie: I'm sorry that I was sick last weekend and could not visit you. Just as soon as I can get a little money ahead, I'm going to come and get you. . . ." interprets this as an irrevocable, hope-to-die promise. He will talk confidently to his peers and to adults in the home about the fact that his mother is going to take him back at the middle of next month. The fully cognitive response of an adult worker to this letter

[2] John Parry, 1968, *The Psychology of Human Communication* (New York: American Elsevier Publishing Company), p. 106. Reprinted by permission of the University of London Press Ltd. and American Elsevier Publishing Company.

is to try to prepare Ronnie for a considerable extension of time. The "I'm sorry . . ." sentence is, judging from similar situations, the real message. Another worker, who has developed a strong liking for Ronnie, experiences the unconscious in terms of emphasizing the message "I'm going to come . . ." and feels concern about her own imminent loss of Ronnie.

Unconscious factors may facilitate communication, but they are easily overlooked because no difficult situations are precipitated and the dynamics are ignored. The facilitating effect of unconscious factors is utilized by advertisers to promote the sale of their products over those of their competitors. Thus, if two soaps are equally effective, the advertisement which enhances the ego of the purchaser is the one that will persuade him to seek, and defend, its product (Packard, 1960).

The psychological defense mechanisms of projection, identification, and repression serve as barriers to accurate communication and are manifestations of the unconscious at work. Projection functions when the actions of another are interpreted in such a way as to serve the perceiver's needs. Thus, Ronnie projected his feelings into his mother's letter. If one dislikes one of the participants in a group, he will interpret what that person says in a manner to confirm his beliefs; this is the familiar self-fulfilling prophecy. Identification is parallel to projection; it means sharing the role and feelings of another. This will lead the receiver to side with the presenter and to reject those elements of the transaction which are inconsistent with the idealized concept he has of the person with whom he identifies. Repression means that unconsciously the receiver rejects those messages which are unwelcome. Thus, normal everyday fears and expectations lead to erroneous conclusions. This is exemplified in cases in which the receiver ignores or distorts segments, both large and small, of the communication transaction.

One of the functions of interpersonal process groups is to call a person's attention to bits of behavior and instances of inaccurate beliefs and perceptions which are characteristic of him. When brought to the conscious level, they become more amenable to modification.

6.   There are modes of oral and written expression which tend to confuse rather than to clarify communication. A persistent problem in the teaching of reading is how to present the material in a manner

both motivating and meaningful. A persistent problem in encouraging pupils to continue to read is also how to present the material. Large print, short sentences, and brevity of total message are factors which tend to make reading purposeful and enjoyable. The authors have supervised students enrolled in counselor education programs who exercise such care and elaboration in asking a counselee a question, using so many forms and words, that the counselee loses track of what was being asked. In consequence, the hypothesis was developed: "The length of the response is inversely proportional to the length of the query." And to illustrate the total point: "The shorter the question, the longer the response." Confusion is increased by much use of such words as *but, despite, otherwise, except, unless, however, nonetheless,* and others, which increase the qualification of a statement.

It is well, in lowering this barrier, to recognize that there are different styles of perception. Some receivers are verbalizers, some are visualizers, and some are spatializers (Parry, 1968, p. 114). Hence, if confusion is to be reduced, it is helpful to use graphic means, illustrations, and models to vary presentation. As in the case of verbal clarification, it is advisable to keep the message simple. As the number of messages which one seeks to convey increases, the clarity of a chart or diagram decreases.

7. Communication is made difficult when there are no established channels for bringing potential senders and receivers together. Reversing the cliché, this is more real than it is apparent. The principal who ends his presentation of the new plan with "Any questions?" may not be opening the process of communication. Gibb (1965) describes what he calls "defensive" management in terms of restricted channels of communication. Low trust causes the management to limit the data that can be transmitted to employees. Much use is made of facade; one pretends to be open but without intent to be candid. The situation is aggravated by the recipient's becoming suspicious of those elements which are honestly presented. Defensive management makes much use of strategy, gimmicks, and tricks to suggest the existence of openness. The result is to increase the difficulty of communication because of ambiguity, distortion, and counterdefensive strategy.

A major cause of the absence of communication channels is that no one is made accountable. Communication is thought to be so natural that it will occur spontaneously. More typically, one becomes so involved in his primary concerns that he fails to take initiative regarding communication. It is a case of "What is everyone's responsibility is no one's responsibility." As organizations become more complex, the necessity for established channels increases. Thus schools with larger and larger enrollments and more and more specialists with a widening range of responsibilities experience the need for a communication specialist. It appears to the authors that this function is a natural for the counselor-consultant.

This barrier — absence of channels — indicates that not all barriers are of the subtle kind requiring attack on causes rather than symptoms. Here direct attack on the symptom seems to be indicated: Provide the channel.

Affiliation — The Formation of Bonds

THE BASIS OF AFFILIATION

The basic aspect of affiliation is to be recognized, to be acknowledged, to be given time. The word means connection — being included. When one knows that his presence makes a difference, he is also led to believe that his ideas make a difference. Fraiberg (1967) contends that the disease of nonattachment may precede neuroses and psychoses. Neuroses and psychoses refer to the breakdown or rupture of human bonds while nonattachment indicates that such bonds were never formed and after a certain age, probably cannot be formed. She calls nonattached individuals "hollow persons." When one attempts to communicate with them, it is as though nothing were there. Such unfortunate, and irritating, beings can experience no joy, grief, or guilt. In the attempt to achieve some feeling, which they vaguely recognize as missing, they may engage in brutal and violent acts to flog a spark of feeling into their relations.

Learning to be human — to have attachments — is carried on through communication. It begins with a smile and a repetitious sound; the mother says, "Oh you little . . . , um, um, um, etc." Children who are not mothered not only show emotional stunting but tend also to be linguistically retarded. Thus, their handicap becomes self-perpetuating. Long before dialogue has meaning in terms of verbal symbols, there is a contact that allows adults to guess at what the baby needs from his cries, postures, and grimaces.

The alienation of youth illustrates a lesser degree of the non-affiliation of unloved babies. Communication of youth with adults is difficult because the experiences of the generations are so different in an era of rapid change (Friedenberg, 1969). Even when the need for communication is recognized and efforts are made to achieve it, the participants are so far apart that frustration is the typical result. The very authority and intransigence which contribute to the lack of understanding are simply intensified when efforts to communicate fail (Schrag, 1969).

APPROACHES TO AFFILIATION

There are no readily accepted explanations of the frailty of human bonds in relation to the conflicts which arise in schools. Human bonds develop out of significant interpersonal relationships which bring meaning and purpose into the life of each member of the affiliation. Sometimes the bonds are due to simple geographic contiguity. At other times the price is a bit higher. Someone must make the effort to reach out — and in so doing risk his own fragile connections already made. Such an example is involved in the following case when a rough-tough former delinquent teen-aged tutor discovered he was needed by a much younger (nine-year-old) fourth-grader.

> The tutorial program was organized by the YMCA and was designed to involve older acting-out youth with younger children having school learning difficulties. We had learned from a pilot demonstration that frequently the older youth were successful where adults had failed to teach a child to read. We could see the benefit for the child but had not noted the significance for a youth who might have been able to experience, directly, his own "being needed."
>
> A sixteen-year-old returned to tutor Billy following a long absence. The young man had worked with Billy on reading assignments for almost six weeks before disappearing. Upon his return, no questions were asked. He was permitted to report directly to the classroom as usual. When Billy saw him, the child broke into a broad grin and put his arms around the young

man. This tough young man dissolved in tears as he caught the emotion of the moment. "He needs me. He needs me!" was all that was said.

Halleck (1968) has described fifteen hypotheses for student unrest, but, while perceiving some as more valid than others, he does not select any as being really inclusive enough. One that he does view with favor is the "neutral hypothesis": No individuals are culpable; rather, the explanation of alienation is that highly complex processes create a need for new modes of psychological adaptation. If a thesis of this book is accepted — that discussing problems diminishes the need for acting-out behavior — then ways to establish communication become a central concern of the counselor-consultant, and certainly of other people too.

One approach to more facile communication, used sporadically by teachers, is sociometry. This is the arrangement of small groups of pupils in accordance with their preferences and needs. Thus, a pupil has the chance to associate with other pupils among whom he feels most comfortable. The process begins by asking the children to list the first and second choices of their classmates with whom they would like to be associated in certain areas. In order to lend reality, this sociometric question should apply to a real situation: "What two pupils would you prefer as chairman of the lunchtime recreation committee?" or "By whom would you like to sit during study periods?" Questions should be of a type pertaining to an interpersonal situation over which the teacher has control. Thus, "With whom would you like to travel in a space capsule?" would be an inappropriate question.

On the basis of the responses to the sociometric questions, it will be perceived that some pupils are unchosen (the isolates); some are chosen by many pupils (the stars); some are chosen by the pupil they chose (the mutual choices). Then a sociogram is drawn — a sort of classroom map on which all pupils are represented, with arrows to indicate the chosen persons. Boys can be represented by a square and girls by a circle if sex is significant — and it probably is, depending on whether the plot is for primary grades or for the middle school. Typically, clusters of pupils can be seen to form on the basis of the question asked. Incidentally, the accuracy of the sociogram can be pictorially indicated by taking a wide-angle photograph from the roof of the school building while children are playing at recess. Some will be by themselves, several will be grouped in pairs or triplets, and one or two clusters will contain five to ten pupils.

It is important that something be done about the sociometric question, but the results should be treated in a confidential manner as far as individual choices made are concerned. The unchosen person need not be embarrassed by having his unpopularity publicized. The grouping should be governed somewhat as follows, and in order of priority. (1) Pupils should, to as great an extent as possible, be placed with the person involved in mutual choice. (2) The unchosen pupil should be placed in a group with the pupil whom he chooses. (3) The more popular one is, the less concern there is about his placement. He has demonstrated, by being frequently chosen, that he is an expert in human relations. He might, in fact, be encouraged to give a little extra consideration to the isolate.

Results of the use of sociometry show that (1) achievement can be enhanced by making pupils sociometrically comfortable, (2) behavior problems can be reduced by such grouping, and (3) social development can be promoted by rearranging the sociometric grouping at various intervals — probably once every two or three weeks at the primary level but at periods two or three times as long in high school. Changing the groupings will allow for new acquaintances and broadened experience. Sociometry also reveals that teachers are largely unaware of the social structure within their classrooms (Mouly, 1968, p. 224). Sociometry indicates that pupils form friendships along socioeconomic class lines and along lines of levels of intelligence. The more distinct the class lines in a community, the more clearly they can be discerned in a classroom sociogram (Edwards and Scannell, 1968, p. 469).

In view of the problems of racial turmoil which characterize our society and in view of the superficial sophistication of high school students today, it would seem desirable that teachers learn how to use the dynamics of communication and the symptoms of its absence. For example, Meyer (1969) has noted that in our "very best" schools, the schools of suburbia, there is a growing provincialism in spite of ease of travel and communication. The basic problem, as indicated in discussion of the formation of human bonds, is to foster the feeling of affiliation. "I make a difference," "I am a cause," "My presence and ideas are noticed."

Direction and Levels of Discourse

DIRECTIONAL FLOW

Neophyte counselors and teachers who have "inherited" the counseling assignment because they have rapport with pupils often perpetuate the one-way flow of communication, as in A of Figure 11-1. This is the pattern which has caused some pupils to tune out or drop out and to assert that school is just a matter of "yakety-yak, yakety-yak." Because of politeness or fear on the part of pupils, the teacher or counselor may think that he is getting his message across because they are quiet. There is no feedback, other than the silence, to confirm this hypothesis.

Part B of Figure 11-1 shows another familiar pattern which is probably representative of some anxiety on the part of the adult. Afraid of losing control, he must be a part of every verbal transaction. He is so insecure that he does not want to be missed during an exchange. (Or, of course, he may simply have developed a habit.) He may be anxious too because he feels that the message of wisdom and experience which he has to contribute is likely to be bypassed. This pattern, the adult domination of verbal transactions, may stem from the "teacher's complex" — the feeling that something has not been said unless it has been put in the words the teacher had in mind before the dialogue began. Perhaps the students have stated the same thing but in other words. The restatement by the teacher of all significant points leads the pupils to be inattentive to all speakers except the teacher. Adult domination is also encouraged by the sense of haste. The pupils are, in fact, "getting there" — but not fast enough.

The counselor-consultant has a chance to test his skills in attempting to alter situations A and B within the classroom or counseling cubicle. Change probably will not be achieved by using either A or B models in the consultation process. Encouraging a visit to another classroom or providing in-service work in counseling may be helpful. A readily available approach is to make use of a tape recorder. The "conversation dominator" has often remarked, upon listening to a tape of himself, "I can hardly believe that I so completely monopolized the scene." The imbalance is so perceptible that no remarks on the part of the supervisor are necessary; the tape is an effective instrument of self-instruction. The art lies in getting the

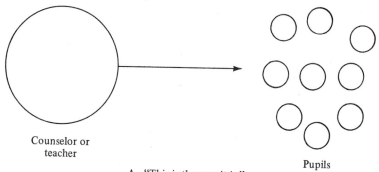

Counselor or
teacher

Pupils

A. "This is the way it is."

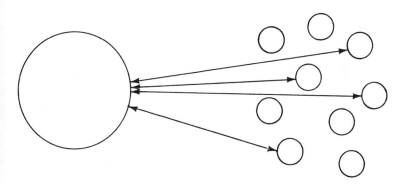

B. Various adult-dominated dialogues.

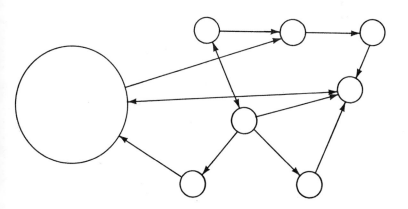

C. Communication within a group.

FIG. 11-1. *Characteristic patterns of verbal transactions.*

tape recorder into the room. It has been noted that in a school where the level of trust is high, the use of video tapes has helped teachers improve their performance. Instead of wondering who is spying on them, the teachers are concerned with finding help in order to do a better job (Harrison, 1970).

LEVELS OF DISCOURSE

Huckins (1971) suggests a schematic device for evaluating the meaning and effectiveness of communication. He distinguishes between discourse and communication, indicating that discourse may be one-way — a lecture or monologue — whereas communication entails mutuality and exchange. The device for assessing the meaning of dialogue consists of five concentric circles (Fig. 11-2); the more the discourse deals with the materials of the two inner circles, the greater is the personal meaning.

Level 5 discourse is widely used in situations in which there is low trust or unfamiliarity and in which one feels the need for protection. Its function is to close the gap of interpersonal distance, but not too much. "How are you?" is an example. This is not a query about health or success in the workaday world. If one does tell how he is, he is regarded as an oddball and the physical distance as well as the psychological distance is increased. This level of discourse is useful because it serves as a facilitator in preliminary meetings. But it is intentionally deceptive — and is understood as such. The message stated is not always the one intended. The words suggest an awareness of the presence of the other person; the message is that of protecting oneself from what is novel and psychologically hazardous. Feelings exist, but the pretense that they do not exist complicates the communication process.

Level 4 discourse is factual. There are no double messages. The task is simply to convey a message with no personal emotions considered. Level 4 messages would suffice to cover the problems of social living if it were true that man is a rational being. The fact is that Level 5 messages do exist — feelings are present even though they are denied. The counselor-consultant should seek to develop awareness of the existence of feelings, which are suppressed and repressed when group meetings occur. While we can offer no formulas for eliminating feelings, we are convinced that much Level 4 discourse is impeded by failure to acknowledge the priority of feelings even in the rational aspects of behavior. At this level little is being done to bring people into psychological closeness. Resulting actions are bland, impersonal, and businesslike. Certainly this kind of transaction has its place and value, but in the society of the young

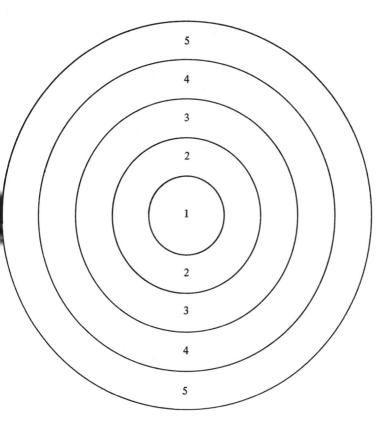

FIG. 11-2. *Levels of discourse*

5. Noninvolvement; purpose is protection.
4. Factual messages; no emotional loading.
3. Messages concern personal meaning and general feelings.
2. Feelings are described which relate to self.
1. Concerns such deeply meaningful processes that verbalization is difficult and often unnecessary.

and in the school, where identity has become a major issue, the wisdom of trying to use Level 4 discourse to the exclusion of more personally meaningful communication may be doubted.

Level 3 discourse tends to decrease psychological distance and bring participants together on a feeling plane. It bears directly on such issues as identity and self-concepts. Topics of a personal nature are considered. Information is transmitted, but, in addition, this type of discourse attempts to make known the feelings of all parties. The fifth-grader who says to his father, "It seems to me that you are friendlier to my pals when I bring them home than you are to me" is at Level 3. Whether Dad answers at Level 3 or Level 4 will depend on whether he needs to protect his "father complex" and whether or not he is aware of the levels of discourse which might ensue. The counselor-consultant will find that his awareness of levels enables him to keep teacher-teacher or teacher-pupil communications at Level 3; he simply calls attention to evasive responses. This level of discourse is ego integrative and tends to promote psychological health. It is necessary to warn, however, that expert control is vital. Birnbaum (1969), Rogers (1968), and Shostrom (1969) are among those who caution that personal revelation of feelings may be at times too rapid and at other times irrelevant.

Level 2 bears much similarity to Level 3, but in this case the feelings described are about oneself rather than about things, processes, and other persons. This level can be either developmental or therapeutic as it supplements Level 3 discourse. Here one increases his appreciation of his place in the world and among people. This is a delicate, tender area with which to deal, and it is probable that escape to Levels 3 and 4 will be sought by those most deeply concerned. Relief is needed to gather or maintain the strength for dealing with feelings about one's protected inner self. This is the level on which interpersonal process groups will operate, and an expert facilitator is needed. The facilitator must be able to make judgments about when the transitory escape has served to refresh and the time has arrived to get back to Level 2. He must be able to tell, during the encounter, when the pressure is too great and it is time to escape to Level 3 or 4 to obtain relief.

Level 1 discourse occurs at what Maslow (1967, pp. 283 ff.) has called peak experiences. Almost everyone has such moments, but they are rare and may escape recognition and acknowledgment.

Hence, one may profit from having them called to attention lest they be dismissed as being too far out. It is unnecessary to describe or analyze the feelings themselves. The communication consists largely in the awareness that an unusual and highly gratifying experience is taking place. Sensation rather than verbalization is the experience being sought. We have felt it occur when some long-standing hostility between counselor trainees has been resolved.

One cannot live and communicate at Level 1 for extended periods. However, Maslow indicates that self-actualized persons have peak experiences more frequently than do the majority of us. And the occurrence of peak moments is stimulated by one's recognition and acknowledgment of their existence.

Implications of Levels of Discourse

There are other schemata for the evaluation of the processes of communication which, like the "levels of discourse" concept, help one evaluate where he is in the communication transaction. But sometimes habit or convenience prevents the full utilization of communication in seeking goals. For example, the introduction of an innovative educational practice might be sought. Level 5 discourse has served its purpose of warming up, and Level 4 discourse is occurring, but with not much progress toward consensual action. The counselor-consultant perceives the value of moving from Level 4 to Level 3 and makes the necessary comments, or asks the necessary questions, or does the necessary confrontation. It may be advisable to move at times to Level 2 — which, if successful, may be so unusual and tempting an experience that it becomes an end in itself (Pierson, 1965, p. 51). While all levels of communication will be sought and utilized, the amount of group or interpersonal time spent at any one level will depend upon the purpose which is paramount at the moment. Sometimes the emphasis will be on getting something done in terms of the innovative practice. At other times it may be most pressing to have a teacher take a look at his own feelings and defensiveness.

Summary

Much that is termed communication is merely a one-way transaction involving no ostensible feedback. Hence, there is value in examining the transactions which are so much taken for granted that substantial parts of the potential value of communication are lost.

One way to conduct such an examination is to study some communications propositions: (1) There is no such thing as noncommunication when people are together. (2) The meaning of communication is largely dependent upon the receiver. (3) Much of the content of communication is controlled by nonverbal rather than verbal factors. (4) Communication is a major process by which individuals define their identity. (5) Much of the manipulation by which one controls others utilizes communication. (6) Persons tend to be rather unaware of the implications of the processes of communication.

Another approach to communications analysis is through the examination of common barriers encountered and "games played." Facades (false fronts) are worn by those who wish to protect their inner selves from clear presentation. Communication is obstructed by the inadequate or inappropriate capacity of the receiver. Distractions of noise and setting limit the amount that can be heard. An unstated assumption may lead to mutual misperceptions. Individual schemata (background, goals, concepts) of sender and receiver may be incompatible. Unconscious and partly conscious factors cause the receiver to misinterpret what the initiator intends to communicate. There are modes of oral and written expression which confuse meaning.

Some unfortunate people have not experienced the communication which enables them to form human bonds. This is a particularly pressing problem of contemporary schools in which role and identity take precedence over goals and achievement. Approaches to achieving affiliation for some and enhancing it for others include such things as sociometry and keeping watch over the direction and levels of communication. Much of the counselor-consultant's work, whether with pupils, professionals, or pupils and professionals, will be in seeing that the level of communication is appropriate to current goals and degree of human involvement requisite to successful educational innovation.

SUGGESTED ADDITIONAL READINGS

Berman, Sanford I., 1962, 1965. *Understanding and Being Understood.* San Diego: International Communication Institute. *The author illustrates by anecdotes derived from experience in business and industry some of the ways in which communication may be blocked or facilitated.*

Bruner, Jerome, 1970. "The Skill of Relevance or the Relevance of Skills," *Saturday Review,* 53(14):66–68+, April 18. *This article is not about communication. However, Bruner emphasizes that curriculum building and curriculum relevancy mean connection between goals and action. Thus, the problems of communication are highlighted without direct reference to such things as are discussed in this chapter. The implications are startlingly, and gratifyingly, direct.*

Parry, John, 1968. *The Psychology of Human Communication.* New York: American Elsevier Publishing Company. *Because communication is such an important aspect of behavior and development, a look into its psychological nature is warranted. This book looks at communication as a problem of personal motivation and adjustment.*

Shostrom, Everett L., 1967. *Man, the Manipulator.* Nashville, Tenn.: Abingdon Press. *The author admits what most of us would like to pretend does not occur. People do try to manipulate others. If manipulators can be transformed into actualizers, the processes of development and communication will have added meaning.*

Thayer, Lee (ed.), 1969. *Communication: Concepts and Perspectives.* New York: Spartan Books. *Twenty-five discussants from five nations deal with the fact that the feeling and cognitive structures of transmitters and receivers differ and that these then constitute communication barriers. Approaches to resolving the difficulties are suggested.*

Chapter Twelve

TEAMWORK IN
STUDENT PERSONNEL
SERVICES

Initiating the consultant process is the major responsibility of the counselor. The strategy of team operation will enhance the probability for success. Team members represent the significant roles to be played, with each significant person sharing the purpose for consulting, which may be any immediate concern or long-term goal that is central to the educational enterprise.

Student personnel services usually employ teamwork methods because of the nature and variability of tasks to be done. Consultation introduces a new dimension of service.

TTT programs,[1] designed to prepare counselors at the consultant level, were initiated by collaborative efforts of colleges, school districts, state agencies, and professional organizations. During the first year it was necessary to determine behavioral objectives and to define

[1] TTT: Training of Teacher Trainers for Counselors; TCT: Training of Counselor Trainers. Two projects, Olympia, Washington, State Department of Public Instruction, Dr. Lawrence Brammer, University of Washington, project coordinator of the Western Washington Project.

the previously nonexistent consultant role, and the experience of the state of Washington may well be utilized in initiating the team-work model being considered here. Bernard and Fullmer (1969) defined the consultant role in the mid-1960's by conducting two second-graduate-year counseling institutes under the old NDEA program. The counselor-consultant was the major emphasis in the institute practicum and fieldwork. It is hoped that this more active role for counselors has become a model for practice in the 1970's. The task of consulting moves beyond the counseling relationship model to definite modification of the social-personal environment for the individual. Chapters 7, 8, and 9 stressed that groups were the basis of consultation. Teams are formed as a specialized type of small group, each team having a task but otherwise being very similar to any other group. The initial thrust of this concern is to discover the nature of the social-personal milieu.

Mapping Communication Processes

SOCIOMETRICS AND HUMAN ORGANIZATION

Sociometry offers a way to measure the nature and condition of human bonds. The graphic representation of these relationships reveals patterns of communication within an organization. The counselor-consultant begins by making a complete sociometric analysis of the team of student personnel workers in a given school, including teachers, supervisors, consultants, psychologists, parents, administrators, and counselors. Variations of this technique may be used with students for ascertaining their attitude toward student personnel services. However, the object in doing a sociogram of the student personnel workers, and all related professional personnel and parents, is to establish the base line for looking at the social bonds and accompanying communication patterns within the existing organization. The counselor-consultant needs this information to lay plans for initiating the consultant process and carrying out the counseling program.

A sociogram illustrates the role of each person in a given group. The sociogram *series* indicates the effects of both interaction over time and the presence or absence of persons originally enrolled or counted in the student group on what takes place among members. The value of the sociogram is its power to reveal the amount, direction, and type of communication in a group. Once the social bonds connecting the individuals in a given group are interpreted, it is possible to help group members learn to be more effective participants. Teamwork requires free communication among individuals under conditions of either low or high stress. The counselor-consultant may share his interpretation of their social bonds with the participating members in an attempt to help them understand the nature of their communication. Because this process is self-conscious, the counselor may find some professionals reluctant to participate. Attention to their individual needs for support and encouragement will help. For others with more severe reactions, it is advisable to use some systematic desensitization procedures to help relieve anxiety.

Using Sociometry in Group Counseling — Example

The purpose of the following report[2] is to demonstrate the use of a sociometric device in group counseling sessions with adolescents. Emphasis is placed on the identification of both verbal and nonverbal cues as expressions of interpersonal behavior.

Hypothesis: Underachievement in academic subjects is one way in which adolescents react to stress situations.

On the basis of this hypothesis, the goal in the group counseling sessions was to help each individual identify his own reaction pattern to stress situations, describe his pattern, and offer alternative patterns. Other areas of concern as part of the group process involved the observation of participants for the quality of their performance in the group. Was there an improvement in the quality of performance? When conflicts arose in the group, was there a move toward tension reduction? Is an experience in tension reduction helpful to a participant in a group situation in understanding why he is underachieving? Is it possible to show interpersonal interaction patterns by using sociometric technique?

The adolescents who participated in the group counseling sessions were selected from two high schools by their high school counselors. It was requested that the students chosen be underachievers. Other

---

[2] The sociometric material was reported during an NDEA Counseling and Guidance Institute in Portland, Oregon, conducted under a contract by the Oregon System of Higher Education.

than indicating that six group counseling sessions would be held, no additional information was given to the high schools.

The First Group Counseling Session. Nine adolescents participated in the first session (see Fig. 12-1). The counselor opened the session with a brief introduction and spent approximately five minutes in aiding the group to learn each other's names. He then began a discussion on underachievement by asking, "How do you account for the fact that you are underachievers?"

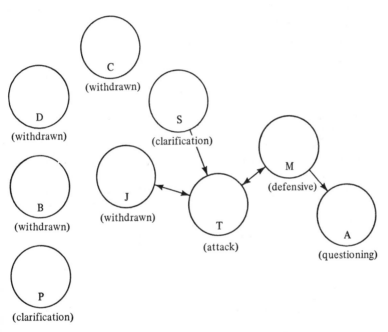

FIG. 12-1. *Sociogram Illustrating the Dominant Role of Each Group Member, Session 1.* Arrows indicate the direction of conversation. Terminology used in describing roles:

Withdrawn: Nonparticipating group member

Defensive: Blocking of ideas presented: restatement of present views

Clarification: What do you mean?

Questioning: What right do we have?

Attack: Describing and ascribing behavior to others

C visibly, not audibly, cried during much of the first half-hour. Sat slightly behind the counselor and out of his line of vision. Smiled when others referred to conflicts with their mothers. Began the session with arms folded but was leaning forward and listening by the end of the session.

D maintained folded arms throughout the session. Spoke for three minutes during the session; defined laziness in response to a direct question; stated his preference for television, sports, and cars.

M participated freely in the group. Spoke for ten minutes: "In our place smoking is not accepted, but I've talked enough. Let someone else talk." "I disagree with his idea. I think there should be restraints." "Brains are drags. Me, I like social activities — not studying all the time." "People call me fat and I know I'm fat. So, I don't let it hurt me."

T the first one to give a verbal response in the group, spoke for thirty minutes of the hour session: ". . . the reason I underachieve in schoolwork is that I have thrown off all restraints and can do as I please."

S made twenty-three verbal responses during the session (asked for clarification of statements). Facial features appeared tense during the session, but no evidence of tenseness in tone of voice.

J responded for one minute near the end of the session: "I've been analyzing what's been going on here. I didn't know I was coming until about an hour ago."

B appeared unruffled in the group. When asked, "What do you think about this?" she responded with "I wasn't really listening" in a weak voice.

P, reserved, poised, and without emotion. Spoke briefly about "grading on a curve."

A, smiling, nodding, agreeable. All comments were brief: "Sometimes I think it is laziness that's keeping me back, sometimes I think it's another force that's in me which holds me back."

What happened to each member of the group during this first session? C withdrew within herself. This was the only session attended by C. Though she did return for a second session, she became ill before entering the room. D and B isolated themselves from the group but at a level which would not show any inner feelings.

T not only dominated the session but did so in such a way as to draw resentment against himself. The content of his discussion was varied and self-centered. The ideas presented were in no particular pattern, nor were the ideas interrelated. The listener was merely pulled through a wide variety of verbiage. When the discourse became personal by way of attacks on other members of the group, resentment was apparent.

M tried to find a place in the group by describing his mode of conduct. T took exception to everything M said and blasted M's adherence to traditional forms of behavior. Nevertheless, M continued to search for a niche for himself in the group.

S was deeply involved in the group process. She made constant attempts to find out more about what statements meant.

J followed the group process closely but hid his feelings until near the end of the session. His remarks brought forth an attack from T.

A was perhaps more involved in the group than any other student. Deep concern and thought was given to the area of underachievement and how this might be resolved.

The Second Group Counseling Session. Between the first and second sessions each student apparently discussed his reactions. Some changing patterns of behavior were evidenced in the second session a week later (see Fig. 12-2).

C, as the group was forming outside the office, asked to be excused because of illness and did not return for any more of the sessions.

D kept arms folded throughout the session and responded only to classmates M and J. Did not have eye contact with other members in the group. Relaxed near the end of the session.

M reacted only to the therapist and general discussion. "I have quite a few responsibilities. I don't choose them." "I don't think I've got a guilty feeling in me." "I don't have any problems at home, none that I know of."

T made thirty-two responses for a total time of fifteen minutes. "The first-period teacher hates me, so I withdraw by checking out and going downtown." "I go out and read poetry or write." "The worst thing is to get emotionally involved in home life." To the counselor, "You ask some wonderfully loaded questions. It's really good the way you do it. It's very good."

S responded to general questions only, hands tightly clenched. "I do enough [schoolwork] to get by. There are other things I would rather do. I like to get by myself and read."

J appeared quite tense during the entire session. "I really wasn't listening." "I was listening with one ear. The idea of a scientific and a creative mind is a bunch of baloney. One should be outstanding in all fields." "I can't stand loud noises. I go to pieces." "I'm interested in TV." "I like to share, but I like to be able to give and not be asked."

B appeared interested in the group but was quite casual. "Things at school, mostly grades, and things at home cause me to get upset."

P spoke a total of ten minutes during the session. She described her home life and its possible effects on schoolwork. "I want to stay away from home or just be with my mother and brother, and not the rest of the family."

A spoke for eleven minutes during the session, responded eighteen times. "People come up against big problems and they usually don't have a defeatist attitude. I am sometimes opti-

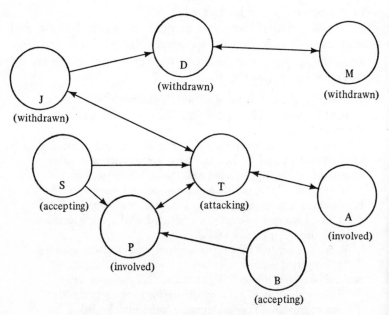

FIG. 12-2. *Session* 2. Terminology (see Session 1):
Accepting: Agreement or reinforcement of group opinion
Involved: Expression of personal feelings about what is
   being said.

mistic when faced with a big problem. I see my big problems as a challenge. My big problem was to be an American, to conform in a few ways. I spent six years in Africa."

The Third Group Counseling Session. In the third session (see Fig. 12-3) the counselor attempted to move the group forward by minimizing his contributions and turning absorbed attention to other's comments. C had now withdrawn from the group and D apparently had decided not to continue. It was reported that D's friends didn't think much of the counseling process.

M in the early part of the session stayed out of contact by bending his head forward and supporting it on his arms. Later he gave a brief reaction, "I will never go to Europe," then moved out of contact again.

T acquired a book during the session which he read and

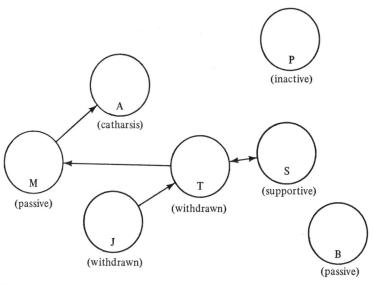

FIG. 12-3. *Session* 3. Terminology (see previous sessions):
Supportive: Agreeing with statements made by others
Passive: Acceptance of ideas without feeling
Inactive: No evidence of acceptance or rejection of ideas
Catharsis: Venting of deep personal feelings

reported on from time to time. Coughed repeatedly, noticeably more intensely when he was not talking. Discussed at length a proposed European tour and marriage.

S chewed gum throughout the session. "My grades have fallen off because I'm dissatisfied with myself and my parents."

J appeared physically uneasy during the session, twisting and turning. "I'd like to be able to give [responses in these sessions] but not be asked [questions]."

B: "I think I'd like to do it [go to Europe]. I've thought of it many times. I plan trips all the time I never go on. My parents stand in my way."

P apparently listened to what was going on in the group.

A: "I can usually face up to big problems; it's the little ones — the sustained tension that takes its toll." Parents are leaving for Africa: "I've known they were leaving for two years. I haven't seen them much during my lifetime. I want them to go back, especially since they thought they liked it so much out there. I'm quite dependent on my parents, financially more than anything; morally and socially, too."

The Fourth Group Counseling Session. The same students were present as at the previous session (see Fig. 12-4). The students tended to take different seats each week.

M sat as far out of the group as possible. "I just sit over here and boil about what he [T] said awhile ago."

T: No book to hide behind today; no coughing. He wrote poetry and drew pictures during the session. Out of the hour session, he spoke for twenty minutes.

S formed a subgroup with T. Wrote notes back and forth with T: "We were just being rude."

J laughed at P's story. Criticized by T for laughing; blamed "T's interpretation."

B interrupted constantly by T. "My reaction [to trying situations] is to shut myself off in my room and draw."

P cool and aloof at the beginning of the session. "I love her [mother] dearly, but she irritates me. She is trying to drive me out of my mind."

A said virtually nothing during the session. Appeared confident; voice was loud but without tension or anxiety. Seemed to prod the group into talking.

D stayed withdrawn from the group.

The fourth session saw a further movement in the group by members who had not been participating freely. The counselor made no attempt to be protective of anyone.

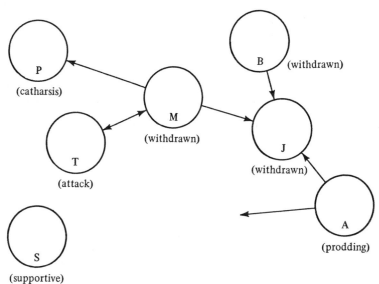

FIG. 12-4.   *Session 4.* Terminology (see previous sessions):
Prodding: Encouraging others to talk

The Fifth Group Counseling Session. The fifth session (see Fig. 12-5) occurred during the regular high school spring vacation. Five of the seven group members were in attendance.

T spoke for thirty minutes of the hour session. "I really feel fine, better than I've felt in quite a long time."

S appeared sleepy throughout the session.

J tried to participate in the group. "He [T] and I have traded characters."

B smiled mechanically throughout the session.

P appeared uncomfortable and tense. "I don't like to be laughed at" (reference to J at the fourth session).

S and B withdrew from the group.

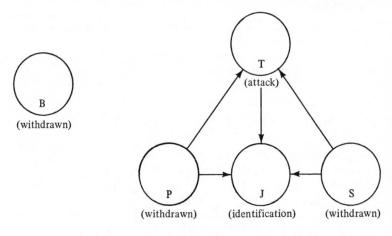

FIG. 12-5. *Session 5.* Terminology (see previous sessions):
Identification: Wanting to be accepted as a partner

The Sixth Group Counseling Session.   The sixth and final session
in this group counseling demonstration (see Fig. 12-6) opened with
a brief statement by the counselor that this was the last meeting.

T appeared serious and sincere. He spoke for twenty minutes
on various subjects.

S chewed gum throughout the session but did not yawn.
Spoke reluctantly and then only to direct questions. "My problems
are too personal to discuss, and I don't trust anyone with them.
Maybe I don't want to forget my problems. Maybe I want to
feel bad about myself."

J said on underachievement in high school, "If I don't do
it here, how can I ever do it in college?"

P responded only to direct questions. Further discussion of
mother: "Makes me feel like she wants me to feel sorry for her
so she can gain emotional release by crying."

A appeared calm and collected. "I am not worth others
giving time to."

Summary of Example.   The purpose of the example, taken from a
group counseling demonstration of sociometric recording, is to provide both verbal and physical representations of the interaction

patterns from session to session. It is important to let the participants see the sociograms to enhance feedback and change in their behavior.

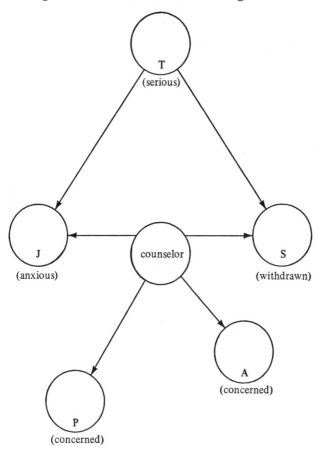

FIG. 12-6.   *Session 6.*

The Use of Group Power

TALENT AND WISDOM

Brim, Glass, Neulinger, and Firestone (1969) contend that we must go beyond the measure of intellectual abilities applied to academic pursuits in meeting the talent-identifying needs of a complex society. Much more is necessary than the primitive level of testing for intelligence and achievement. The measuring of attitudes, values, peer relationships, and motivational characteristics has been neglected. In view of the complexity of our society, discovering some means of identifying talents and encouraging their development through the application of knowledge already acquired must become a matter of concern for the counselor-consultant. Active talent search is augmented by active participation in an attempt to enhance the development of talents through teamwork.

Wisdom is generated through the systematic application of exising knowledge in the teamwork of a group of student personnel professionals; however, wisdom is not automatically acquired as a consequence of pooling the knowledge of the student personnel professionals. It stems rather from experience related to direct evaluation of specific endeavors over time — endeavors that have yielded the kinds of results desirable and necessary in the fully functioning student personnel program.

The counselor-consultant may establish his own talent center and create the opportunity for development of common wisdom among the members of the student personnel services group. The wisdom initially may be only the accumulation of shared experiences. However, over time the evaluation of experiences will result in the systematic identification of those aspects that can be classified as wisdom, a natural sequence in counseling.

Collective wisdom is a possibility in teams. Though there is no guarantee that the mere formation of teams will create wisdom, it does enhance the opportunities to gain access to both talent and wisdom.

DEFINITION OF COUNSELOR-CONSULTANT

The counselor is the only professional educator concerned primarily with the individual student's personal knowledge, or learning about his self (Kehas, 1969). Teachers are interested in teaching subject matter knowledge to the individual self. Other professionals, in social work, psychology, and medicine, for example, practice their respective professions in connection with the school without becoming involved with the classroom teaching-learning situation. The teacher works with *established* knowledge. The counselor works *to establish* knowledge. Though the shared concern is instruction, the sources, content, and methods are different. The ideal goal for counseling, like education, is to "know thyself." The development of the individual's intelligence about his self is the purpose of counseling.

Why is consulting needed? Why not concentrate the counselor's efforts on the central purpose of counseling? The answers are complex. Americans have never managed to close the gap between what is known and what gets done. Regretfully, this is still very much the case in education. Schooling is only one institutionalized part of education. It is primarily concerned with teaching subject matter and perhaps secondarily concerned with the individual. Consulting is a strategy and a method for equalizing the instrumental effort.

Consulting seems to promise an alternative means for counselors to encounter the teacher, parent, administrator, and student, in a way designed to achieve closure of the gap between teaching and individual personal learning. If the counselor succeeds in creating a team of collaborating professionals, parents, and students, it may be possible to tackle the central purpose of counseling. Consequently, consulting is the strategy for active and aggressive counselor behavior in a profession characterized in the 1960's as passive, receptive, and ancillary (Kehas, 1969). The 1970's should see a renaissance in counseling practice because of increasing recognition of the need for individual human relations skills (see Chapter Two). The social-personal process in education means two things. First, the content of established knowledge is external to the individual and is transferred to him by teaching; teaching is the central purpose of schooling (Kehas, 1969). Second, the person of the learner is the content of personal-social knowledge and is internal and unique to *each* individual; this second area is the concern of counseling. In Chapter Two, Bruner, Maslow, Rogers, and Combs are cited as examples of contemporary leaders who have emphasized both person and process in effective learning. Whenever learning is the subject, the person of the learner has number one priority. Whenever teaching is the subject, the content of established knowledge has higher priority than learning. Learning is quite different from teaching. Traditional literature on schooling focuses upon the situation created when *teaching-learning* is considered as a unit. The teaching-learning "situation," really a third phenomenon created by the two units, is a fiction. Teaching exists, and learning exists; the *situation* is something else.

The pedantic nature of the above is essential to the idea of consulting. The counselor is an agent of change only insofar as he influences the quality of learning. The interventions necessary to carry on the active-aggressive counseling role are the responsibility of the professional counselor-consultant.

COUNSELOR EDUCATION FOR CONSULTATION

Consulting is limited by the counselor's level of sophistication. The counselor practices the services he can perform well and often diminishes or downgrades those he has limited skills to provide (Bernard and Fullmer, 1969). The professional counselor-consultant is the only practitioner qualified to handle the consulting function. His preparation will entail at least two years of full-time graduate study in a program which will need to be of recent origin. Continuous renewal of the program is also essential because the rate of obsolescence is accelerating. In the concern for continuity and stability in counselor-consultant preparation programs, speed is a problem. The changes come fast (Carey, 1969).

If the full-time graduate student completes a two-year program in three or more years, there may be a problem because of new concepts. Doctoral candidates rarely complete a program in less than three years. The only answer seems to be in continuous self-renewal, as discussed in Chapter Two. Some recently developed programs have built in a provision for emphasizing self-renewal. At the University of Hawaii, the process is tied in with supervision of counselors and counselor educators. It is a team model designed to do two things: (1) A small group is created and maintained for each counselor-consultant; (2) the counselor-consultant always arranges to be supervised by others. Supervision provides feedback for evaluation and learning. Renewal is a consequence of continuous exposure to supervision. The range and frequency of exposures to new or standard practice in counseling and consulting will define the areas of competence the professional is maintaining (Fullmer, 1969c).

Current practice in school counseling falls short of public expectations for the counseling profession (Pearl, 1969). Counseling and guidance functions are expanded in this text to include consultation, which as carried on by a professional counselor represents an interim stage in the development of a new kind of professional practitioner. Rogers (1968) projects that the eventual development will lead to the creation of a new professional role for the teacher. The teacher will evolve into a facilitator, a type of learning resources expert who manages a team of professionals, paraprofessionals, technicians, and learners. Whatever the future may bring, the counselor-consultant function is the new model for the professional counselor in the 1970's. History will decide whether the counselor-consultant is the forerunner of anything or merely an intelligent response to the needs of the school and students in a change-saturated moment. The assumptions implied by the above statements may be considered controversial in terms of the more traditional premises on which American schooling is based. The following lists of assumptions are intended to show the nature of relationships underlying the key differences between counseling and teaching.

Assumptions About the Present Structure of Education

EXPLICIT

1. Education is equated with teaching.
2. The basic concern is with the teaching-learning situation (external knowledge).
3. The only relationship of any major consequence is that of teacher to student.

IMPLICIT

4. There is only one type of educator in the schools — teacher. Other professions are kept out of school or allowed circumscribed access in limited ways (Kehas, 1969, p. 68).

Proposed Counseling Assumptions

EXPLICIT

1. Counseling is learning about one's self.
2. Personal knowledge of self is the primary concern (personal IQ).
3. Primary relationship is that of counselor to counselee.
4. Education is counseling, learning, and teaching.

IMPLICIT

5. No other educator is concerned primarily with the individual's personal IQ learning (the teacher is concerned with teaching subject matter — external knowledge).

6. The goal of counseling, individual or group, is to help the student examine the meanings he experiences in his world — indeed, the world and experiences he creates for himself (Kehas, 1969, p. 62).

THE SOCIOLOGY OF ASSUMPTIONS

Counseling, teaching, learning, and instruction — each has been established within professional theory and practice, especially in regard to the school. All of these processes are expected to be an integral part of the school, which is a social system as well as a social institution. All practitioners in the schooling model may be characterized as "captive" within the parameters of the system. The claim here is merely that at present teaching is paramount in the priority system, all other professional specialties being considered supportive, ancillary, or collaborative.

NEW DIRECTION

We can no longer safely ignore the structure, context, or environment of our counseling profession. We should not ignore the necessity of educating the counselor thoroughly in the skills and techniques of developing the consultation model as a step toward creation of a new teacher role. In the role of educational manager the teacher will deal with people in much the same way a coach deals with a team or a drama troupe, i.e., as a leader whose expertise lies in the exposure of the talents of others who possess special skills. This facilitator may have no other special skill of his own.

Study of the ecology of students (Danskin, Kennedy, and Friesen, 1965) may be a way to enhance the learning climate in the classroom. Family consultation is one way of influencing the student's home and community environments (Bernard and Fullmer, 1969). Krumboltz and Thoresen (1969) think behavior modification methods will help students.

New direction is necessary to reconstruct the interpersonal relationships system within the classroom and school so that the student may retain the emphasis on humanizing his education and at the same time be exposed to the newer technologies applied to his subject matter instruction.

Although similar in the processes used to accomplish each, instruction and counseling are defined as entirely separate functions. *In-*

struction means any activity in which there are specific goals and specific subject matter content to be learned by the youngster. *Counseling* is that process which is engaged in to determine (1) what the goals might be, and (2) what the subject matter may become. Instruction, then, is used when we know what we want to teach and have a way of knowing when we have taught it. Counseling with other persons is used when it is not known, in any specific case, what the goals are or the content should be. When counseling has determined what the goals and content of personal-social character development should be, instruction follows in natural sequence. The differentiation of instruction and counseling allows for a sequencing of learning theories and learning principles to accompany instruction rather than being a part of the initial counseling process. Counseling and instruction are based on entirely different sets of theories. These distinctions must be clearly stated and kept in mind in reading the material concerning the new role of the teacher in Chapter Fourteen.

The consultation process is exemplified in the idea of the community talent center, where people come together to do specific tasks, including defining problems and concerns and planning actions which may become the innovations of the future. One of these innovations is the development of talent.

Another idea is to fashion a whole instructional program using consultation methods and counseling group processes in the fostering of job search techniques. Creating opportunities is perhaps one of the major learning areas for the counseling-consulting professional, as he works through the use of group processes, especially through teams.

In initiating the consultant process, one must recognize the polarity in behavior represented by the urge to grow and the urge for stability. This implies that the consultant must seek the counselee, whether he is a teacher, a pupil, a parent, or an administrator, instead of waiting for the counselee to seek counseling. The traditional wisdom of the 1960's is no longer valid. The old cliché: One can be helped only if he seeks help, is repudiated by the consultant who admits the existence of the polarity of homeostasis and heterostasis. The important factor is rapport; personal feelings are understood, shared, and respected. This, in turn, means listening. The respect of listening provides an avenue to developing involvement of counselees, to building self-reliance and accepting cooperative responsibility.

TEAM MEMBERS

The team members consist of supervisors, consultants, psychologists, parents, and administrators, who by serving on the team augment the counselor's functions as consultant, in terms of the assumptions listed above. The Kehas (1969) model is particularly well suited to communicating to the reader the central idea in counselor consultation.

Involvement comes from committing oneself to a specific task. When the task is shared by others significant to the achievement of the goals of the enterprise, the expectations come from the group and are met because of the social pressure to gain respect. The motivation for each participant is a part of the expectation held for each other member. A team is a special kind of group whose purpose is task oriented. It may consist of the counselor-consultant and one other significant person from the professional groups listed above, or it may consist of representatives of all the professions concerned with the problem of the moment. Teams may be formed for brief periods of time and then disbanded, or they may be formed for continuing periods of time, changing members as necessary. However, the counselor-consultant works most often with teachers, supervisors, and psychologists, and occasionally with parents, administrators, and other consultants, depending upon the particular array of complex variables operating in the school situation.

Activating Consultation Processes

TEACHER-INITIATED CONSULTATION

Teachers most frequently initiate counselor-consultant contacts when something goes wrong in the intellectual functioning of a child or when social control factors are jeopardized in the classroom. When the teacher becomes aware of ambiguous or somehow disturbing events, there may be a referral. Rarely, if ever, does the teacher make a referral to the counselor-consultant that is not of the remedial or corrective type. It should be noted that all testing program materials, consisting of individual achievement profiles in each subject area for each child in each classroom, are available routinely to the teacher, as are individual and/or group intelligence test scores. However, beyond these general measures of intellectual health little information finds its way routinely into the hands of the teacher as a part of a growth and development emphasis. The counselor-consultant can take the action necessary to alert the teacher before crises arise.

COUNSELOR-INITIATED CONSULTATION

The counselor-consultant encounters each teacher in her classroom. During this encounter it is established that the counselor will actively seek the participation of the teacher as a member of the team of specialists, parents, and administrators concerned with improving the learning environment of the school. One of the significant aspects of the counselor-consultant function is the conducting of professional services in the classroom with teacher and pupils present. Whether the counselor is working with one child, a small group of children, or the teacher in relation to a given child, everyone in the classroom shares in the experience, which may benefit all those concerned. This general statement is an example of how the counselor-consultant strives to affect the structure and the context of the classsroom environment.

The ecology of the student and the teacher is part of the central concern in consulting, as mentioned earlier in this chapter. The counselor may also wish to utilize methods of modifying environments that have come out of recent developments in clinical sociology, behavior modification and operant conditioning, and cultural milieu planning (Lennard and Bernstein, 1969; Krumboltz and Thoresen, 1969).

The counselor-consultant gets involved with parents and families according to the nature of his preparation. More than ten years have been devoted to the development of family consultation in groups, which has been found particularly useful in the prevention of some developmental problems. However, schools usually follow the traditional pattern of utilizing the counselor in a corrective and remedial mode. The goal of family group consultation is to reshape the relationships existing among significant family members and thus effect changes in the environment of the student. Family group consultation is a method of altering the cultural milieu through the social system of the family group.

Consultation Initiated by Others

Almost anyone connected with a school setting can initiate a consultation relationship. It is simply a matter of calling together a number of persons whose concerns and expertise place them in the position of offering assistance in resolving certain problems and/or forming a training milieu for the development of personal IQ. The level of an individual's personal intelligence about his own self, whether he is a team member or a student, is included in the model for counselor-consultant teams. The regularized approach to forming teams of consultants and other significant specialists within the school may take the form of a continuing institute of studies made up of individual team members and/or students and parents. Students and parents constitute a special category simply because of the numbers of persons involved in a particular school. The counselor-consultant may begin by organizing the professional staff into ongoing teams for conducting the several activities to achieve the above-mentioned purposes.

Supervisors and administrators may be included as team members in the consultation process. Because of the time commitment of professional people it is essential that the counselor-consultant set up the most efficient and effective possible schedules. Small groups that function as encounter groups or sensitivity and awareness training groups are in a special category and are not included in this type of operation. However, the counselor-consultant may wish to utilize the encounter group method as part of the program initiated under the continuing institute for staff development.

Whether the counselor-consultant works in an individual one-to-one relationship or as a coordinator of groups, the purpose in consultation is the same. The idea is to go beyond the interpersonal relationship and affect the environment in positive ways that will result in improved personal IQ's of those connected with the enterprise. It is assumed that if the counseling-consulting program could operate efficiently and effectively in the above model, it would enhance the instructional tasks and improve teaching also.

The essence of the counselor-consultant process is to define a strategy leading to the creation of a model of human organization in which each person is engaged in business for himself at the same time that he is involved with others to heighten the total effect of the enterprise.

INITIATING THE CONSULTANT PROCESS

The consultant process is characterized by active seeking on the part of the counselor as, going beyond the interpersonal relationship in the traditional counseling model, he performs some action which has a direct impact upon the environment of another person. Such action, whether or not it is successful, may result in a high level of rapport with that person. This is in sharp contrast to traditional counseling, in which rapport must precede any significant action taken within the counseling relationship.

DECISION MAKING: THE TEAM

The team is the effective agent in the consultation process. Decision making is central to all group action, but it requires rules which regulate the interaction of the members of the team. The counselor-consultant will establish these with each team and see that they are derived from the membership. No imposed rules from an external source will in any way serve to enhance the operation of the team. On the contrary, the members will resent being coerced by external forces. Decision making is a matter of group interaction and can be regarded as one of the major formulas in the life of a group.

ACTION: TREATMENT

All treatment is a result of action. The action to be taken does not follow, nor is it restricted to, the traditional formula for counseling. In order to initiate the consultant relationship it is necessary to establish its credibility. The counselor-consultant will do this most effectively by actually involving himself with a team and undertaking a specific task related to improving the personal knowledge of an individual student, teacher, administrator, parent, or other significant person in the school milieu.

The counselor-consultant must possess the personal characteristics considered desirable in the professional practitioner. He should be ascendant rather than submissive. The emotional climate he establishes is essentially the same as in any other group work. He must be open, firm, flexible, and competent. His confidence is antecedent to his credibility. He must be able to elicit and maintain respect at the level at which a counselor maintains rapport if he is to function at all. Any compromise with the quality of personal-social encounter will transform the consulting process to something else. This is no job for a weak and dependent milquetoast type. The counselor-consultant is hard-nosed like any professional.

Summary

Teamwork in student personnel services is a major concern for the counselor-consultant. In the 1970's and beyond, education will broaden its expectations of counseling to include consulting (Ferguson, 1968). The consultant studies process by observation and systematic data taking. Sociometry offers a technique useful for objectifying data usually identified as subjective. The group or team interaction patterns can be described in detail to reveal the pattern within the interaction process. The professional counselor-consultant will have the necessary skills to deliver the consulting services indicated above.

Wisdom is essential for successful consulting, and the source of wisdom is other people. The counselor-consultant maintains a talent pool consisting of persons with widely divergent talents engaged in different primary tasks within the school and in the community. A community talent center may be instituted through the leadership of the counselor-consultant. Such a center will generate a continuing supply of talent but will not guarantee wisdom.

The counselor-consultant role and responsibility are closely tied to the action model for counseling in groups. The consultant helps clarify the issues in any controversial area and encourages the release of emotional pressures through open verbal and nonverbal expression. He must reestablish and/or maintain a healthy psychosocial climate for team members where they can organize and encounter at their own level of functioning. The consultant is frequently the communications linkup within otherwise divergent areas in the organization.

Team members involved in consultation include teachers, supervisors, consultants, psychologists, social workers, parents, administrators, and, in some cases, students. Services performed by the consultant and team should enhance development of self-reliance and cooperative responsibility as contrasted with dependency.

Initiating the consulting process has been and is the major problem for the counselor-consultant. He must begin on a small scale with one other person and build his competence and extend his confidence. This active seeking behavior (consultation) leads inevitably to direct intervention. Here we see the need for rapport as a consequence of action. Before, the counselee knew nothing of the counselor-consultant's action; the action brought new awareness. The traditional counseling model relied upon rapport as an antecedent to action. Consulting may be the reverse because rapport frequently follows the consultant's action.

Treatment is the result of decisions made within the consulting team. The treatment is the action taken to effect change in the learning environment.

SUGGESTED ADDITIONAL READINGS

Bjerg, Kresten, 1968. "Interplay-Analysis: A Preliminary Report on an Approach to the Problems of Interpersonal Understanding," *Acta Psychologica*, 28(3):201–243. *Bjerg presents a classification system for interaction. He uses the term* agon *to depict the social interaction context within which resources are used. He then relates this to specific types of interaction and their products (power, love, esteem, reproach, pleasing, entertainment, etc.). His conceptualization is intended to clarify descriptions of complex human interaction.*

Corrigan, Dean, 1969. "Educational Personnel Development: What's Ahead," *Journal of Research and Development in Education*, 2(3):3–11, Spring. *Present plans for education of personnel necessitate long-range assessment of the future world. Corrigan identifies some changes that will take place and their probable influence on training of education personnel. Explosion of knowledge and the growing emphasis of human interaction will greatly affect the form of the future's educational program. Technology will influence the process of education, especially as regards the use of systems analysis and cybernetics. Creativity will be a must in one's work. Education will need to teach people how to be comfortable and deal with complexity and change.* Continuing education *and more emphasis on the* process *of learning will be crucial. Man's sense of importance rests less on the kind of work he does than on the* kind of life he leads. *Education will help people to develop and clarify their values and focus on personal feelings.*

Kehas, C. D., 1969. "Toward a Redefinition of Education: A New Framework for Counseling in Education," in S. C. Stone and B. Shertzer (eds.), *Introduction to Guidance: Selected Readings.* Boston: Houghton Mifflin Company. Pp. 59–71. *The major issue is to bring learning about personal-social development of each individual to equal status with academic subject matter learning. This is a refinement on the theme that process is more important than content, because process is learning to learn and content is concerned with teaching. In an era of rapid change, continuous learning is necessary. The primary priority is development of personal meaning in each individual's life.*

Miller, Norman, 1969. "The Ineffectiveness of Punishment Power in Group Interaction," *Sociometry,* 32(1):24–41, March. *Individuals rely on their ability to bestow reward and inflict punishment in order to influence others. Miller's study looks at effectiveness of social (reward, punishment) power in group interaction. He found that those with greatest social power bestowed rewards rather than inflicting punishments. Those with the greatest reward power are most likely to receive rewards in turn.*

Newsweek, 1969. "The Group: Joy on Thursday," 91:104–106, May 12. Newsweek *describes some of the more sensational aspects of the group movement along with its rationale, according to Maslow, Bindrim, Sampson, Sager, and others.*

Chapter Thirteen

EVALUATION OF

EDUCATIONAL PROCESSES

A number of years ago Paul Woodring wrote a book called *A Fourth of a Nation* (1957). The title indicated that 25 percent of the population of the United States was engaged in the business of education — as pupil, teacher, or administrator and supporting staff. The baby boom of the 1940's had not yet swelled school enrollments at the time Woodring's book was published. Today, with the median age of the population established at twenty-five years (and the average at 27.7 years), and with the increasing popularity of education, it is probable that an even larger portion of the population is concerned with formal schooling.

Larger school populations and rising demands — e.g., for early childhood education, community schools (in which parents may enroll), and part-time classes — mean higher costs, which are vigorously protested, particularly during a period of inflation. The costs of education are so visible — higher tax bills or increased tuition costs — that finances are a source of constant criticism. The question usually is "What are we getting for our money?" In the wake of repeated defeats of school funding issues at the polls in recent years, educators have begun to be concerned with proving their worth. There is talk about such things as responsibility and accountability. There is talk about measuring the outcomes of education. There is talk about assessing the intangible aspects of education. It has long been assumed that education was "good" for one. Now some critics of education such as Paul Goodman, Jonathan Kozol, John Holt, and Edgar Z. Friedenberg have voiced doubts about just how good for the individual present educational processes are — and whether education has sufficient viability to make the changes necessary for survival.

Counselors for the 1970's will inevitably face the issues of the controversial purposes of schools. Will evaluation of schools be in terms of whether they meet the needs of students, or in terms of whether the student "fits" the school? Obviously, the latter policy, despite teacher protestations, is predominately in effect in educational institutions from nursery school to graduate university level. Major efforts at compensatory education to make the children of the poor fit the school have largely failed, according to Arthur Jensen and to James Coleman (testifying before the Labor-Education Committee of the U.S. Senate on May 13, 1970). The counselor-consultant will need to evaluate the forces in the school which are making it unusable for such a large percentage of students currently enrolled or currently alienated.

An approach to the resolution of some of these problems lies in the purposes and techniques of evaluation. We do not presume to have the necessary answers for the many issues involved. We do feel that the counselor-consultant, whose work involves the personal view, the present milieu, and the proactive aspects of behavior, has special concerns and responsibilities for rather unique involvement in matters of evaluation.

Purposes of Evaluation

Conventional Functions of Evaluation

Within the contemporary school milieu there is considerable criticism of the use of intelligence tests, achievement tests, personality questionnaires and inventories, and of that part of evaluation which most intimately affects the pupil — the grading system. Heated debates and much acrimony result from various interpretations of the merit of tests and the purposes of evaluation. Most persons would immediately think of evaluation in terms of pupils' achievement in academic skills and knowledge. Evaluation in terms of scores to be recorded in a pupil's permanent record or submitted to a college registrar or prospective employer makes the process a terminal activity and therefore renders it dubious in the eyes of those who are concerned about student welfare rather than the convenience of employers and admissions officers. Yet the former, in practice, is the function of much evaluation activity. Theoretically, at least, evaluation also includes the comparative effectiveness of teachers, curricula, and school systems. Evaluation which is a part of guidance, counseling, and the individualization of instruction comes closer to the essential purposes of education. In this case it aims to assess pupil strengths as well as weaknesses so that decisions, at least tentative ones, can be made about what pupils and school personnel should do next. It is a matter of discovering latent talent which might warrant cultivation. If the talent appears to have no immediate commercial value, it still might serve as reason for recognition by others and thus make for a healthy ego concept.

In schools of the 1970's the major function of evaluation is to facilitate and maximize the processes of learning. Having learned this, where does one go next? Why is it difficult for Gordie to learn this particular arithmetic problem? What emotions are getting in the way of Tom's gaining an appreciation of literature? What is Christine learning about herself? What sparks a little more interest in Randy than usual? What enthusiastic interests does Burt have that could be used to develop the skills this class seeks to develop — writing, computation, research, history, social living? What makes Jack sullen when an assignment is made? What sets off Mike's always ready belligerent mechanisms? When a teacher has learned to view behavior and misbehavior as phenomena to be understood, he is conducting evaluation — an activity which is part and parcel of instructional and learning processes. When teachers seek to find the best "next steps," they are using evaluation in a professional manner.

Thus the real functions of evaluation are to encourage and facilitate the processes and habits of continuous learning. These are the matters that can and should be the basis of communication between home and school. Final grades, reports to parents of relative rank, achievement of comparative standards, college admissions, and the providing of school marks to prospective employers are really secondary. The question must be asked, and frequently asked, because of conventional practices: "Is the school made for the pupil or is the pupil made for the school?" None will debate the correct answer, ethically or morally. *But* there will be many "Yes, but's . . ." in the staff meetings which are held to formulate better evaluation practices.

THE PURPOSES OF EDUCATION

The purposes of education have been periodically defined in formal statements, the best-known of which is probably the "Seven Cardinal Principles of Secondary Education." There have been statements of the aims of elementary education. The Educational Policies Commission of the National Education Association (1939) listed the aims of education under four major headings, each with eight to twelve subheads. The aims may have been quite suitable in a society which changed slowly and in which curricula could prepare people for a somewhat predictable future. Evaluation that demanded measurable achievements had merit in school systems committed to sorting and classifying pupils. In a technological society in which the unskilled and uneducated person is a liability to himself and society, education must serve all pupils rather than sorting them. The sorting function has declined in the last half-century, but it still exists, and the evaluative techniques persist despite changes in school purposes. For example, although intelligence tests are fair measures of intellectual ability, they do not probe artistic, musical, social, or leadership abilities (Havighurst and Neugarten, 1967, pp. 71–73).

In a society marked by an accelerated rate of already rapid change, the emphasis in education and evaluation must shift from mastery of content to the processes of learning. Evaluation must turn from exclusively academic achievement to embrace interest in, and the habit of, continuous learning. This does not need to mean that pupils will study only things which are of interest to them or that academic achievement is of no consideration. It means that evaluation, rather than being a terminal activity, will have to emphasize the development of intrinsic motives — self-confidence, feelings of worth, respect for one's own uniqueness — which will stimulate continuous learning *after* the grade has been passed, the certificate received, the diploma tucked away (Miller, 1967, p. 23).

Evaluation and Measurement

MEASUREMENT

Existing tools for "measurement" are such that only a few aspects of the human individual can be measured. We can weigh the pupil, tell how tall he is or how fast he can run a hundred yards, and record his brain waves on an electroencephalograph. His intelligence, his motivation, his honesty, his social orientation, his personality — these cannot be measured, yet they may have much more to do with his humanity than height, weight, speed of reflex, or blood pressure. We are still trying to figure out what those brain waves mean in terms of behavior.

In the process of trying to make living, and education, and psychology, and learning more scientific, more predictable, and hence, we hope, more effective, various aspects of behavior have been tentatively quantified. IQ, mental age, basal metabolism, blood pressure, corpuscle count, percentile rank, age-grade equivalents, standard scores (and standard errors), and coefficients of correlation have supplied a statistical confirmation which seems to be reassuring to some researchers. To the skeptical, probable errors and coefficients of correlation do not mean much if the instrument for the original measurement was unreliable or does not sample widely enough the function being evaluated. Measurement is, for example, an inadequate approach when it comes to ambition, love, and self-realization.

EVALUATION

Evaluation means to judge the worth, to "put a price on." The amount of money it took to build a house is not an evaluation of the market value of that house. If it is built over a thermal spring and heated from subterranean sources, it may be a case of "It's not the original cost, it's the upkeep." A whole town in a desert area where there was once a gold rush may be purchased at a fraction of the cost of a single lot with no house on the coast of Kona.

It has been demonstrated repeatedly that even if IQ were considered to be a measurement (which it is not by many people) it does not tell how one now behaves or predict how one will perform, academically or in any other area, in the future. Strauss (1969, p. 127) has presented a study of eighty-nine Ph.D.'s in science and mathematics at Cornell and the Universities of California and Ohio. He found that 3 percent of them had IQ's of less than 100 while in high school; 6 percent had IQ's between 101 and 110, and 29 percent had IQ's between 111 and 120. Thus, over a third of the Ph.D.'s in this study had IQ's while in high school that seemed to be barely high enough for "respectable high school work of the traditional kind." Strauss indicates the role of evaluation as contrasted to measurement in some remarks about the early education of the Ph.D.'s-to-be. In effect he says, the personal interest, the faith and confidence in these boys expressed by some elementary, high school, or college instructor made a deep impression and constituted a driving force.

Almost every teacher has at some time or other doubted the validity of a test score because it did not accord with the way pupils achieved. Two pupils with the same score on a test of intelligence — let us say the Stanford-Binet — do not, and should not be expected to, perform the same in their English and mathematics classes. Among other reasons, the components, or subdivisions, of intelligence may be quite different in the two persons with apparently equivalent scores, as is well illustrated in the several "multi-factor" tests which have appeared on the educational market in the last couple of decades. The profile of test scores of a student is shown in Figure 13-1. It demonstrates a phenomenon which is too little appreciated by parents and teachers. We have always known that pupils differed from one another. It has not been so thoroughly perceived that pupils also differ from themselves, *intellectually*. In Figure 13-1, for example, Rocky is at about the fiftieth percentile on the verbal reasoning test. From test data, his performance in interpreting written messages would be expected to be average. However, his numerical aptitude score shows he is at the ninety-ninth percentile and, again basing predictions on the aptitude test scores, we would expect him to do outstanding work. He *should* be able to perform in the upper 5 percent of students like those on whom the test was standardized.

Because there is so much disparity between what a test score suggests and what teachers perceive, some teachers have become skeptical and others downright hostile. The latter feel that test results so becloud the expectancy picture that scores do more harm than good. They, along with uninformed lay citizens, are in favor of discarding the whole system of tests. One who has an individualistic and humanistic orientation is tempted to join those in favor of the tossing out. However, tests (and measurements) can become a part of processes of evaluation.

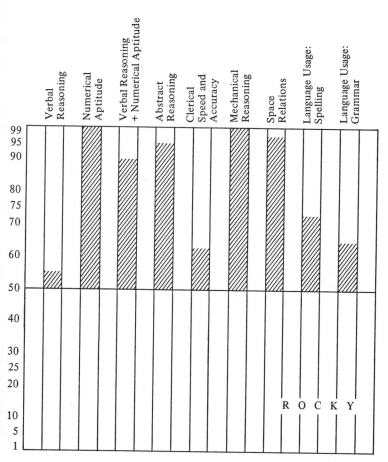

FIG. 13-1. *Profile of test scores on the Differential Aptitude Test. From Harold G. Seashore, 1963, "The Identification of the Gifted,"* Test Service Bulletin, No. 55. *New York: The Psychological Corporation.*

CREATING THE MEASUREMENT-EVALUATION TEAM

Lip service is paid to processes of evaluation, yet most textbooks on evaluation deal with tests, statistics, and standardized scores. They repeatedly admonish that the results are to be used with due caution and as supplementary information, but little time is spent on matters of informal observation, interviews, anecdotal records, sociometry, dynamics of small groups, socioeconomic class, peer group influences, and teacher-pupil transactions.

Models of what good evaluation practice might look like are almost nonexistent. Even the so-called professionals, i.e., the consultants on evaluation, have failed to provide adequate help (witness the section on evaluation of any federal program guidelines), and they have not been able to design evaluations which will meet their own standards of excellence. When evaluations are conducted they typically result in findings of "no significant difference," a conclusion often sharply at variance with the perceptions of the participants or even of outside observers. We have so far failed to evolve a pervasive theory of evaluation that can cope with these problems and which is backed by useful instruments and designs. Finally, we have been unable to find a way to train the personnel necessary to these tasks.

At another level of analysis we may say that contemporary evaluation practice and theory suffer from several severe deficiencies. There is, first of all, the unreasoning emphasis on measurement. Indeed, in many instances evaluation is defined as equivalent to measurement, and an evaluation program is reduced to one of finding appropriate measures. Kaplan has warned us of the law of the hammer, viz., give a small boy a hammer and he will find that everything needs pounding (Kaplan, 1964, p. 28). Within the rubric the only things that are worth measuring are those for which measures exist; everything else is intangible and hence not worth evaluating. The fact that many variables which have recently come to be of prime importance to educationists (e.g., social consciousness, cultural differences, disadvantaged learning) easily qualify as intangibles has not eased the situation.[1]

[1] Egon G. Guba and John J. Horvat, 1970, "Evaluation During Development," *Viewpoints,* Bulletin of the School of Education, Indiana University, 46(2):22–23, March. Reprinted by permission of the publisher.

The ideas expressed by Guba and Horvat — overdependence on *measures* and the value of intangibles — have not become an educational trend. It is suggested herewith that the counselor-consultant develop, with concerned staff members, a plan for the use of measurement in a system for *continuous* evaluation which would have the purpose of stimulating optimum learning from day to day. This would be in sharp contrast to the use of measurement as a terminal device determining one's place in the permanent record and the graduating class and his chances in the files of the college admissions office.

MORE TESTS

Perhaps it would be wise to use more tests instead of being increasingly selective of those which are used. The proposition is that the more devices and approaches used for studying the individual, with all his complexities, the more conscious we will become of his uniqueness. The greater will be the chance of discovering some distinct talent that will be worth cultivating — and that will therefore become a lens for magnifying his feeling of significance. A little stimulus is provided for moving from safety and love needs to the levels of esteem and self-actualization needs.

One exciting stimulus to the use of more tests is provided by Guilford (1967) in his theory of the structure of intelligence. His studies over the years, with particular emphasis on the many facets of creativity, led him to postulate that there were at least 120 different kinds of intelligence. The theory is conceptualized as a sort of periodic table of intelligence — which may lead to the directed search for specific kinds of intellectual functioning. He suggests that there are three major categories of intelligence: *Content* has four subdivisions, *operations* has five subdivisions, and *products* has six subdivisions. Multiplied together in their interactive processes, these result in a possibility of 120 factors (4 × 5 × 6) in intelligence (Fig. 13-2). Many of the factors had been identified prior to Guilford's postulation, but more have been discovered since. Even the multi-factor tests which are used in schools probe only about a dozen intellectual factors. Many intelligence tests lump all aspects of intelligence together in what is called a global score. This single score is about as effective in terms of understanding an individual as it would be to take a high-powered rifle and shoot in the general direction of a bear. The effectiveness of the general approach is indicated by the burdens which are placed on pupils by global scores — and by the effectiveness of a hunter who shoots at the flock of quail instead of aiming at one.

Of the theoretically possible 120 factors of intelligence, about eighty had been discovered up to 1967, when Guilford's theory

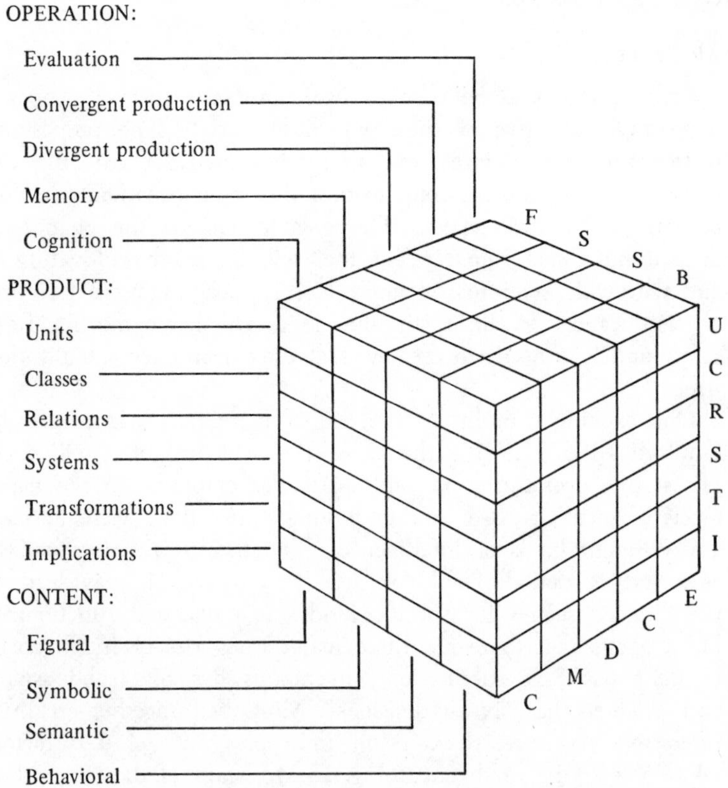

OPERATION:

Evaluation
Convergent production
Divergent production
Memory
Cognition

PRODUCT:

Units
Classes
Relations
Systems
Transformations
Implications

CONTENT:

Figural
Symbolic
Semantic
Behavioral

FIG. 13-2. *The structure-of-intellect model, with three parameters (other parameters may need to be added). From* The Nature of Human Intelligence *by J. P. Guilford. Copyright 1967 by McGraw-Hill Book Company. P. 63. Used with permission of McGraw-Hill Book Company.*

was published. Thus, it would appear to be feasible to test about two-thirds of intellectual potential; in school practice (with multifactor tests probing only about a dozen intellectual functions), one-tenth of the total is probed. And, as noted previously, one test score sometimes represents all 120 factors.

A hint of the potentialities of this scheme is given in the publications of Getzels and Jackson (1962) and Torrance (1962) with their interest in and suggestions on the phenomenon of creativity and the contrasts between convergent and divergent thinking (see the second and third factors under "Operations" in Fig. 13-2). Authorities in the field of creativity have been calling attention for a long time to the fact that high global intelligence is not synonymous with creativity — creativity may be a concomitant of high or average intelligence. This single emphasis on creativity may indicate some of the future value and implications of using many more tests. This would mean probing more latent talents, recognizing diversity, and giving more than lip service to the concept of individual differences.

Taylor (1968b) asserts that identifying numerous talents is a new way to reach the culturally different pupil. However, it seems that the implications go much farther. This is an approach to more effective ways to motivate the many pupils who do no more than "get by" in obediently, but indifferently, meeting minimum requirements for academic progress. In addition, there are many pupils, advantaged as well as disadvantaged, who will simply not acquiesce in what they regard as useless routines and exercises. As noted in Chapter One, Taylor has shown that virtually all pupils will be above average in some category if as many as eight quite unrelated talents are tested.

> These calculations yield a beatuiful phenomenon and a most promising picture for educators: Not only do new star performers emerge from almost all levels of the previous talent ladder, but those who had not been flourishing in the old talent areas will rise toward the middle of their class in each new talent area in turn. Moreover, nearly all students will have the rewarding experience of being above average in one or another talent area if we cultivate enough different talents in the classroom. In addition, about a third of the students will be found to be highly gifted in at least one major talent area.

This is a very heartening outlook in terms of motivation of students and the potential in our human resources. The subgroup heretofore classified as educationally deprived will almost approach an average group in a new gifted area, and individually they will spread widely up and down this new type of gifted ladder — certainly not highly concentrated at the bottom. A third or more of them will tend to be above average, and a somewhat different third of them will be above average, and a somewhat different third of them will be above average in each new area of giftedness focused upon.

The implications of this phenomenon are exciting because, if a variety of talents are tested and trained for, a student can learn a great deal about himself and his abilities and consequently become self-directed. He can steer himself throughout his life into activities that call for his best talents — a course that can well lead to optimum self-actualization and productivity.[2]

Taylor's contentions seem to be supported by Seashore. In connection with Figure 13-1, which shows Rocky's test profile on the Differential Aptitude Test, he says, "If we could convince someone that Rocky is talented, really gifted, somebody might latch on to his best talents and make them a motivating force for upgrading even his lagging language skills."[3] Fantini (1970) makes a similar plea in asking for emphasis on diversity rather than sameness.

More tests are needed in daily teaching — more achievement tests, diagnostic tests, survey tests — if instruction is to be individualized and the pupil is to have reading, social studies, and arithmetic books appropriate to his level of development. Corey (1970) states that the first month of school in an ungraded school is spent teaching pupils how to behave, be independent, and be reliable and determining where each child is. *Then* books are handed out which contain material suited to the pupils' needs. With the use of many tests, given frequently, the pupil need deal only with those tasks in which he is capable of success. He need not, with frequent tests, waste his time learning things he already knows.

---

[2] Calvin W. Taylor, 1968, "Cultivating New Talents: A Way to Reach the Educationally Deprived," *Journal of Creative Behavior*, 2(2):86, Spring. Reprinted by permission of the publisher and the author.

[3] Harold G. Seashore, 1963, "The Identification of the Gifted," *Test Service Bulletin*, No. 55 (New York: The Psychological Corporation), p. 3.

Informal and Semiformal Techniques

TEACHER-MADE EVALUATIONS

In addition to standardized achievement and ability tests, the teacher, sticking to subject matter evaluation, can devise his own tests to indicate progress. These may include essay-type tests, short-answer tests (T–F items, matching, and multiple choice), and performance tests in shop, home economics, physical education, or in competition for positions in the orchestra. The procedures will be meritorious or culpable, depending on how they are used. One of the tasks of the counselor-consultant might be to ask teachers in their professional staff meetings what impact the way they use classroom tests has on personality, on ego concepts, on attitudes toward continuous learning. Most teachers, because they must manage a classroom and because of their concern with individual pupils, are also concerned with the affective phases of education. Besides, there are many approaches to evaluation other than tests.

Interviews can help teachers to understand the attitudes and behaviors of pupils in day-to-day study and in their peer relations. These are the kinds of evaluations which need to be brought to the conscious level, in view of the purposes of facilitating learning and the development of the pupils' appreciation of satisfactions to be derived from growth.

Sociometry can be used to ease peer relations, thus freeing the pupil from the unnecessary tensions which impede learning. Sociometry is the schematic plotting of likes and attractions. These exist, whether or not they are recognized, and can be used as the basis for seating arrangements, formation of committees, or composition of small groups for special assignments.[4]

Incomplete sentences can be presented to stimulate imagination and creativity. Clues to some of the worries and anxieties that pupils feel chronically or from time to time may be uncovered. In addition, language activities and processes of socialization take on the zest of games.

Q-sort techniques on such matters as "This is how I am" and

---

[4] Harold W. Bernard, 1970, *Mental Health in the Classroom* (New York: McGraw-Hill Book Company), pp. 340 ff., describes the advantages and techniques of sociometry.

"This is what I'd like to be" can be used to make pupils aware of themselves as persons having some control. Q-sorts can bring pupils to perceive that education is something other than application to academic tasks.

Guess who (peer nominations) approaches can be used to develop the realization that one has a social impact. The bully will wake up to the impression he creates, the show-off will become cognizant of his image, and the reticent person can recognize that he does not, after all, escape notice. Awareness of self takes on particular value when teachers can help pupils develop plans for change when the "Guess who" hits too close to home.

Role playing can be used to mitigate problems of classroom decorum, rivalries, and color and socioecenomic prejudice, in addition to helping teachers and pupils achieve better mutual understanding.[5]

Projective techniques can reduce the social distance when interviews are likely to be strained because of a superior-inferior relationship. For example, one teacher asked her third-grade pupils to describe what they saw in Figure 13-3 and then draw a more complete scene around the structure provided. The drawing was then described. One boy added three additional arms and wrote, "The Airport Raydar"

> Once upon a there lived a man his name was Mr. Brown, He was young man about 33, years old. He is mairred. His wife was named Hese. Every day he came home for lunch and dinner after dinner he stayed home but after lunch he had to go back to work. He worked at the airport, he was insarts of the mechings. One day he didnt come home, so his wife went to the airport they got a raydar thats why he didn't come home.

Another teacher reported that she gained understanding and rapport

---

[5] Role playing gained national visibility when (May 11, 1970) the television program "Eye of the Storm" showed a fourth-grade teacher in Riceville, Iowa, having her pupils role-play being different in color. On one day brown-eyed pupils had to sit in the back, have a shorter recess, not drink at the fountain, keep off the playground equipment, and not have seconds at lunch. On that day blue-eyed people were better: They were smarter, cleaner, more attentive, less pugnacious, etc. The next day the roles were reversed — and it was *not* play. The emotions were very real. The teacher then asked questions about Negroes, Mexicans, and Indians.

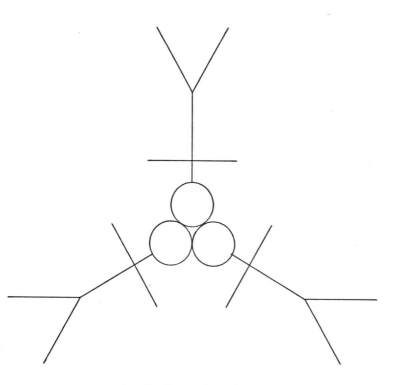

FIG. 13-3.   *Teacher-made projective device.*

with pupils by asking them to describe a number of stick figures such as are shown in Figure 13-4.

These and similar approaches have the advantage of not being standardized, thus escaping the hazards of quantifying into a global score behaviors which are highly complex and have many ramifications. They have the advantage of being openly subjective, so that the user is aware of the need for supplementary and corroborative data in the formulation of conclusions and hypotheses. They have the advantage of calling to attention the proposition that education may — many would say must — be concerned with the affective as well as the cognitive aspects of behavior.

FIG. 13-4.   *Stick-figures used to stimulate pupil descriptions.*

Observation of Specific Behaviors

Very difficult to answer is the question "How effective is counseling?" Counseling with students does not typically result in higher grade point averages or elimination of undesirable symptomatic behavior. A minimum criterion we have used in counselor education programs is "Does the counselee keep coming back?" Even if there is no more discernible change, the fact of faithfulness in voluntarily appearing for the session gives evidence that some need is being met. The need may not be accurately perceived by others (perhaps the counselee wants to miss a particular class or study hall), but some need is being met. Similarly, evaluation is based on behaviors, even though guesses must be made as to what the behaviors mean.

Absence is an obvious behavior indicating dissatisfaction with school, i.e., evidence that felt needs are not being satisfied. However, the cause of the absences must be confirmed; they may be due to peer or parental pressures rather than to personal dissatisfaction.

Appointments which are *forgotten* or deliberately *broken* may indicate lack of regard for the person to be met, apprehension about what will transpire at the meeting, or disguised hostility.

Nonparticipation in athletic events, class meetings, library activities, or conversation with peers or teachers provides clues to inclusion in the school's social structure but, like a reading on a fever thermometer, does not identify the ailment (another illustration of a difference between measurement and evaluation).

Changes in program may be an indication of growth and expanding perceptions and interests or of the pupil's trying to run away from his own unhappy self.

Citations — both those which are of a commendatory nature and those which are referrals to the principal's office for disciplinary decision — are symptomatic of inner drives.

Punctuality in doing assignments, getting to school, being ready for consecutive activities may be a sign of fear of authority or of a cheerful respect for others, for self, and for the concept of growth.

Book usage — books checked out of the library, types of books being taken home and brought from home, paperbacks purchased, etc. — may provide a very exacting criterion of the extent to which schools are accomplishing the thrust toward the habit of continuous learning.

Agency referrals to police, detention facilities, or delinquency homes, and suspension or probation from school merit investigation and evaluation. Sexual deviation, intoxication, drug usage, fighting, etc., must be evaluated in terms of pupil tension vs. removal (as parents would remove a child displaying a temper tantrum) for the protection and comfort of others.

Leisure activities afford clues for the evaluation of habits and attitudes related to the habit of continuous learning. This item may well apply to the evaluation of professional as well as pupil behavior; i.e., what about teachers who regard pupil conversation and byplay in the halls and library as a waste of time, if not a downright nuisance? (High schools are being built with extra-wide hallways *and* benches to provide stimulus to socialization processes.)

Vandalism and graffiti are symptomatic of pupil hostility to authority, report cards, teacher rigidity, invidious comparisons, and many other personal interpretations of being unwanted, out of place, or insignificant. Viewed as symptoms, these evidences of hate, fear, or insecurity may lead staff members to rigorous examination of what they are doing to block achievement of sturdy ego concepts and the goal of enjoyment of learning.

TEACHER SELF-EVALUATION

Staff meetings held to devise better techniques of evaluation should desirably include assessment of what teachers themselves are and do to promote continuous learning as a way of life. Some of this is a matter of the teacher's independent study, but the self-evaluation can be made more accurate when supplemented with group meetings in which participants describe what they read into the behaviors of their peers. Self-evaluation with the aid of colleagues can help to avoid the hazards of too critical or too lenient judgments of what one is and does.

Grading Systems

CRITICISM OF COMPARATIVE GRADES

Criticism of comparative, competitive grading systems is not just a recent development stemming from studies of dropouts, children who run away from home, culturally different pupils, and the increasing popularity of humanistic psychologies.

Parker (1937, pp. 271 ff.) asserted that schools are immoral when marks and prizes are used in such a way as to cultivate selfishness, invoke punishment, or degrade the spirit. Insistence on grades deprives the child of spontaneous originality.

Burton (1944, p. 52) says that a prevalent misconception of learning is that "the symbols of learning are often confused with and mistaken for the outcomes of learning."

Mursell (1946, p. 290) suggests that as attention is devoted to matters of appraising the effectiveness of teaching and learning, "One should work for an abandonment of all marking below the senior-high-school level, where the question of transfer credit does not arise."

Holt (1964) contends that children's love for learning is destroyed when they are encouraged and compelled to work for petty and contemptible rewards — gold stars, grades on papers, letter grades on report cards, dean's lists, and Phi Beta Kappa keys — in short, for the ignoble satisfaction of feeling that one is better than others.

DuPue (1967), commenting on the grading system based on

the normal curve of distribution, remarks that it is an extremely jaundiced person who thinks that half our doctors are quacks, half our lawyers are shysters, half our teachers are incompetents, and half our pupils are failures. He applies to the conventional grading system such words as *senseless, chaotic, ridiculous* [not an appropriate appellation in the view of pupils who get an F], and *specious.*

Goodlad (1967, p. 47), speculating about the schools which are needed in the 1970's, asks whether we really respect the human client, seek to give pupils experiences of success, and permit students to make decisions, and whether the schools really grip and hold the learner. He states that the evidence is to the contrary; for example, the fact that 25 percent of the pupils receive 75 percent of the failing grades encourages them to leave school as soon as the law allows.

Dyer (1968) asserts (and he is a representative of a test publishing company) that the important thing about evaluation is the *total* personality of the pupil, not his percentile standing on a standardized achievement test or comparative score on a teacher-made test.

Glasser (1969, pp. 95 ff.) proclaims that children do not learn to succeed by being failed in school. From the time a pupil enters school he must think in terms of success. "We cannot achieve this goal using the present grading system."

Thus grades have been protested for decades. A few schools are moving away from an outmoded and ineffective practice, but they can hardly be seen as representative of a trend. Perhaps a few more school personnel will be impelled to do something by a statement that is more than half a century old.

> In antediluvian times, while the animal kingdom was being differentiated into swimmers, climbers, runners, and fliers, there was a school started for their development. Its theory was that the best animals should be able to do one thing as well as another. If an animal had short legs and good wings, attention should be devoted to running, so as to even up the qualities as far as possible. So the duck was kept waddling instead of swimming, and the pelican was kept wagging his short wings in the attempt to fly. The eagle was made to run and allowed to fly only for recreation, while maturing tadpoles were unmercifully guyed for being neither one thing nor another.

The animals that would not submit to such training, but persisted in developing the best gifts they had, were dishonored and humiliated in many ways. They were stigmatized as being narrow-minded specialists. No one was allowed to graduate from the school unless he could climb, swim, run, and fly at certain prescribed rates; so it happened that the time wasted by the duck in the attempt to run had so hindered him from swimming, that his swimming muscles atrophied and he was hardly able to swim at all, and in addition, he had been scolded, punished, and ill-treated in many ways so as to make his life a burden. In fact, he left school humiliated. The eagle could make no headway in climbing to the top of a tree, and although he showed he could get there just the same, the performance was counted a demerit since it had not been done according to the prescribed course of study.

An abnormal eel with large pectoral fins proved that he could run, swim, climb trees, and fly a little. He attained an average of sixty per cent in all his studies. He was made valedictorian of the class.[6]

EVALUATION TO REPLACE GRADES AND MARKS

Many teachers say, "Getting rid of the grading system cannot be done. What about parents, employers, college admissions?" These, of course, are questions which must be considered. However, Principal Wendell Corey (1970) introduced into a fourteen-teacher elementary school in The Dalles, Oregon, a nongraded organization *and* no grades. In the first year (1969–1970) only *one* parent came in to protest the absence of grades. Corey told the parent that teachers could grade the child or she could be sent to another school. The parent said, "Let's let it ride for now," and later the child was registered in the same (Joseph G. Wilson) school, for the 1970–1971 year. The motto of the school is "Every child in this school succeeds [at the level of his needs]. No child in this school is failed." In the meetings preliminary to instituting nongraded organization, one teacher put the whole matter succinctly: "I can utilize the nongraded organization and I can individualize instruction as soon as we eliminate grades." Also in The Dalles, the dean of girls in high school, back from a state

[6] J. Adams Puffer, 1913, *Vocational Guidance* (Chicago: Rand McNally & Co.), pp. 22–23.

meeting of high school counselors and college admissions personnel, commented that the frame of reference of the latter was "Do what you want. We want good students no matter how their work was evaluated."

Some alternatives to grades are already in existence. One which is used rather widely in the primary grades and to some extent at the upper elementary and junior high school level is the parent-teacher conference. Time to hold such conferences is found by combining classes, by excusing pupils from school for half a day, and by using funds already available for substitute teachers to man the classroom while teachers are "conferencing."

The meaningful evaluation is that which occurs in daily teacher-pupil dialogue as part of the teaching-learning transaction. At the high school level the fulfillment of contracts or achievement of levels of accomplishment is the end — with no grades attached. For college admissions officers the pupil's rank on scholastic achievement tests provides sufficient data — without the overkill of six- or nine-week report cards to convince the pupil that he is or is not fitted for college.

It is probable that *the* substitute for grades has not been found; perhaps it never will be. Progress may be made and locally useful plans may be devised by consensus of teachers, parents, and pupils in meetings specifically designed to improve instruction. The practices described above in the section on "Informal and Semiformal Techniques" can be used as a starting point in staff meetings devoted to the topic "What our school can do to improve evaluation and facilitation of the teaching-learning process."

The dilemma of evaluation may be highlighted by a puzzling category of students. These are the boys and girls who achieve well on what achievement tests measure but fail in terms of the conformity required to earn them good marks in school. Perhaps such students should be encouraged to leave school — to drop out — and take the General Educational Development tests to secure a high school graduation equivalency certificate. Perhaps school personnel should examine the practices which raise such a consideration; however, it seems defensible that the mere fact of institutionalization is enough to turn off some students. Community colleges exist in most parts of the United States where many such youth are being salvaged by ingenious programs that simply do not, somehow, put the student down.

Summary

Pupil assessment is an ever present and ever changing aspect of education. Basically the purpose of evaluation is to improve the teaching-learning process. The consultant needs to develop expertise in assessment as he works with pupils and teacher toward the end of individual growth and pupil adjustment to rapid change. The purpose of the school has changed to include the development of a healthy ego concept and a love of the process of continuous learning as well as the acquisition of knowledge and skills. These goals are supplementary rather than dichotomous.

Measurement of outcomes is a helpful ingredient of evaluation but should serve the purpose of guidance for next steps rather than the designation of some mysterious and ambiguous end product. More rather than less measurement is needed to achieve the shift from measurement per se to evaluation.

Teacher-made evaluation devices can be used to supplement standardized test data and day-to-day observations. It should be remembered that self-evaluation by teachers should be a part of the school assessment program, because they are the model and the adult human factor in the teaching-learning experience. Their influence is probably greater than that of curriculum, organization, and socioeconomic status in what the pupil learns about himself.

Elimination of competitive grades appears to be a necessity if individual differences are to be respected, if educational symbols are not to be the goal, and if continuous learning is to become an autonomous and enjoyable activity. Unfortunately substitutes for the all too familiar grading pattern have not yet been devised. Teacher-parent conferences, self-evaluating learning packages, and self-evaluation are approaches. Such things as sociograms, computer feedback, and pupil contracts are also being tried. But there is a whole area of personality, intuitive judgments, and social effectiveness for which instruments and scales are lacking. The creative talents of a school, perhaps stimulated by a consultant who emphasizes humanistic concerns, will bring about some of the needed development.

SUGGESTED ADDITIONAL READINGS

Gross, Beatrice, and Ronald Gross, 1970. "A Little Bit of Chaos," *Saturday Review*, 53(20):71–73+, May 16. *An examination of British infant schools shows some of the necessary "new" dimensions needed in evaluation and, by implication, suggests approaches which might be used.*

Guba, Egon G., and John J. Horvat, 1970. "Evaluation During Development," *Viewpoints*, Bulletin of the School of Education, Indiana University, 46(2):21–45, March. *The authors emphasize the fact that there are different purposes and stages of evaluation. Hence different modes of assessment are needed. They assert that many of the important outcomes of education are neglected because lack of instruments to assess them leads to the belief that they are not worthwhile.*

Hoffman, Banesh, 1967. "Psychometric Scientism," *Phi Delta Kappan*, 48:381–386. *The article reveals, perhaps in more detail than is needed, certain considerations about objective and standardized testing which cause one to wonder at the huge faith reposed in tests.*

Saylor, Galen, 1970. "National Assessment: Pro and Con," *The Record, Teachers College*, 71:588–597, May, *Although some of the protest against national assessment has quieted down, many of the issues of "How?" still remain — and the issues are much like those faced by individual schools. It seems advisable for the federal government to help local schools improve their assessment programs.*

Sobel, Harold W., 1969. "The Anachronistic Practices of American Education as Perpetrated by an Unenlightened Citizenry and Misguided Pedagogues Against the Inmates of the Public Schools," *Phi Delta Kappan*, 51:94–97. *The processes of evaluation might be improved if we are made aware of some of the aspects of the schools which deserve change. Sobel highlights a few of those aspects.*

Chapter Fourteen

EMERGENT ROLE
OF THE TEACHER

The behavior of a whole system is unpredicted by the way any separate part or subgrouping of parts behaves. This is synergism. It is not a new idea that the whole is greater than the sum of its parts. It may be new to apply the concept to the counselor-consultant while we proceed to define the emergent role of the teacher (Bernard, 1957).

Predictions are important in American social systems because they form a standard or a norm (Kowitz, 1969). Without established traditions and other stability-producing guidelines, prediction is crucial whenever it leads to self-fulfilling practice. Institutions in America, including the federal government, will *forecast* and then proceed to fulfill (Green, 1968). Planning and development have been used in educational institutions and government to define or "divine" the future. What is done or not done today does place limits on tomorrow. The next ten-year plan is frequently revised and projected another ten years — following its first year of operation. Since the tempo of growth is usually more rapid than the planners anticipate, revision is necessary, with the prospect of redoing it again and again.

The process for carrying on the *new* thinking about the future is much like the process of the counselor when he is consulting (Kowitz, 1969). The most striking similarity is simply analytic. There is no way to *know* the future. There are no facts to gather because facts belong to the past or the present, never the future. There can be no data! Again, similarity between planning the future and consulting comes out of the Green (1968) material. The counselor-consultant makes no claim to know the future. He begins his work with teachers, parents, students, and others without asserting that he knows any answers. He has, instead, a way of forecasting, much like a weatherman. No matter whether he is exactly right; the near miss is useful too. The keystone is to look at the future and avoid extrapolating the present, for on the basis of the present, we get more and bigger quantities of the same. The counselor-consultant avoids such pitfalls by remembering that between here and now and ten years into the future new inventions will be made. The point is to use the newer idea or invent one if the new task requires something altogether different.

Educational Challenges of the 1970's

New Teacher Roles

Teachers will become more like the forecasters, dealing less and less with data and more and more with creating new inventions. Initially, there will need to be invented a way of teaching or learning the process of inventing! In previous publication (Fullmer and Bernard, 1964), we called this learning how to learn. By whatever label, the issue is a major one.

Education has been defined as preparation for life. Farson (1968) and Rogers (1968) think the teacher will become a *facilitator* of living; the experience of life in the here and now is the central purpose of education. When these two contrasting purposes are carried into practice, they lead to very different kinds of teaching. Gibb (1968) claims the best learning experiences happen when people are involved in an immediate activity. The here and now is contrasted with living in the past or escaping to the future. Persons who live in the past are not very effective. Future-oriented people do not have to be effective now. ("Mañana is good enough for me.") Gibb (1968) thinks the differences between education and therapy are disappearing. It may be that teaching and counseling are becoming more like consulting — thus are becoming more similar. This is already a fact of past origin where group processes are employed.

Toward a New Definition of Education

Learning to live is the act of living, for the acceleration of change has brought the future into the present. Paradoxically, tomorrow is still mañana, and we cannot *know* the future. But we can forecast, and on the assumption that what happens in the future is limited by what happens or does not happen today, we have the rationale. Research (data gathering about past events) is available to evaluate the efficacy of the process described above. One of the differences postulated here is that traditional methodology of *predicting* the future on the basis of extrapolations from the past (data gathering) can be replaced by *forecasting* the future on the basis of what we would like to have (Green, 1968). As methodology in teaching moves from the learner as passive receiver to the learner as active seeker, how best to *prepare* for living in the world of tomorrow is laid aside like the boomerang it is. Instead, each person picks up the courage to be alive now, in this moment of history. If now is eternal, it is always now. Let the psyche be titillated because humans cannot long escape from remembering a yesterday and anticipating a tomorrow. Therefore, we propose a shift in emphasis in order to capture the best of both worlds without castrating either. As in living between two cultures, the real hazard is in not being a part of either.

Kehas (1969), writing about a new framework for counseling, has argued for the establishment of a dichotomy for teaching and counseling based upon a defined area of responsibility for learning. Established knowledge defined by academic disciplines is the major single emphasis in schooling. Schooling is identified with teaching; teachers are responsible for what they teach — not for what is learned. Kehas would have this emphasis change to a focus on learning. The thought comes that teaching, too, would change to accommodate a new purpose. It follows that teachers would change roles. However, Kehas does not dwell on the teacher or teaching but pushes on to the counselor role. The counselor will become the professional in the school responsible for one's *learning* about one's self. The personal-social-character-internal inquiry will gain equal status with external subject matter learning. If such a change did come to pass, it would create some monumental problems for the reeducation of teachers, teachers of teachers, and teachers of teachers of teachers, not to mention teachers of counselor-teachers.

BACK TO REALITY

The world of education does include schooling as a major part of the planned and systematic intervention system. The teacher will continue to be the keystone in all schooling. The counselor-consultant is presented as one model for bringing counselor and teacher into a more meaningful relationship. If this venture is successful, the teacher will modify the traditional pattern of behavior but will probably not change her model. For example, the model of one teacher in one classroom has been modified in Hawaii with the three-on-two program, in which three teachers take two classrooms of children into a single unit. Time will evaluate the efficacy of this modification, but early observation (after two years) indicates each teacher still has her very own group (class) of youngsters in her own territory (classroom). The school may be able to absorb many new innovations and retain its basic integrity. The question remains: Can the school be changed? Likewise, can the teacher be changed? Present practice would lead to the perpetuation of the current system of schooling, which allows for change without chaos. There is the distinct possibility that a parallel school system will be developed, and its impact might be profound enough to get more rapid change in the traditional school system.

Whatever happens in the way of educational innovation — e.g., with counselors as instruments of change — teachers will remain focal. Team teaching, continuous progress, computer-assisted instruction, independent study, modular scheduling — these will depend less on organization and structure than on the attitude toward pupils and skills of the teacher in the teaching-learning transaction. Ultimately, teachers must face the fact that they are, inescapably, models. They will be models for emulation of continuous learning or they will be anti-models of what not to do or be. They must know not only what turns pupils on (creativity, independence, recognition, achievement, success) but what turns pupils off (facades, authoritarianism, hypocrisy, envy, sadism). Adelson's (1961) research indicates that anti-models are in their own charismatic way influences on student behavior. One breeds disciples or enemies. Adelson believes that the positive model can be developed by disclosing the negative model and exercising the power of choice of what teachers will be and become. It seems that there is no more challenging task for the counselor-consultant.

TECHNOLOGY APPLIED TO EDUCATING

Education has been the very last major social institution to apply the newer technologies to its central function, namely, teaching. Teaching machines appeared in the recent past. The new hardware of the newer media came along, but the school remained basically the same (Loughary, 1966, p. 225). Industry, business, the military, and government agencies have moved relatively quickly to apply the new technologies to problems of training, teaching, counseling, and educating generally. Why? Does the school, designed for an earlier era, fit into any meaningful relationship with modern society? These difficult questions remain unanswered in practice because no substitute has been advanced at this writing. The problem of making an old system do the new task calls for education methods to help people learn what they do not know as well as how to use what they do know.

To apply and use what is known is a legitimate enterprise at every level of the social system. This assumption seems safe enough. Conflicts emerge at those points where new aplications will materially alter current practices. The future is here now in the sense that forecasts made in 1966 (Loughary, 1966) indicated the acceptance of man-machine systems as natural or established practice in education.

Implementation of new technologies in educational practice is conflict area I and arises out of the changed status of teachers, counselors, students, parents, and administrators. The status and communication models used in the traditional school social system are replaced by a different model, which requires a transition period for the process of implementation. Social control systems do not change without certain assurances based upon a complete plan with controls of its own. For the person caught up in the change from traditional to machine systems technology, the experience is tantamount to learning a new language before continuing to do the same work. What happens to the individual? Are freedom and privacy assured? How do we know the machine will serve us instead of enslaving us? Dundes (1969) thinks man is afraid of machines because he may be responsible if something in the machine should go wrong, go wrong . . . The folklore or commonly held beliefs support the fear, as if Big Brother is watching. The task seems to be to make machines more humane instead of making man behave more and more like a machine (robot).

These changes are of a magnitude equivalent to those in changing cultures. The advanced parties are viewed by extremists as extremists; they may even be engaged in a subversive plot. The generations may differ in the ability to accept machine technology. Youngsters born in the fifties and sixties are likely to expect the electronic hardware to be available to serve them. The television screen changed from black and white to living color while teaching them. It showed them about the sex life of the gray whale and the living desert. The drug addict had his trip in full view of all. Why not expect the machine to go on serving knowledge without the hazards of direct exposure? Programming so much data into materials for machine use in instruction has its own perils. There is not space here to do justice to the topic, but just consider the problem of deciding what subject matter to include and what to omit. Who will decide for you or me? Safeguards for the individual and the group must be placed on priorities within the total social system. The pecking order will probably be changed; if it is, expect resistance.

Can the Teacher Be a Problem?

Gattegno (1970) claims that learning to speak is the most complex and difficult learning achieved by any human being — and each of us did it by ourself before we reached three years of age. Lashley (1958) has reminded us that psychologists unwisely omit one-trial learning from serious consideration in favor of the pedagogue's drill or repetition. To repeat, there seems to be little evidence to support the assumption that repetition has a positive effect on learning. What is supported, particularly in the teaching of reading, was reported by Liddell (1956). Classical and operant conditioning used in the reinforcement schedules for teaching reading may lead to learning disabilities. Traditional teacher behavior may produce emotionally bankrupt students. Behavior disabilities can become chronic. Some school systems currently mount a special education effort to treat learning disabilities. If the above be accurate in its representation of the long-term effect of an untested assumption regarding the learning process, imagine the consequences awaiting *new* teacher behavior! Surely behavior should focus on learning as well as teaching. Personal variables in the learner should become the primary concern; then, secondarily, after a secure and safe relationship exists, some conditioning techniques may be employed.

An example of the above professional brief is readily available in the child who no longer responds to the reward or punishment given by the teacher. He takes a low grade or a smile of approval without any visible response. *Emotionally bankrupt* may be too extreme a term for this humble example, but *turned off* is a quite accurate label. The counselor-consultant frequently must enter the classroom to help the teacher learn to "turn on" a formerly "turned off" student.

Strategies to Meet the Challenges

Programmed Instruction

The materials developed for machines and programmed textbooks have had some outstanding virtues, among them the virtue of self-help or self-administration. The teacher is unnecessary. The materials are divided into sufficiently minute steps to permit independent study. This sets up the self-determining phenomenon so essential to the learning process as we have come to know it in counseling. The teacher, being changed from information processor to technical consultant, no longer stands between the student and what he is to learn. The student is nearer the condition experienced in the first three years of life, when he learned to speak.

Independent Study

How frequently does the school achieve the goal of continuous independent study? The teacher could be the key to the lifelong pursuit of knowledge, but at present independent study is used as a reward. What is happening? Independent study of what?

The teacher may become a manager or a technician with independent study and programmed instruction. How will the teacher and the team work?

To avoid the obvious emphasis on subject matter, the right focus on independent study should be the personal development of the individual. Personal intelligence about the self would lead to meaning systems which relate self-knowledge to the idiosyncratic world of each other person significant to the learner. The new teacher in the school of the future with a counselor-consultant could make this idea a reality. Present practices will otherwise turn independent study into yet another teaching method.

TEAM TEACHING

The newer technologies most certainly will be applied to instruction. In this case the teacher will be faced by new needs, demands, and expectations for leadership from all varieties of technicians, paraprofessionals, human behavior specialists, and others, some of whom are not yet named. Leadership will be in the form of management or consultation, perhaps both.

There are a number of team teaching models in use, a review of which is beyond the scope of coverage here. Rather, it is proposed to establish a model for teamwork that will accommodate up to six or seven members (Kowitz, 1969). One great hazard in team operation, generally, is the tendency toward alienation among members. The loss of identity with the products of teamwork may be one reason.

Alienated people give us a clear view of the problems in society (May, 1969). The team is a mini-society — like a family, if the team stays intact for a long period. The model of organization is crucial; whether a given person makes it as a team member depends on the organization. This is in contrast with the common wisdom that individuals are troublemakers. Rollo May (1969) points up the idea that a troublemaker — an alienated member of society — may be signaling a problem in the basic structure of the human organization. Fullmer (1969a) has found alienation to be a symptom of faulty organization in the family. The symptom bearer is like the automatic fire alarm — the signal may trip the sprinklers and avert the big fire. The ecology of the team may be a more productive focus than has been the individual member in revolt, if we really wish to learn how to make a team go.

INDIVIDUAL STUDENT EVALUATION

Among Hawaiian youngsters there is a concept called "make shame," an overriding criterion of performance. Literally, it means to lose face by being wrong. There are other ramifications, but chiefly it means that low-risk performance is the rule. To make a mistake or to be the center of attention is equal to "make shame" (Howard and Gallimore, 1968).

The mainland United States may be more accurately characterized by behavior expressing guilt. Shame is on the individual, but the concept is different. Guilt and loss of face are two basic belief systems, and merging of the cultures may cause both to operate in a given individual.

Evaluation is based on the belief system. If face saving is primary, the behavior will be avoidance of risk. If guilt drives the person, risk taking may become foolish. The individual student can be helped to understand the basic belief on which he operates. He can then anticipate his behavior and the feelings he will have as a result of his performance and its evaluation (Gleason, 1967).

KNOWLEDGE

The concept of knowing is central to the emergent role of teachers, for teaching is founded on facts based upon established knowledge. In the good old days when schooling was preparation for life, the traditional teaching function held. But tomorrow is another matter. Schooling is no longer preparation for anything. Facts will be new and made available only to those who have learned to collect them. Rogers (1962, pp. 311–314) claims that innovations do not easily diffuse among the population because opinion leaders are caught in the paradox of conformity. See the simple sentence? Followers of opinion leaders wait for the signal to change. The opinion leader is hung up on what is. Thus, the paradox and some fifty ramifications were identified by Rogers.

Adelson (1961) ties knowledge to beliefs in a most unusual way. Teaching is explained by relating the style of a teacher to the five methods of healing devised by mankind. The methods were taken from a cross-cultural study and are approximately accurate in covering the characteristic modes of teacher behavior in American schools. The five models are:

shamanism
magic
religion
mysticism
naturalism

The shaman is personally powerful, even charismatic, as a teacher.

The magician is like the psychodramatist — following rules and rituals precisely.

The priest is only an agent of power; the modern scholar says, "Believe me because of what authority I represent."

The mystic relies on wisdom and insight like the counselor of the fifties and sixties; the cure is for a sick soul.

The naturalist is impersonal, empirical, and task oriented just like a modern physician.

The emergent mode for the teacher may well be any one of these. The transmission of knowledge is obviously only one part of the massive function in teaching.

Rhodes (1969) explained a new awareness of the difference between *teaching* and *learning*. As Kehas (1969) also mentioned, the need to understand instruction from the external point of view of subject matter and the internal view of the person learning leads to different models and methods of schooling. The teacher seems destined to stay in the school and to manage teams (Bushnell, 1969) and individualized learning environments. New knowledge does not always find application with the existing methods and conceptualizations. The new wine needs new jars unless we are to have more of the same (Havelock, 1969).

Cleveland (1969) claims that simplicity has been the goal of science and technology. Success with small parts of the urban environment has led to the production of more dirt, smoke, and other wastes. The massive threat to physical survival by man is not a simple problem, and its solution cannot be simple. The whole is more complex than the sum of the parts. Synergism (see opening statement of this chapter) characterizes the problem, an explanation of which will require the unlocking of secret principles heretofore unknown in relation to the behavior of the parts. Then it may be possible to apply knowledge to produce a solution.

Teaching is no less like Cleveland's (1969) idea of modern society than is the counselor-consultant. Together they may identify the problem, but the solution is a whole new problem. All we can forecast is that, whatever the problem of integrating complex differentness in social-cultural ecology, the great institutions will have to be accountable for adequate behavior. What will be the school's response? The choice seems to lie between psychotherapy (adjustment to life) and competent behavior to meet the future with more than good mental health. The mental hygiene goal has been lost for some years (Cleveland, 1969), yet it is still to be hoped that we will move toward more competent behavior (Fullmer, 1969a).

Change and dislocation are the norm for modern urban society. Only teamwork will suffice to manage the complex energies and forces combining to create the living present (Cleveland, 1969).

Counseling as Educative Process

Bronfenbrenner (1967) claims that American schools have never made a serious effort at character education. The emphasis has been on developing verbal and quantitative intellectual skills, and this has been equated with developing the mind. Character education is personal, social, and emotional development. The process can be made explicit. Hall (1959) maintains that most American character learning is left nonexplicit but it is very much a real part of everyone's biology. Character education would lead to systematic diversity, a goal long claimed in American education. However, conformity and sameness may have been the major achievement of schooling.

The means and ends problem in education remains. What are we teaching with schools built on the prison model (Kimball, 1967)? Schools are among the most hierarchical power structures in the entire American social system. The fact that many of the immediate problems in education are created by the school was pointed out in the story about a pali (cliff). The story tells of a beautiful view along the very edge of the cliff, but tragically, people kept falling over the edge. Because a wall or fence would spoil the view, a hospital was built in the valley. By and by a stranger came along and proposed a preventative measure: just use glass to protect the strollers. Can you imagine the reaction of the community built up around that hospital?

Perhaps the story understates the case for the teacher and the counselor-consultant during the 1970's. Guidance for the 1970's should be more than transparent walls to eliminate the need for a hospital. A place must be prepared for those displaced by new innovations, inventions, and social-physical solutions. The hope for tomorrow is still born today.

Summary

Teaching and schooling have developed as identical twins in American education. Identical twins are as similar as two persons may be; however, each is unique in his personal-social development. The synergism of the whole system is seen here. Identical twins are strongly competitive. Because of their symmetrical relationship, each must strive to define a difference, a uniqueness. Simultaneously, they are the most powerful of sibling peer groups, bound together by loyalty in a cohesive, living survival pact.

The counselor-consultant forms a team with the teacher. Together they seek the possible. The possible learning may be enhanced by applications of the newer technologies to instruction. The team strives to make machines more humane instead of making people behave more like machines.

The future will surely be characterized by change. To achieve any management over the destiny of our social and physical environments, we will need to combine our talents in ways yet unheard of. The task will be more complex instead of more simple. The psychotherapy goal of education may be discarded to provide for a living-in style of education leading to competent behavior. Competent behavior is appropriate behavior by whatever criteria are applied. Continuous learning is the only answer given. Only through continuous learning will the inventions and dissemination of innovations occur fast enough to avoid disaster.

Schooling is but one form of educating. The family is a more powerful form. The mass media, the community, and time are powerful interveners. The ultimate intervention may be self-study done independently. The school may reach the student who wants to learn, but the youngster who has turned off is another story. The teacher as shaman, magician, mystic, priest, or naturalist may not bring about successful learning but only responsible teaching.

The emergent role of the teacher will reverse the status quo. The teacher responsible for what he teaches will become the teacher responsible and accountable for what is learned.

SUGGESTED ADDITIONAL READINGS

Bigge, M. L., 1964. *Learning Theories for Teachers*. New York: Harper & Row, Publishers. *Learning theory may come of age in counseling through the consultation process with teachers and parents. Teachers may need reeducation about learning theories. Here is a very good resource.*

Bushnell, D. S., 1969. "An Educational System for the '70's," *Phi Delta Kappan*, 51(4):199–203, December. Gleason, G. T. (ed.), 1967. *The Theory and Nature of Independent Learning*. Scranton, Pa.: International Textbook Company. *One-hundred-plus pages report a conference held at the University of Wisconsin, Milwaukee. The trick may be to keep independent learning from becoming a new form of teaching.*

Jacobs, P. I., M. H. Maier, and L. M. Stolurow, 1966. *A Guide to Evaluating Self-Instructional Programs*. New York: Holt, Rinehart & Winston. *This brief survey of programmed instruction and the selection of a program brings together a set of ideas which should be useful to the evaluator. Nearly one-half of the text is devoted to evaluation study directions.*

Lashley, Carl, 1958. "Cerebral Organization and Behavior," pp. 1–18 in Harry Solomon, Stanley Cobb, and Wilder Penfield (eds.), 1958, *The Brain and Human Behavior*, Vol. 36. Baltimore: The Williams & Wilkins Co. *One-trial learning and repetition are not widely understood concepts among teachers and counselors. Psychologists, most recently the behaviorists, have mostly misunderstood the learning process. They have been mainly pedagogues rather than behavioral scientists. The net result is that a bright child may be emotionally bankrupted by the classical or operant conditioning schedules used in reading instruction, for example.*

Liddell, Howard, 1956. *Emotional Hazards in Animals and Man*. Springfield, Ill.: Charles C Thomas, Publisher. *Experimental neurosis or emotional bankruptcy can produce chronic learning disabilities in school youngsters. Liddell gives an important commentary on the behaviorists and school learning.*

Popham, J. W., 1969. "Focus on Outcomes: A Guiding Theme of ES '70 Schools," *Phi Delta Kappan,* 51(4):208–210.

Rhodes, L., 1969. "Linkage Strategies for Change: Process May Be the Product," *Phi Delta Kappan,* 51(4):204–207. *The three articles by Bushnell, Popham, and Rhodes in* Phi Delta Kappan *report on the Educational System nationwide experiment to discover whether systems analysis has a legitimate role in educational reform. The questions of process and outcomes remain central issues to the project. Do we need to determine the outcome (closed system) or the process (open system)? What is to become of the new wine of computers if put in the old jars of the school system?*

Simpson, R. H., 1966. *Teacher Self-Evaluation.* New York: The Macmillan Company. *The evaluation of any professional must become self-actualized at some stage of development. This resource may help the new and experienced counselor, consultant, and teacher mobilize for productive evaluation.*

GLOSSARY

Acculturation The process of acquiring a culture with all of its values, social-physical conditioning, and symbol systems.

Affiliation The level of involvement that denotes connection for coordinated effort without veto power over others in a partnership.

Alienation The condition of separation from intimate involvement in significant relationships at the personal or social level; lacking identity with the culture.

Ambivalence The condition of unresolved attraction to two or more mutually opposed points of view or alternatives to action. Contemporaneously having feelings which are polar opposites: love-hate, interest-boredom, longing-aversion, approach-avoidance.

Arenas of Encounter The home, the office, the encounter group, the classroom, or any place where significant persons come together for the specific purpose of coordinating efforts and mutually accommodating interpersonal feelings.

Autonomy The condition in a life event in which the individual can act alone. There is a measure of chosen isolation and perhaps a positive value loading connected to the concept of autonomy.

Becoming The concept of growth and development in competent behavior better to carry out the tasks of life. It is frequently used to indicate the process of a person's becoming himself through group encounter. *Doing* the school tasks may be branded as irrelevant while *becoming* is a purpose with a future and consequently relevant.

318

Behavior modification The particular application of schedules of reinforcement to modify the behavior of a target person or population.

Behavior specialist Any one of a number of professional level persons who possess special skills and knowledge about how to utilize social control, deal with interpersonal feelings, and manage learning environments for and with others.

Behaviorism An area of the psychology of human behavior reflecting an emphasis upon the simple learning process called conditioning. Reinforcement principles are central concerns to the learning principles derived from the basic theory. Behaviorism is basically a response oriented psychology.

Birth order Sequence of oldest to youngest child in a given family. It is used in Adlerian individual psychology for postulating behavior patterns.

Body tactile The form of group therapy in which each participant, usually man and wife, engage in body contact, without words, to express to each other a range of emotional conditions.

Catharsis The expression of feelings by verbal or dramatic reliving of past life events. Usually this requires a listener, who provides empathic recognition of what is being communicated.

Change The dislocation of persons due to the restructuring of the social or economic environment as a consequence of new learning applied to the behavior of one or more persons in a group.

Closure The Hawaiian word *Pau* (pronounced "pow") has a final phonetic sound. Closure is such a final completed cycle concept.

Coefficients of correlation A numerical index which indicates the degree of relationship between two phenomena. Such coefficients range from perfect negative, -1.0 (the more of one thing the less of another; e.g., gas volume in relation to pressure) through no relationship, 0.0, to perfect positive, $+1.0$ (the more of one thing the more of another; e.g., volume of gas in relation to temperature).

Communication The exchange of messages and meanings between persons.

Communication flow The transmittal of messages and meanings between and among members of a group.

Communication, noncontextual The context of a behavior is linked to the culture's definition of appropriate behavior. Inappropriate behavior is a form of noncontextual communication because the meaning has reference to happenings outside the current context. Neurotic behavior is an example of noncontextual behavior because the reference is to causes outside the current context.

Communication, nonverbal The exchange of messages and meanings without verbal confirmation.

Communication, verbal Message exchange by use of language.

Confrontation groups The groups established to help persons learn to manage their feelings under increasing degrees of stress created in interpersonal encounters with persons who may not consistently agree. See Interpersonal process group.

Congruent The condition of being parallel or convergent in feelings, one with another. Congruency is a prerequisite to achieving mutual empathy.

Consulting Bringing together and encouraging communication between the human members of a total developmental milieu. As contrasted to supervising and "guidance," it is not an advisory role but recognizes the contributory role of all those involved.

Corporate group The established management agency or institution in which human groups operate. There is always a superior-subordinate pattern. The concept of equals cannot apply to superior-subordinate relationships within a corporate group. Outside the corporate group — in a training group, for example — equal status and conditions may be invoked.

Counseling A relationship, individual or group, designed to increase self-understanding, self-reliance, and the ability to cope with problems of living or working.

Counselor-consultant The professional role of the counselor characterized by his working with persons significant to the client instead of with the client directly — e.g., family consultation directed to the welfare of a pupil, teacher-administrator consultation for the benefit of pupils. See Profession.

Credibility gap The margin of trust within a relationship which the reality of experience seems to warrant; it is a personal perception, not a fixed distance.

Cross-cultural study The simultaneous study of specific phenomena in more than one culture. It is especially useful for the teacher whose classroom population represents multiple cultures.

Cultural conditioning The process of experiencing circumstances repeatedly and consistently creates internal changes which are so firmly established that they seem to be a part of one's basic personality.

Cultural conditioning is such that physical discomfort is felt when one is exposed to a different cultural pattern.

Cultural inertia   The tendency of the culture to stabilize and maintain continuity creates a potential for inertia or the inability to change.

Culture   The rules and parameters symbolized in behavior characterizing a person as distinct from persons in a different culture.

Desensitization   Progressive exposure, under controlled conditions, to an anxiety-producing life situation which results in a reduction of anxiety.

Dialogue   Genuine communication in which participants are able to "speak their piece" and are listened to by those seeking to understand.

Dislocation   The concept of change is expressed in the dislocation of persons in a society. A relocated population is not necessarily dislocated but often it is. Dislocation refers to the loss of one's place or identity in a population.

Eclecticism   The use of techniques and ideas for more than one system of psychology or counseling. It is the opposite of *classicism*, which means strict adherence to a specific system.

Ecology of the student and the teacher   The environmental conditions and/or forces affecting life in the classroom and school.

Empathy   The emotional linkage that characterizes relationships between individuals; the sensing and appreciation of the feelings and needs of others.

Encounter group   See Interpersonal process group.

Environment for learning   The established conditions designed for the neophyte to learn from the experienced person. Examples include the teacher-classroom model, the family group model, and the general peer group models.

Evaluation   The process of deciding the value or merit of a person or thing. In education, *grading* and *evaluation* are not correctly used as synonymous terms.

Experience   The unique meaning given to a specific life event by a person. Experience is differentiated from experiencing by a time line or dimension indicating an ongoing, perhaps continuous, experience.

Facilitator   The teacher or leader who coordinates efforts systematically to expose a pupil to learning environments; the one who is primarily responsible for the direction which interpersonal process groups take.

Family group consultation Consulting with all members of two or more families and two facilitators to improve mutual understanding and acceptance. Although a family may be counseled as a unit, two or more mothers, fathers, children often may "teach" more than a consultant can.

Feedback The computer-oriented term used to indicate information on how one is doing and what impact on others he is creating. Feedback may be verbal or nonverbal but it supplies one with data on who he is and how he comes across to others. Basically it means that part of the output of a system is reintroduced as a factor in regulation.

Free association A psychoanalytic technique in which a client speaks the first word which comes to mind upon the presentation of a stimulus word; also talking freely to a therapist without questions, prompting, or stimulus words.

Generation gap The difference between parents and children in terms of values and orientations, magnified by the accelerating rate of social and technological change. The "gap" is essential at the family level but has been used to designate misunderstanding at the public adult-youth level. Misunderstanding is at once normal and potentially tragic.

Group The universal form of human organization found in nearly every culture (more than 460) throughout the world to carry on the tasks and processes essential to systematically managing human affairs. Group is an information service in a real sense because other persons are the resources used by most people to validate information and confirm their decisions to act.

Guidance The necessary processes for managing environments in which individuals may learn and/or earn. Formerly it meant managing individuals.

Halo effect The tendency to project positive or negative characteristics beyond those actually possessed by the subject.

Heterostasis The urge or tendency to explore and to satisfy one's curiosity; the desire to grow, to be active, and to become. See Homeostasis.

Hidden agenda The unexpressed goals or purposes, the covert reasons, for a person's acting in a given way.

Homeostasis The tendency to preserve a stable or constant internal state, despite fluctuations of bodily conditions or external physical or psychological stimulations.

I-Thou concept The concept expressed by theologian Martin Buber to show the human relationship necessary for the meaningful existence of each person; subjective, personalized relationship as opposed to seeing a person as an object or thing.

Interaction models The relationship and communication patterns which characterize a particular group or which typify a particular interaction concept.

Interpersonal process group A group of eight to twelve persons which meets with the intent of self-examination in terms of seeing how one "comes across" to others. By honestly airing feelings and perceptions of self and others, with the aid of a facilitator, members seek improved social effectiveness. As the term is used in this book, the interpersonal process group leads toward the developmental rather than the therapeutic orientation. See Feedback and Sensitivity groups.

Inventory A compilation of an individual's assets and liabilities for school records and for the purpose of facilitating development.

Involvement Identification with an individual or process created through the feeling that one has an effect or influence. One is involved when he feels that his presence makes a difference.

Learning climate The emotional tone of a learning environment. The interpersonal stress level between teacher and student could be used to measure the quality of the learning climate.

Learning to learn In learning to learn, the person is taught or catches on to the necessary process and events essential to his own learning. Parts of these processes are unique and some are widely shared.

Level of aspiration The relative difficulty of long-range goals toward which one aspires or toward which he will strive.

Margin of comfort An individual is placed under stress in any learning experience. The margin is the amount of stress he can tolerate before breaking off a personal-learning relationship.

Micro-labs The simulated method for training individuals in group process by having them engage in a specific formula of giving and getting feedback in a small group; "micro" because they condense much experience in a small unit of time.

Milieu The environment, including all forces in the social system affecting a given life event.

Modeling The patterning of behavior after a model.

Myths The beliefs of a system which make possible certain prophecies, the self-fulfilling nature of which maintains a measure of predictability. E.g., awkwardness is attributed to puberty; adolescents rebel against authority; threat of failure is an incentive to learning.

Nongraded organization   A school in which the age-grade lines are expanded to cover more than one year or one grade level.

Nonpower-power posture   The behavior of helplessness which grants one control over another person; e.g., sick, lonely, helpless mother; delicate, sensitive girls; the innocence of natives as they exploit the foreigner.

Nonverbal, contextual cues   A nonverbal cue is any behavior, other than verbal, that a person acts out: scratching, distancing, body posturing, etc. Contextual cues are those connected to the context; e.g., the president's office is the largest in the company.

Paradigm   The complete analysis and/or schematization of parts-whole relationships showing the relative order and organization of the parts.

Paraprofessionals   Individuals who are trained to do a particular part of the professional's duties and who thereby free the professional to handle the more demanding aspects of a job.

Practicum   Supervised practice in a professionally applied area — e.g., counseling, guidance, consultation, and teaching.

Proactive, humanistic psychology   The learner or organism is seen as acting upon his environment as an active seeker in addition to being the sum of his past life. He can foresee consequences and behave accordingly. Proactive psychology includes the response phenomenon plus the idea that the human being can act to seek a particular consequence or response.

Process-product concept   The concept of "Which" is more important — process or product? The child is frequently more interested in the process of an event than in what is produced by his efforts. The same holds for peer groups and many events in a family.

Profession   An occupational category in which one performs a unique service, based on scholarly understanding and specific training, which cannot be conducted adequately by one who is not thus specifically prepared. See Technician.

Professional competence   The special skills of the professional practitioner are combined with his clinical experience and understanding of theory to produce a level of flexible competence.

Programmed instruction   The intentional plan to systematize information to be learned by individualized and step-by-step instructional techniques. Such plans are usually characterized by immediate feedback on the accuracy of each performance.

Prolonged adolescence phenomenon The extension of economic dependence due to time-consuming education programs, especially in the major professions. A physician may be thirty years old before he completes his educational and postdoctoral residencies and becomes self-supporting.

Psychoanalysis A category of therapeutic treatment based on concepts and theories of, primarily, Freud, Jung, and Adler.

Psychotherapeutic model The belief that psychological therapists have methods which should be emulated by others in the helping professions. Hence, the psychotherapeutic model led to treating counseling clients as sick persons or patients. It may be that this model for teaching improved behaviors, popular in the fifties and sixties, will gradually be replaced or supplemented by family and interpersonal process group models.

Rapport The existence of a significant interpersonal relationship with a client or pupil, one characterized by openness, mutual awareness, and mutual concern.

Reference groups The groups which influence the ideas, behaviors, and attitudes of others without one's necessarily having a direct physical connection with those influenced; groups to which one "refers" for his values and behaviors.

Relationship A human contract in which mutual understanding, helpfulness, and dependency exist or in which such mutuality is sought.

Self-actualization Developing one's latent capacities and talents; learning to accept and be oneself; becoming the best of whatever one can be.

Self-defeating behavior Actions and statements that enhance the perpetuation of circumstances which in reality one wishes to avoid.

Self-fulfilling prophecy The tendency for one to be or become that which is expected of, or attributed to, him by others.

Self-help group Any group operating without external leadership; one designed to give and receive feedback between and among peers.

Sensitivity groups The groups associated with short-term exposure to training in interpersonal transactions. They are meant to increase one's awareness of his impact on others and others' impact on him. See Interpersonal process group.

Short-term intimacy The closeness and involvement achieved in a sensitivity group by helping group members experience their emotions. It may result in alienation if there is no long-term intimacy in a stable relationship.

Sibling rivalry The alleged and sometimes real competition between siblings or children in the same family.

Simulation The act of replicating reality without risking the consequences of reality; role playing; games designed to teach certain skills and processes.

Social engineering The procedures connected with manipulation of environments to increase the probability that a preselected choice or choices between alternatives will be made; planning future social environments as opposed to just letting things happen by chance or accident.

Social isolates Persons who, through their own actions or through the inferences drawn about them by other people, are without connection to a particular reference group. Sociometric procedures reveal that such persons are not chosen by others in the group.

Social system forces The influences within a given group or individual personality which result in particular patterns of behavior. Usually the behavior matches the cultural pattern; otherwise the behavior may be labeled deviant.

Socialization process The social conditionings and learning which lead one to the behavior of a given social system or culture.

Sociometry A graphic or columnar representation of interpersonal attractions or avoidances in group situations; the study of reactions and avoidances between individual members of a social group — pursued through tabulations or the plotting of lines of attraction, indifference, or dislike.

Stages of development Each person grows through stages or levels of development from birth to old age. Each stage assumes a prior stage as a necessary antecedent.

Synanon game Kind of group therapy involving a particular contract between the client and the group defined in advance and enforced by specific techniques.

Technician One who, with varying degrees of success, applies the needed approaches and uses specialized techniques to solve a problem but who does not necessarily understand the theory underlying the techniques. He therefore tends to be less flexible and resourceful than a professional.

Territory and territoriality Every living thing requires space of his own in which to live. In humans, each culture specifically defines the space or distance which separates strangers, passing acquaintances, friends, lovers, or parent and child. These space definitions are usually different in each culture.

Theory   An idea expressed as a set of relationships connecting characteristics, attributes, or principles in a pattern of meaningful and observable phenomena. Theory in regard to human behavior is an attempt to understand the underlying principles which make it predictable and comprehensible.

Three I's of counseling   The Interruption of a client-counselor meeting is connected to the Intervention given as treatment by the counselor to the counselee or client and the Influence felt as a consequence of the counselor's work. It is claimed by Fullmer and Bernard that all personal encounter — especially counseling — results in at least the three I's.

Venture groups   A specific type of self-help group interested in personal development.

BIBLIOGRAPHY

Adams, J., 1957. "Laboratory Studies of Behavior Without Awareness," *Psychological Bulletin*, 54:383–405.

Adelson, Joseph, 1961. "The Teacher as a Model," *American Scholar*, 30:383–406.

Ahmann, J. Stanley, and Marvin D. Glock, 1967. *Evaluating Pupil Growth: Principles of Tests and Measurements*, 3rd ed. Boston: Allyn & Bacon.

Aldridge, John W., 1969. "In the Country of the Young," *Harper's*, 239 (1433):49–64, October.

Allport, Gordon W., 1968. *The Person in Psychology: Selected Essays*. Boston: Beacon Press.

Almy, Millie, 1968. "Intellectual Mastery and Mental Health," in W. H. MacGinite and S. Bell (eds.), *Readings in Psychological Foundations of Education*. New York: McGraw-Hill Book Company.

American Personnel and Guidance Association, 1969. "1969 Senate Resolutions," *The Guidepost*, 12(1):10–13, September.

Anastasiow, Nicholas, 1969. "Educational Relevance and Jensen's Conclusions," *Phi Delta Kappan*, 51:32–35.

Arbuckle, Dugald S., 1962. "A Semantic Excursion," *Personnel and Guidance Journal*, 41:64–66.

Bakan, D., 1967. *On Method: Toward a Reconstruction of Psychological Investigation*. San Francisco: Jossey-Bass.

Barbula, M., 1967. *Life Career Games.* San Diego: San Diego County Schools.

Barry, Ruth, and Beverly Wolf, 1962. *An Epitaph for Vocational Guidance — Myths, Actualities, Implications.* New York: Teachers College, Columbia University.

Bealer, Robert C., Fern K. Willits, and Peter Maida, 1969. "The Myth of a Rebellious Adolescent Subculture," in H. W. Bernard (ed.), *Readings in Adolescent Development.* Scranton, Pa.: International Textbook Company. From *Rural Youth in Crisis: Facts, Myths, and Social Change.* Washington: U.S. Department of Health, Education and Welfare, 1965. Pp. 54–61.

Beck, Carlton E., Normand R. Bernier, James B. Macdonald, Thomas W. Walton, and Jack C. Willers, 1968. *Education for Relevance.* Boston: Houghton Mifflin Company.

Becker, Ernest, 1962. *The Birth and Death of Meaning.* New York: The Free Press of Glencoe.

Beggs, David W., III, and Edward G. Buffie (eds.), 1967. *Nongraded Schools in Action.* Bloomington: Indiana University Press.

Beier, Ernest G., 1967. *The Silent Language of Psychotherapy.* Chicago: Aldine Publishing Company.

Bernard, Harold W., and Daniel W. Fullmer, 1969. *Principles of Guidance: A Basic Text.* Scranton, Pa.: Itnernational Textbook Company.

Bernard, Harold W., and Wesley C. Huckins, 1967. "Technical Report, Institute for Teachers and Counselors of the Disadvantaged." Portland: Oregon State System of Higher Education (mimeographed).

Bernard, Harold W., and Wesley C. Huckins, 1968. "A Rationale for Educational Innovation." Dayton, Ohio: Institute for Development of Educational Activities (I/D/E/A), Kettering Foundation (typed report).

Bernard, Jessie, 1957. "Parties and Issues in Conflict," *Journal of Conflict Resolution,* 1(2):111–121.

Berne, Eric, 1961. *Transactional Analysis in Psychotherapy.* New York: Grove Press.

Berne, Eric, 1964. *The Games People Play.* New York: Grove Press.

Bettelheim, Bruno, 1969. As reported in "Youth: Confused Parents, Confused Kids," *Time,* 94(10):58, September 5.

Beymer, Lawrence, 1970. "Confrontation Groups: Hula Hoops?" *Counselor Education and Supervision,* 9:75–86.

Billard, Jules B., 1970. "The Revolution in American Agriculture," *National Geographic,* 137(2):147–185.

Bion, W. R., 1952. "Group Dynamics: A Re-View," *International Journal of Psychoanalysis,* 33:235–247.

Birnbaum, Max, 1969. "Sense About Sensitivity Training," *Saturday Review,* 52(46):82–83 ff., November 15.

Blachly, Paul H., M.D. (ed.), 1970. *Drug Abuse: Data and Debate.* Springfield, Ill.: Charles C Thomas.

Bonner, Hubert, 1965 . *On Being Mindful of Man.* Boston: Houghton Mifflin Company.

Boy, Angelo V., and Gerald J. Pine, 1969. "A Sociological View of the Counselor's Role: A Dilemma and a Solution," *Personnel and Guidance Journal,* 47:736–740.

Brim, O. G., Jr., D. C. Glass, J. Neulinger, and I. J. Firestone, 1969. *American Beliefs and Attitudes About Intelligence.* New York: Russell Sage Foundation.

Bronfenbrenenr, U., 1967. "Introduction" in A. S. Makerenko, *The Collective Family: A Handbook for Russian Parents* (translated by Robert Daglish). New York: Doubleday & Company.

Bruner, Jerome, 1963. *The Process of Education.* Cambridge, Mass.: Harvard University Press.

Bruner, Jerome S., 1968. "Culture, Politics, and Pedagogy," *Saturday Review,* 51(20):69–72 ff., May 18.

Buber, Martin, 1958. *I and Thou.* New York: Charles Scribner's Sons.

Buber, Martin, 1965. *Between Man and Man.* New York: The Macmillan Company.

Burton, William H., 1944. *The Guidance of Learning Activities.* New York: D. Appleton-Century Company.

Bushnell, D. S., 1969. "An Educational System for the '70's," *Phi Delta Kappan,* 51(4):199–203, December.

Calhoun, J. B., 1962. "Population Density and Social Psychology," *Scientific American,* 206(2):139–150.

Carey, R. W., 1969. "Student Protest and the Counselor," *Personnel and Guidance Journal,* 48(3):185–191, November.

Cleveland, Harlan, 1969. "Commencement Address." Honolulu: University of Hawaii, December 21.

Cohen, E. A., 1953. *Human Behavior in the Concentration Camp.* New York: Grosset & Dunlap.

Cole, W. E., 1958. *Urban Society*. Boston: Houghton Mifflin Company.

Coleman, James S., 1965. *Adolescents and the Schools*. New York: Basic Books.

Conant, James B., 1959. *The American High School Today*. New York: McGraw-Hill Book Company.

Corey, Wendell, 1970. "The Essence of the Nongraded School," lecture, The Dalles, Oregon, May 12.

Cottle, Thomas J., 1969a. "Bristol Township Schools: Strategy for Change," *Saturday Review*, 52(38):70–71+, September 20.

Cottle, Thomas J., 1969b. "Parent and Child — The Hazards of Equality," *Saturday Review*, 52(5): 16–19+, February 1.

Danskin, David G., Carroll E. Kennedy, Jr., and Walter S. Friesen, 1965. "Guidance: The Ecology of Students," *Personnel and Guidance Journal*, 44:130–135.

Darley, John M., and Bibb Latané, 1968. "When Will People Help in a Crisis?" *Psychology Today*, 2(7):54–57 ff., December.

Downing, Lester N., 1968. *Guidance and Counseling Services: An Introduction*. New York: McGraw-Hill Book Company.

Drucker, P. F., 1968. "A Warning to the Rich White World," *Harper's*, 237:67–75, December.

Dundes, Alan, 1969. "Folklore in the Modern World," address at California Personnel and Guidance Association Convention, Anaheim, Calif., February 15.

DuPue, Palmer, 1967. "The Great Fault of School Marks," *Journal of Secondary Education*, 42:217–222.

Dyer, Henry L., 1968. "Nine Common Misconceptions About Tests and Test Results," in Don E. Hamachek (ed.), *Human Dynamics in Psychology and Education*. Boston: Allyn & Bacon.

Ebel, Robert L., 1970. "The Social Consequences of Educational Testing," in B. Shertzer and S. C. Stone (eds.), *Introduction to Guidance: Selected Readings*. Boston: Houghton Mifflin Company.

Educational Policies Commission, 1939. *The Purpose of Education in American Democracy*. Washington: National Education Association.

Edwards, Allen J., and Dale P. Scannell, 1968. *Educational Psychology*. Scranton, Pa.: International Textbook Company.

Ellis, Albert, 1966. "Requisite Conditions for Basic Personality Change," in Ben N. Ard, Jr. (ed.), *Counseling and Psychotherapy*. Palo Alto, Calif.: Science and Behavior Books.

Engebretson, D. E., 1969. "Cross Cultural Variations in Territoriality," unpublished doctoral dissertation, University of Hawaii, August.

Erikson, Erik H., 1964a. *Insight and Responsibility*. New York: W. W. Norton & Company.

Erikson, Erik H., 1964b. "A Memorandum on Identity and Negro Youth," *Journal of Social Issues*, 20:29–42, October.

Erikson, Erik H., 1968. *Identity, Youth and Crisis*. New York: W. W. Norton & Company.

Evaluative Criteria, 1960. Section G, "Guidance Series," in *National Study of Secondary School Evaluation*. Washington: Cooperative Study of Secondary School Standards.

Fantini, Mario D., 1970. "Institutional Reform — Schools for the Seventies," *Today's Education*, 59(4):43–44+.

Farson, R. E., 1968. "The Education of Jeremy Farson," address in John A. Guthrie (ed.), *IMPACT*, Invitational Meeting on the Preparation of Administrators, Counselors, and Teachers, Phoenix, Arizona, April. Pp. 22–51. (National Seminar conducted by the University of Pittsburgh under contract with the U.S. Office of Education, Department of Health, Education, and Welfare, April 27–May 2, 1968.)

Faust, Verne, 1968. *The Counselor-Consultant in the Elementary School*. Boston: Houghton Mifflin Company.

Ferguson, Charles K., 1968. "Concerning the Nature of Human Systems and the Consultant's Role," *Applied Behavioral Science*, 4(2): 179–193.

Flanders, Ned A., 1965. *Teacher Influence, Pupil Attitudes, and Achievement*. Washington: Office of Education, U.S. Department of Health, Education, and Welfare.

Flexner, Abraham, 1910. *Medical Education in the United States and Canada*. Boston: D. P. Updike Company, The Merrymount Press.

Fraiberg, Selma, 1967. "The Origins of Human Bonds," *Commentary*, 44(6):51–57, December.

French, J. R. P., Jr., 1956. "A Formal Theory of Social Power," *Psychological Review*, 63:181–194.

Friedenberg, E. Z., 1965. *Coming of Age in America: Growth and Acquiescence*. New York: Random House.

Friedenberg, Edgar Z., 1969. "The Generation Gap," *The Annals of the American Academy of Political and Social Science*, 382:32–42.

Friedenberg, Edgar Z., 1970. "The University Community in an Open Society," *Daedalus*, 99:56–74.

Fullmer, D. W., 1963. Report of Directors, U.S. Office of Education Report, Cambridge, Mass. Counseling and Guidance Institute Branch. Washington: U.S. Office of Education.

Fullmer, Daniel W., 1969a. "Alienation in the Living Room," *Proceedings,* California Personnel and Guidance Association, Anaheim, California.

Fullmer, D. W., 1969b. "A Report on Pre-Employment Preparation Program: Group Therapy and Interaction Model," Manpower Training, Rehabilitation Center of Hawaii, January 20 to August 31.

Fullmer, D. W., 1969c. "Future of Supervision," *Educational Perspectives,* 3(3):29–32, October.

Fullmer, D. W., 1971a. "Counseling with Parents of Students," in *Encyclopedia of Education.* New York: The Macmillan Company.

Fullmer, Daniel W., and Harold W. Bernard, 1964. *Counseling: Content and Process.* Chicago: Science Research Associates.

Fullmer, D. W., and Harold W. Bernard, 1968. *Family Consultation.* Boston: Houghton Mifflin Company.

Gaddis, Thomas, 1955. *Birdman of Alcatraz.* New York: Random House.

Gardner, John W., 1963. *Self-Renewal.* New York: Harper & Row, Publishers.

Gattengo, C., 1969. *Towards a Visual Culture: Educating Through Television.* New York: Outerbridge & Dienstfrey.

Gattengo, C., 1970. *What We Owe Children: The Subordination of Teaching to Learning.* New York: Outerbridge & Dienstfrey.

Gazda, G. M., 1968. *Innovations to Group Psychotherapy.* Springfield, Ill.: Charles C Thomas, Publisher.

Gazda, G. M. (ed.), 1969. *Theories and Methods of Group Counseling in the Schools.* Springfield, Ill.: Charles C Thomas, Publisher.

Gephart, William J., and Daniel P. Antonoplos, 1969. "The Effects of Expectancy and Other Research-Biasing Factors," *Phi Delta Kappan,* 50:579–583.

Getzels, J. W., and P. W. Jackson, 1962. *Creativity and Intelligence.* New York: John Wiley & Sons.

Gibb, Jack R., 1965. "Fear and Facade: Defensive Management," in Richard E. Farson (ed.), *Science and Human Affairs.* Palo Alto, Calif.: Science and Behavior Books.

Gibb, Jack R., 1968. "Using Groups in an Educational Setting," address in John A. Guthrie (ed.), *IMPACT,* Invitational Meeting on the Preparation of Administrators, Counselors, and Teachers, Phoenix, Arizona, April. Pp. 52–73. (National Seminar conducted by the University of Pittsburgh under contract with the U.S. Office of Education, Department of Health, Education, and Welfare, April 27–May 2, 1968.)

Ginott, Haim G., 1965. *Between Parent and Child*. New York: Avon Books.

Glasser, William, 1966. "Reality Therapy: A Realistic Approach to the Young Offender," in Ben N. Ard, Jr. (ed.), *Counseling and Psychotherapy*. Palo Alto, Calif.: Science and Behavior Books.

Glasser, William, 1969. *Schools Without Failure*. New York: Harper & Row, Publishers.

Glasser, William, 1970. "Exploring the World of the Adolescent," lecture, Portland, Oregon, January 17.

Gleason, G. T., 1967. "Technological Developments Related to Independent Learning," in *The Theory and Nature of Independent Learning*. Scranton, Pa.: International Textbook Company. Pp. 65–78.

Gonyea, G., 1964 "The Ideal Therapeutic Relationship and Counseling Outcome," *Journal of Clinical Psychology*, 19:481–487.

Goodlad, John I., 1967. "The Educational Program to 1980 and Beyond," in Edgar L. Morphet and C. O. Ryan (eds.), *Implications for Education of Prospective Changes in Society*. Denver: Designing Education for the Future.

Goodlad, John I., 1969. "The School *vs.* Education," *Saturday Review*, 52(16):59–61+, April 19.

Goodman, Paul, 1962. *Compulsory Mis-Education*. New York: Vintage Books.

Goodman, Paul, 1968. "Freedom and Learning: The Need for Choice," *Saturday Review*, 51 (20):73–75, May 18.

Green, Thomas F., 1968. "Program Plannings and Process: Can History of the Future Be Written?" address in John A. Guthrie (ed.), *IMPACT*, Invitational Meetings on the Preparation of Administrators, Counselors, and Teachers, Phoenix, Arizona, April. Pp. 144–173. (National Seminar conducted by the University of Pittsburgh under contract with U.S. Office of Education, Department of Health, Education, and Welfare, April 27–May 2, 1968).

Guba, Egon G., and John J. Horvat, 1970. "Evaluation During Development," *Viewpoints*, Bulletin of the School of Education, Indiana University, 46 (2):21–45, March.

Guilford, J. P., 1967. *The Nature of Human Intelligence*. New York: McGraw-Hill Book Company.

Gunther, Bernard, 1968. *Sense Relaxation*. New York: The Macmillan Company, Collier Books.

Guthrie, John A., (ed.), 1968. *IMPACT*, Invitational Meeting on the Preparation of Administrators, Counselors, and Teachers, Phoenix, Arizona, April. (National Seminar conducted by the University of Pittsburgh under contract with the U.S. Office of Education, Department of Health, Education and Welfare, April 27–May 2, 1968.)

Hall, E. T., 1959. *The Silent Language*. New York: Doubleday & Company.

Halleck, S. L., 1968. "Hypotheses of Student Unrest," *Phi Delta Kappan*, 50:2–9.

Hallman, Ralph J., 1967. "Techniques of Creative Teaching," *Journal of Creative Behavior*, 1:325–330.

Harrison, Charles H., 1970. "South Brunswick, N.J.: Schools Put a Town on the Map," *Saturday Review*, 53(8):66–68+, February 21.

Hart, Leslie A., 1969. "Learning at Random," *Saturday Review*, 52 (16):62–63, April 19.

Havelock, R. G., 1969. "A Comparative Study of the Literature on the Dissemination and Utilization of Scientific Knowledge," Final Report No. 7-0028. Washington: Bureau of Research, U.S. Office of Education, July.

Havemann, Ernest, 1969. "Alternatives to Analysis," *Playboy*, 16:133–134+.

Havighurst, Robert J., and Bernice L. Neugarten, 1967. *Society and Education*, 3rd ed. Boston: Allyn & Bacon.

Hayakawa, S. I., 1968. "Television Commentary: Who's Bringing Up Your Children?" *ETC*, 35:299–308, September.

Heilbroner, Robert L., 1970. "Priorities for the Seventies," *Saturday Review*, 53 (1):17–19 ff., January 3.

Heine, W., 1953. "A Comparison of Patients' Reports on Psychotherapeutic Experience with Psychoanalytic, Non-directive, and Adlerian Therapies," *American Journal of Psychotherapy*, 7:16–23.

Herriott, R. E., 1963. "Some Social Determinants of Educational Aspiration," *Harvard Educational Review*, 33:157–177.

Herzberg, Frederick, 1966. *Work and the Nature of Man*. Cleveland: World Publishing Company.

Hickerson, Nathaniel, 1966. *Education for Alienation.* Englewood Cliffs, N.J.: Prentice-Hall.

Hollingshead, August B., 1949. *Elmtown's Youth: The Impact of Social Classes on Adolescence.* New York: John Wiley & Sons.

Holt, John, 1964. *How Children Fail.* New York: Pitman Publishing Corporation.

Howard, A., and R. Gallimore, 1968. "Studies in a Hawaiian Community," *Na Makamaka O Nanakuli.* Honolulu: University of Hawaii.

Howe, Harold, II, 1968. Quoted in P. W. Hutson, "Counselor-Teacher Relations," *Idaho Guidance News and Views.* Boise: Idaho State Department of Education.

Hoyt, Kenneth B., 1962. "Guidance: A Constellation of Services," *Personnel and Guidance Journal,* 40 (8):690–97, April.

Hubbard, L. Ron, 1951. *Dienetics: The Modern Science of Mental Health.* New York: Random House.

Huckins, W., 1966. "The Nature and Power of Acceptance," address, Counseling Institute, Portland, Oregon.

Huckins, Wesley C., 1971. "Interpersonal Relationships and Communication," in H. W. Bernard and W. C. Huckins, *Dynamics of Adjustment.* Boston: Holbrook Press.

Innovation and Experiment in Education, 1964, A Report of the Panel on Educational Research and Development. Washington: The President's Science Advisory Committee.

Irish G., 1966. "Behavioral Changes in Participants in Family Group Consultation," unpublished doctoral dissertation, Oregon State University (Corvallis).

Jensen, Arthur R., 1969a. "How Much Can We Boost IQ and Scholastic Achievement?" *Harvard Educational Review,* 39:1–123.

Jensen, Arthur R., 1969b. "Input — Arthur Jensen Replies," *Psychology Today,* 3 (5):4–6, October.

Jersild, Arthur T., 1955. *When Teachers Face Themselves.* New York: Teachers College, Columbia University.

Jersild, Arthur T., and Eve Allina Lazar, 1962. *The Meaning of Psychotherapy in the Teacher's Life and Work.* New York: Teachers College, Columbia University.

Joel, W., and D. Shapiro, 1949. "A Genotypical Approach to the Analysis of Personal Interaction," *Journal of Psychology,* 27:9–17.

Johnson, Wendell, 1946. *People in Quandaries*. New York: Harper & Row, Publishers.

Joint ACES-ASCA Policy Statement Concerning the School Counselor for Superintendents of Schools and School Boards, 1969. Washington: American Personnel and Guidance Association.

Jones, Maxwell, 1953. *The Therapeutic Community*. New York: Basic Books.

Kaplan, Abraham, 1964. *The Conduct of Inquiry*. San Francisco: Chandler Publishing Company.

Katz, E. W., M. M. Ohlsen, and F. C. Proff, 1960. "An Analysis of the Interpersonal Behavior of Adolescents in Group Counseling," University of Illinois.

Kehas, Chris D., 1969. "Toward a Redefinition of Education: A New Framework for Counseling in Education," in S. C. Stone and B. Shertzer (eds.), *Introduction to Guidance: Selected Readings*. Boston: Houghton Mifflin Company. Pp. 59–71.

Kelley, Earl C., 1962. *In Defense of Youth*. Englewood Cliffs, N.J.: Prentice-Hall.

Kemp, C. Gratton, 1969. "Communication in Group Counseling," *Focus on Guidance*, 1(8):1–7, April.

Keniston, Kenneth, 1960. *The Uncommitted, Alienated Youth in American Society*. New York: Dell Publishing Company.

Keniston, Kenneth, 1967. "College Students and Children in Developmental Institutions," *Children*, 14:3–7, January–February.

Kiesler, C. A., and S. B. Kiesler, 1969. *Conformity*. Reading, Mass., Addison-Wesley Publishing Co.

Kimball, Solon T., 1967. "Contributions of Anthropology to Counseling," lecture, Portland, Division of Continuing Education, Oregon State System of Higher Education, June 26.

King, Paul T., 1965. "Psychoanalytic Adaptations," in Buford Stefflre (ed.), *Theories of Counseling*. New York: McGraw-Hill Book Company.

Kowitz, G. T., 1969. "Trends in Elementary School Counseling," *Educational Forum*, 30(1):87–93.

Krumboltz, John D. (ed.), 1966. *Revolution in Counseling*. Boston: Houghton Mifflin Company.

Krumboltz, J. D., and C. E. Thoresen (eds.), 1969. *Behavioral Counseling: Cases and Techniques*. New York: Holt, Rinehart and Winston.

Kushel, Gerald, 1967. *Discord in Teacher-Counselor Relations.* Englewood Cliffs, N.J.: Prentice-Hall.

Lashley, Carl, 1958. "Cerebral Organization and Behavior," in *The Brain and Human Behavior,* Harry Solomon, Stanley Cobb, and Wilder Penfield (eds.), Vol. 36. Baltimore: The Williams & Wilkins Co., Association for Research in Nervous and Mental Disease. Pp. 1–18.

Lennard, H. L., and A. Bernstein, 1969. *Patterns in Human Interaction: An Introduction to Clinical Sociology.* San Francisco: Jossey-Bass.

Liddell, Howard, 1956. *Emotional Hazards in Animals and Man.* Springfield, Ill.: Charles C Thomas, Publishers.

Lieberman, Myron, 1956. *Education as a Profession.* Englewood Cliffs, N.J.: Prentice-Hall.

Lipsman, Claire K., 1969. "Revolution and Prophecy: Community Involvement for Counselors," *Personnel and Guidance Journal,* 48(2): 97–100, October.

Loughary, J. W. (ed.), 1966. *Man-Machine Systems in Education.* New York: Harper & Row, Publishers.

Lowry, Ritchie P., and Robert P. Rankin, 1969. *Sociology: The Science of Society.* New York: Charles Scribner's Sons.

Lynd, Robert S., and Helen M. Lynd, 1929. *Middletown.* New York: Harcourt, Brace & World.

Lynton, R. P., 1960. *The Tide of Learning: The Aloka Experience.* London: Routledge and Kegan Paul.

McCully, C. Harold, 1962. "The School Counselor: Strategy for Professionalization," *Personnel and Guidance Journal,* 40(8):681–689, April.

McCully, C. Harold, 1969. *Challenge for Change in Counselor Education,* compiled by Lyle L. Miller. Minneapolis: Burgess Publishing Company.

McDermott, John W., 1969. "Creativity," *Proceedings,* Personnel and Guidance Association, Honolulu, University of Hawaii.

Mahler, Clarence A., 1969. *Group Counseling in the Schools.* Boston: Houghton Mifflin Company.

Maslow, A. H., 1954. *Motivation and Personality.* New York: Harper & Brothers.

Maslow, Abraham H., 1967. "Self-Actualization and Beyond," in

J. F. T. Bugenthal (ed.), *Challenges of Humanistic Psychology*. New York: McGraw-Hill Book Company.

Mathewson, R. H., 1962. *Guidance Policy and Practice*, 3d ed. New York: Harper & Row, Publishers.

May, Rollo, 1969. "The Psychodynamics of Alienation," address, East-West Philosophers Conference, Honolulu, University of Hawaii.

Mead, Margaret, 1970. "Youth Revolt: The Future Is Now," *Saturday Review*, 53(2):23–25 ff., January 10.

Mead, Margaret, and K. Heyman, 1965. *Family*. New York: A Ridge Press Book, The Macmillan Company.

Menninger, Karl, 1968. "The Crime of Punishment," *Saturday Review*, 51(36):21–25+, September 7.

Menninger, Karl, with Martin Mayman and Paul Pruyser, 1963. *The Vital Balance: The Life Process in Mental Health and Illness*. New York: The Viking Press.

Meyer, James A., 1969. "Suburbia: A Wasteland of Disadvantaged Youth and Negligent Schools?" *Phi Delta Kappan*, 50:575–578.

Miller, Lyle L., 1969. "On Approaching Professional Maturity," in C. Harold McCully, *Challenge for Change in Counselor Education*, compiled by Lyle L. Miller. Minneapolis: Burgess Publishing Company.

Miller, Paul A., 1967. "Major Implications for Education of Prospective Changes in Society, One Perspective," in E. L. Morphet and C. D. Ryan (eds.), *Implications for Education of Prospective Changes in Society*. Denver: Designing Education for the Future.

Moore, Dan, 1969. "In the Midst of Revolution," lecture, American School Board Association, Portland, Oregon, January.

Mouly, George J., 1968. *Psychology for Effective Teaching*. New York: Holt, Rinehart & Winston.

Mowrer, O. H., 1968. "Loss and Recovery of Community," in G. M. Gazda (ed.), *Innovations to Group Psychotherapy*. Springfield, Ill.: Charles C Thomas, Publisher. Pp. 130–189.

Murphy, Gardner, 1965. "Where is the Human Race Going?" in R. E. Farson (ed.), *Science and Human Affairs*. Palo Alto, Calif.: Science and Behavior Books, Inc.

Mursell, James L., 1946. *Successful Teaching*. New York: McGraw-Hill Book Company.

Mylecraine, Walter E., 1965. "Public Domain," *American Education*, 1(10):7–8, November.

Nations, Jimmy E., 1967. "Caring for Individual Differences in Reading Through Nongrading," lecture, Seattle Public Schools, May 3.

Packard, Vance, 1960. *The Hidden Persuaders*. Harmondsworth, England: Penguin Books.

Parker, Francis W., 1937. *Talks on Pedagogics*. New York: The John Day Company.

Parry, John, 1968. *The Psychology of Human Communication*. New York: American Elsevier Publishing Company.

Patterson, C. H., 1966. *Theories of Counseling and Psychotherapy*. New York: Harper & Row, Publishers.

Patterson, C. H., 1969a. "A Current View of Client-Centered or Relationship Theory," *The Counseling Psychologist*, 1(2):2–25, Summer.

Patterson, C. H., 1969b. "Pupil Personnel Services in the Automated School," *Personnel and Guidance Journal*, 48(2):101–108, October.

Pearl, A., 1969. "Educational Change: Why-How-for Whom," address, San Francisco, California. Repeated at California Personnel and Guidance Association, Anaheim, Calif., February 1969.

Penfield, Wilder, 1967. "The Uncommitted Cortex, The Child's Changing Brain," in H. W. Bernard and W. C. Huckins (eds.), *Readings in Human Development*. Boston: Allyn & Bacon.

Pierson, George A., 1965. *An Evaluation: Counselor Education in Regular Session Institutes*. Washington: Office of Education, U.S. Department of Health, Education, and Welfare.

Prescott, Daniel A., 1957. *The Child in the Educative Process*. New York: McGraw-Hill Book Company.

Rae-Grant, Q., T. Gladwin, and E. Bower, 1966. "Mental Health, Social Competence, and the War on Poverty," *American Journal of Orthopsychiatry*, 36:652–664.

Raths, James, 1966. "Mutuality of Effective Function and School Experiences," in Walter B. Waetjen and R. R. Leeper (eds.), *Learning and Mental Health in the School*. Washington: Association for Supervision and Curriculum Development, NEA.

Rhodes, L., 1969. "Linkage Strategies for Change: Process May Be the Product," *Phi Delta Kappan*, 51(4):204–207.

Riessman, Frank, 1964. "The Strategy of Style," *The Record, Teachers College*, 65:484–489.

Rogers, Carl R., 1942. *Counseling and Psychotherapy*. Boston: Houghton Mifflin Company.

Rogers, Carl R., 1966. "The Necessary and Sufficient Conditions of Therapeutic Personality Change," in Ben N. Ard, Jr. (ed.), *Counseling and Psychotherapy*. Palo Alto, Calif.: Science and Behavior Books.

Rogers, Carl R., 1968. "Interpersonal Relationships: U.S.A. 2000," *Journal of Applied Behavioral Sciences*, 4:265–280.

Rogers, Carl R., no date. "The Process of the Basic Encounter Group," La Jolla, Calif., Western Behavioral Sciences Institute (mimeographed).

Rogers, Carl R., and F. J. Roethlisberger, 1952. "Barriers and Gateways to Communication," *Harvard Business Review*, 30(4):46–52, June–August.

Rogers, E. M., 1962. *Diffusion of Innovations*. New York: The Free Press of Glencoe.

Rosenthal, Robert, and Lenore Jacobson, 1968. *Pygmalion in the Classroom*. New York: Holt, Rinehart & Winston.

Rousseve, Ronald J., 1969. "Counselor, Know Thyself," *Personnel and Guidance Journal*, 47:628–633.

Ruesch, Jurgen, and Weldon Kees, 1961. *Nonverbal Communication*. Berkeley: University of California Press.

Saterstrom, M. H., and J. A. Steph (eds.), 1969. *Educators Guide to Free Guidance Materials*, 8th ed. Randolph, Wis.: Educators Progress Service, August.

Scheflen, Albert B., 1961. *A Psychotherapy of Schizophrenia: Direct Analysis*. Springfield, Ill.: Charles C Thomas, Publisher.

Schein, Edgar H., 1969. *Process Consultation: Its Role in Organization Development*. Reading, Mass.: Addison-Wesley Publishing Company.

Schrag, Peter, 1969. "School Administrators and Angry Students: Gloom at the Top," *Saturday Review*, 52(33):50–51+, August 16.

Seashore, Harold G., 1963. "The Identification of the Gifted," *Test Service Bulletin*, No. 55. New York: The Psychological Corporation.

SECAW, 1969. Western Association for Counselor Education and Supervision, Newsletter, Eugene: College of Education, University of Oregon, Fall. Pp. 14–15.

Seixas, Kim G., 1969. *The Rehabilitation Center of Hawaii*. Manpower Project, October.

Sherif, M., and C. W. Sherif, 1964. *Reference Groups: Explorations into Conformity and Deviation in Adolescents*. New York: Harper & Row, Publishers.

Sherman, Robert, and Ida Shapiro, 1969. "Teacher-Counselor Communication," *The School Counselor,* 17:55–62.

Shertzer, Bruce, and Shelley C. Stone (eds.), 1970. *Introduction to Guidance: Selected Readings.* Boston: Houghton Mifflin Company.

Shoben, Edward J., 1966. "Personal Worth in Education and Counseling," in John D. Krumboltz (ed.), *Revolution in Counseling.* Boston: Houghton Mifflin Company.

Shostrom, Everett L., 1967. *Man, the Manipulator,* Nashville, Tenn.: Abingdon Press.

Shostrom, Everett L., 1969. "Group Therapy: Let the Buyer Beware," *Psychology Today,* 2(12):36–40, May.

Silberman, C. E., 1970. *Crisis in the Classroom: The Remaking of American Education.* New York: Random House.

Skinner, B. F., 1954. "The Science of Learning and the Art of Teaching," *Harvard Educational Review,* 24:86–97.

Skinner, B. F., 1959. "A Case Study in Scientific Method," in S. Koch (ed.), *Psychology: A Study of Science,* Vol. 2. New York: McGraw-Hill Book Company.

Smith, B. Othanel, 1967. "Conditions of Learning," in E. L. Morphet and C. O. Ryan (eds.), *Implications for Education of Prospective Changes in Society.* Denver: Designing Education for the Future.

Spitz, R. A., 1949. "The Role of Ecological Factors in the Emotional Development of Infancy," *Child Development,* 20:145–146.

Stefflre, Buford, 1966. "Counselor's Role," lecture at NDEA Counseling and Guidance Institute, Portland, Oregon, May.

Stewart, Naomi, 1947. "A.G.C.T. Scores of Army Personnel Grouped by Occupations," *Occupations,* 26:5–41.

Stoller, F. H. 1968. "Marathon Group Therapy," in G. M. Gazda (ed.), *Innovations to Group Psychotherapy.* Springfield, Ill.: Charles C Thomas, Publisher. Pp. 42–95.

Strauss, Samuel, 1969. "Looking Backward on Future Scientists," in H. W. Bernard (ed.), *Readings in Adolescent Development.* Scranton, Pa.: International Textbook Company. From *The Science Teacher,* 24:385–387, 1957.

Street, Paul, 1970. "Compensatory Education by Community Action," *Phi Delta Kappan,* 51:320–323.

Swan, R. J., 1966. "The Counselor and the Curriculum," *Personnel and Guidance Journal,* 44:689–693.

Taylor, Calvin W., 1968a. "Be Talent Developers . . . As Well as Knowledge Dispensers," *Today's Education*, 57:67–69, December.

Taylor, Calvin W., 1968b. "Cultivating New Talents: A Way to Reach the Educationally Deprived," *Journal of Creative Behavior*, 2(2):83–90, Spring.

Thayer, Lee, 1968. *Communication and Communications Systems*. Homewood, Ill.: Richard D. Irwin.

Thorndike, Robert L., 1969. "Pygmalion in the Classroom, a Book Review," *The Record, Teachers College*, 70:805–807.

Tiedeman, David V., 1961. "The Training and Role of a Counselor," *Guidance News Letter*. Chicago: Science Research Associates, March.

Torrance, E. Paul, 1962. *Guiding Creative Talent*. Englewood Cliffs, N.J.: Prentice-Hall.

Torrance, E. Paul, 1969. "What Is Honored: Comparative Studies of Creative Achievement and Motivation," *Journal of Creative Behavior*, 3:149–154.

200 Million Americans, 1967. Washington: U.S. Department of Commerce, Bureau of the Census.

Varenhorst, B. B., 1969. "Behavioral Group Counseling," in G. M. Gazda (ed.), *Theories and Methods of Group Counseling in the Schools*. Springfield, Ill.: Charles C Thomas, Publisher.

Washington, K. S., 1968. "What Counselors Must Know About Black Power," *Personnel and Guidance Journal*, 47:204–208.

Watzlawick, Paul, Janet H. Beavin, and Don D. Jackson, 1967. *Pragmatics of Human Communication*. New York: W. W. Norton & Company.

"What's Wrong with the High Schools?" 1970, *Newsweek*, pp. 65–69, February 16.

Whorf, B. L., 1956. "Science and Linguistics," in J. B. Carroll (ed.), *Language, Thought, and Reality*. New York: John Wiley & Sons. Pp. 207–219.

Williams, Frank E., 1967. "Intellectual Creativity and the Teacher," *Journal of Creative Behavior*, 1:173–180.

Williams, T. H., 1964. "Conditioning of Verbalization: A Review," *Psychological Bulletin*, 62:383–393.

Wolpe, J., 1969. *The Practice of Behavior Therapy*. New York: Pergamon Press.

Woodring, Paul, 1957. *A Fourth of a Nation*. New York: McGraw-Hill Book Company.

Woodring, Paul, 1968. "Some Thoughts on the Sexual Revolution," *Saturday Review*, 51(3):62–63, January 20.

Wrenn, C. Gilbert, 1962. *The Counselor in a Changing World.* Washington: American Personnel and Guidance Association.

Wyzanski, Charles E., Jr., 1969. "A Federal Judge Digs the Young," in H. W. Bernard (ed.), *Readings in Adolescent Development.* Scranton, Pa.: International Textbook Company. From *Saturday Review*, 51(29):14–16+, July 20, 1968.

Zeigler, R., 1969. "Creative Job Search Techniques," Portland, Ore.: State Bureau of Labor.

INDEX OF NAMES

INDEX OF SUBJECTS